THE EXAMINED LIFE JOURNAL

A Literary Publication of the
University of Iowa
Carver College of Medicine

Cover art by Wenjie Yu, PhD, Lung & Cystic Fibrosis Research Center

About the image: Airways secrete mucus to protect the lung from environmental injury caused by pathogens and particles in inhaled air. However, in diseases such as asthma, cystic fibrosis, and chronic obstructive pulmonary disease (COPD), mucus hypersecretion and accumulation obstruct the airway and limit breathing. The image shows mucus hypersecretion and accumulation in an asthmatic distal airway. Airway cells are labeled in light blue with nuclear staining. Goblet cells in airway produce two types of mucin proteins, MUC5AC (red) and MUC5B (green); they are the most important components of airway mucus. The airway lumen is collapsed and filled with mucus instead of air.

The Examined Life Journal is published by The University of Iowa Carver College of Medicine in Iowa City, Iowa.

THE EXAMINED LIFE JOURNAL

A Literary Publication of the
University of Iowa
Carver College of Medicine

VOLUME 8 | FALL 2020

THEEXAMINEDLIFEJOURNAL.COM

Foreword

FALL 2020

Thanks again to all our wonderful, submitters, contributors, subscribers and readers. As most of you know, we have transitioned to producing one journal issue per year with our newsstand date in October. For this issue, and we hope for many future issues, we welcome two new staff members:

Cate Dicharry is our new managing editor. Cate graduated from Lewis & Clark College in Portland, OR with a BA in Political Science in 2003, moved to China to teach English at Dalian Nationalities University and discovered a love for creative writing. She obtained an MFA in Creative Writing from the Low Residency Program at the University of California, Riverside. Her first novel was published by Unnamed Press in 2015. Cate also directs the Writing and Medical Humanities Program for The University of Iowa Carver College of Medicine.

Brittany Bettendorf is our new nonfiction editor. Brittany is a Clinical Assistant Professor in Rheumatology at The University of Iowa. She completed her Internal Medicine and Pediatrics residency as well as her Rheumatology fellowship at Medical College of Wisconsin. She joined the faculty at University of Iowa in 2017. In addition to her clinical practice, she is currently enrolled in the nonfiction program at The Iowa Writer's Workshop and works with Cate in the Medical Humanities Program teaching and mentoring medical students.

Highlighted in this issue is the text of a speech, "Recapturing the Joy of Surgery," which our fiction editor, Dr. Carol Scott-Conner, was chosen to give as the annual Olga Jonassen Lecturer at the 2019 American College of Surgeons Meeting. Here too is the text of an interview with Carol that Kerri Goers, one of our dedicated neonatal nurse practitioners and budding young writers, conducted which describes Carol's journey to becoming a prominent national figure in the field of surgery.

As usual, this issue is filled with a wide range of lovely medical writing you will not see published elsewhere; writing that includes several medical student pieces and a number of COVID-19 pieces. In fiction, you will see a physician's frustration in our current era of "Quality Control." In nonfiction, there is a bittersweet remembrance of a pediatric cardiac surgeon and his pediatric intensivist wife as they shepherd a newborn through the course of a TAPVR repair, the same deformity that took the life of one of their own babies. In poetry there are lovely medical student reflections on several critical stages of their exhausting training.

Thanks again for supporting us. Stay safe.

Bruce P. Brown MD
Editor-in-Chief

THE
EXAMINED
LIFE
JOURNAL

Recapturing the Joy of Surgery

CAROL SCOTT-CONNER

2019 OLGA JONASSON LECTURE SPONSORED BY THE WOMEN IN SURGERY COMMITTEE OF THE AMERICAN COLLEGE OF SURGEONS

When Dr Olga Jonasson was a medical student at the University of Illinois at Chicago during the late 1950s, she told her chief, Dr Warren Cole, that she wanted to be a surgeon. He thought this was an absurd idea.

By sheer determination, hard work, and excellence, she joined the house staff at the University of Illinois, where Cook County Hospital was the prime attraction. After his initial skepticism subsided, Dr Cole became her mentor, advising her to obtain additional training in research to prepare for an academic career. She spent a year at Walter Reed studying immunohistochemistry and another year at the Massachusetts General Hospital studying transplantation immunobiology. She obtained N.I.H. funding to establish a tissue typing laboratory that was ultimately used by six transplantation centers in Chicago. In 1969, she performed the first kidney transplantation in the state of Illinois.

When she was named Chief of Surgery at Cook County Hospital in 1977, she was the first woman to hold such a position at a major medical center and considered the preeminent woman among academic surgeons in the United States at the time. She retained her preeminence for the rest of her life and continues to influence the course of surgery and the careers of surgeons to this day.

In 1987, she left Cook County Hospital to become the Robert M. Zollinger Professor of Surgery and Chair at the Ohio State University, the first woman to hold such a position in the US. While there, she coauthored an editorial that provided the first rational discussion of child-bearing during surgical residency, including a practical way to accommodate this very natural process. Photographs of Dr. Jonasson show a serious-faced woman with a transcendently warm smile. She was a woman who not only served as an inspiration, but also clearly took joy in her chosen profession.

Before I speak to the title of my lecture, "Recapturing the Joy," we need to delve into the darkness. The medical profession is beset by numerous stressors, and it seems that we surgeons, because of our very active and direct involvement in patient care, are stuck in the "pain point" between our patients and the system.

What do I know of this, after a lifetime spent in the cloisters of academia? My own academic career took me from the East coast megalopolis where I grew up and trained, to three predominately rural states: West Virginia, Mississippi, and Iowa. I stay in contact with former residents in both academic and private practice and with surgeons in mostly rural practice around my area. I am also an avid follower of the American College of Surgeons (ACS) Communities, an electronic discussion forum where surgeons of all specialties post and comment upon problems of individual and mutual interest. Reading those posts, it is impossible not to be struck by the sense of unhappiness and frustration engulfing many of my surgical colleagues. This misery stands in stark contrast to the sense of joy and vocation that called many of us to the practice of surgery. And let me add that we in academia also experience and must respond to these pressures.

Let's name some of the problems.

Among these are: drastically declining reimbursement, the rapid pace of technological innovation, increasing specialization within general surgery, closure of small hospitals, consolidation of hospital systems, conversion to employed status for many in private practice, threat of litigation, what I call "weaponized" peer review, dysfunctional electronic medical records, closed insurance networks, and many others. Dr. Danielle Ofri, an attending physician at Bellevue Hospital, published an editorial in the New York Times pointing out, "One resource seems infinite and free, the professionalism of caregivers" (1).

Let's talk for a few minutes about how these issues affect us, and discuss tactics to circumvent them. Changes are needed nationally, internationally and within our own individual medical communities. We also need to take action individually, to allow ourselves to experience and project joy – the joy that drew us to this amazing vocation in the first place.

Without these changes to revitalize our joy, we will continue to see what has become an epidemic of burnout.

Burnout was initially defined in 1975 by Freudenberger as "a constellation of symptoms – malaise, fatigue, frustration, cynicism, and inefficacy – that arise from excessive demands on energy, strength, or resources in the workplace." Key symptoms include a feeling of emotional exhaustion, and a tendency to treat colleagues or patients as objects (2). Burnout is the currently most accepted term used to describe clinician distress in an inherently dysfunctional system.

The problem with the term burnout is that it seems to imply that if we were just stronger, smarter, better, we wouldn't burn out. As a surgeon, I don't like the concept. Maybe you don't either. What burns out? A defective light bulb. A candle guttering to its end. We'd like to think that surgeons do not burn out. Yet the very nature of our work and our ethos in the current environment predisposes us. We take on tough cases, and expect excellent outcomes. We suffer, find workarounds, and continue to advocate for our patients until the burden becomes unendurable. The very dedication and perfectionism we surgeons prize render us more susceptible.

It is crucial to recognize that burnout is a symptom of a problem in the workplace, not a weakness of the clinician. Burnout and disruptive behavior are on a continuum; when too much pressure accumulates over time, the clinician erupts. At the breaking point, surgeons may consider early retirement. Clinical depression is common. Suicide can be an extreme consequence.

System-wide change as well as individual strategies to develop the personal resilience are required to survive these assaults (3).

I prefer the term "moral injury" to describe the deep distress many of us are feeling. Moral injury is a term that was initially used to describe some of the symptoms of soldiers returning from the Viet Nam war; those with a constellation of symptoms that appeared to threaten a soldier's moral fiber, rather than threats to their own life (as in classic post-traumatic stress disorder). Wendy Dean, in a recent editorial, described it as resulting in the medical environment from "the challenge of simultaneously knowing what care patients need but being unable to provide it due to constraints that are beyond our control (4)."

Let's take a few minutes to think about it. A patient needs an operation, but the insurance company won't cover it. A patient needs a particular medication, but can't afford it (and the insurance company won't cover it). You request a particular kind of instrument during an operation – maybe just a stapler or a particular suture, or possibly a particular implantable device – and are told that you have to use something else, something that someone somewhere has judged to be "equivalent," because the hospital has a contract with the manufacturer.

To paraphrase Dean and others, surgeons are smart, tough, durable and resourceful. If we could have MacGyver'ed ourselves out of this situation "by working harder, smarter, or differently," we would have done it. In fact, our constant efforts to MacGyver ourselves out of one or another bind, and to get the care our patients need, may add to our evolving burden of moral injury – the continued erosion of our moral fiber. Think of a rope, fraying against the edge of a rocky cliff, strand by strand parting, until it finally breaks.

Because I believe that precisely naming the problem helps develop solutions, I want to give you another concept that also applies to surgeons, and that is the concept of the "second victim." Whenever there is a complication, a medical error, or a death, the "first victim" is the patient. The "second victim," often forgotten, is the surgeon who feels responsible for the event (5).

Remember the old saying that every surgeon carries a graveyard around in their head; that we each walk through this graveyard periodically, thinking about deaths and complications that might have been averted? Who among us does not do that?

When the complication or death is due to a medical error, or a malpractice suit has been filed, the suffering for the surgeon is intensified. Hence the term, "second victim." Because we intervene so directly and decisively in the lives of our patients – that is, we are uniquely privileged and allowed to inflict the controlled trauma of an operation – the inherent imperfections of our own art and the deep sense of personal responsibility inculcated in us by our mentors comes back to haunt us in this way.

Both the system and the surgeon need to take action to combat these assaults. At the systemic level, we need tort reform and a more rational system for compensating victims of errors. At the individual level, we must support each other when such an event occurs. Too often the "second victim" retreats into a self-imposed isolation at a time when both collegial and institutional support are needed.

Added to these are individual stressors such as the high burden of student debt, care for children, care of elderly parents, and the need to plan for retirement. Many of these burdens fall disproportionately upon women because of our natural role as caregivers.

But let's talk about joy and how we can recapture that sense in our own lives as surgeons. I have told you that I will talk about three spheres of action – individual actions or strategies we can all incorporate; local action, at the hospital staff, county, or state level, and global action through our professional societies, including those that the ACS and the AMA, are undertaking and must expand on our behalf.

First, let's acknowledge that what we do is miraculous and should give us joy. Let's talk some more about joy. Let me tell you a story.

I need to explain first that I've been studying Narrative Medicine lately. When I retired from clinical practice, I sought a way to communicate the joys and challenges of surgical practice to the lay public. So, Narrative Medicine.

What is Narrative Medicine? You can think of it as the intersection between the humanities and medical practice, and also as a set of tools that facilitate incorporation of the humanities into medical training. It is both of these and more (6).

I recently led a Narrative Medicine session for a group of pediatrics residents. I use a Narrative Medicine session format that incorporates three elements: close reading of a short piece of literature, a period of quiet reflective writing – that is, writing in response to a prompt, and then time to share what is written. Sharing is completely voluntary. No preparation is required, and there is no homework. All this is done in a little under an hour.

For this particular session, I used a stanza from the William Carlos Williams poem: "The young doctor is dancing with happiness/in the sparkling wind, along/at the prow of the ferry!" The stanza concludes with just one more sentence. The entire stanza is just two sentences, each ending with an exclamation point.

We discussed this poem for about 15 minutes, speculating about the setting, and the source of the doctor's happiness. Where was he going on the ferry? Perhaps to meet a loved one. Maybe to a new job. Possibly on vacation. Why dancing? Why a doctor? Why alone?

Then I gave them the writing prompt, "Write about a time when you felt like dancing with happiness." Some wrote from the hospital environment, but most wrote about profound personal experiences, such as the birth of a child. We shared what we had written. As usual, some shared, but others did not. There's no pressure to share.

At the conclusion of the hour, one resident said, "We don't talk about joy enough."

Think about that. "We don't talk about joy enough."

It seems to me as surgeons we have two sources of joy – our personal lives and our professional ones. Within the hospital environment, we surgeons find joy in what we do for patients and in the exercise of our skill. A surgeon whom I respect greatly put it this way in a recent email, "It's the great results that are joyful, whether a cosmetic surgery or a life-saving one. Seeing the patients' results is a joy for me."

I recently asked a pediatric surgery colleague what his favorite operation was. What operation did he enjoy doing most? I thought about all of the difficult and life-saving operations he must perform on tiny infants, and I wondered if he would choose one of these. Perhaps the repair of a diaphragmatic hernia, esophageal atresia, or malrotation. He told me that he gets the most satisfaction from doing a simple pyloromyotomy for hypertrophic pyloric stenosis. The improvement is dramatic, immediate, and life-changing for both the small patient and the family. Everyone is happy.

I became curious, so I queried our American College of Surgeons discussion group members, asking, "What is your absolutely favorite operation? And, if you have time, why?" It was a totally unscientific survey. I primed the pump by confessing that I had always loved to drain pus.

I was amazed by the results. Some surgeons wrote of delicate or technically demanding operations such as a Whipple or a parathyroidectomy or carotid endarterectomy. Several wrote eloquently of their satisfaction with life-changing operations, particularly for patients who had no other recourse. These were not necessarily dramatic "saves," rather they were operations that made a significant difference in a patient's life. One surgeon said that on a global outreach mission he repaired a scrotal hernia that "went down to the knees" and then he recounted the satisfaction of seeing the man walk away, unencumbered, afterwards. Some mentioned that their favorite operation was whatever they were doing at the time. One surgeon cited the pleasure of helping a resident do their first case.

Many wrote to remind us that regardless of each surgeon's favorite operation or expertise, of course, the focus is not on the surgeon, but on the patient. This leads directly to my first recommendation: Focus on the patient, not on yourself. In the early 1900s, Berkeley Moynihan of Leeds said, "The most important person present at an operation is the patient. This is a truth not everywhere and always remembered."(7)

Focus on task, not self. This simple advice was given, year after year, to our surgical residents by our program director at the University of Iowa, Dr William "John" Sharp. This helps avoid endless rumination about how much you wish you could get a cup of coffee, get home on time, grab a bite to eat, or even a quick pit stop. I've invoked it myself during long nights on trauma call.

Don't lose sight of the miraculous. The unexpected save, or the everyday things we take for granted. Cultivate a quality of mindfulness.

A hospital chaplain, allowed to observe a kidney transplant, later told me that urine started to come out of the ureter as soon as the blood vessels were attached and the surgeon said, "Look, it is making pee!" She said that she felt she was standing upon sacred ground.

Talk with your patients. Find out their priorities and their concerns. We surgeons speak truth. Blunt and plain-spoken to a fault, we are sometimes criticized for that. Yet who among us has not been called to the bedside of a patient and taken on the hard duty of explaining, to patient and family, that intervention is futile? The very concept of palliative care has grown from this sort of honest discussion of alternatives. When you make evening rounds, take the time to sit down at the bedside. Hold out your hand. Often, the patient will reach out and grasp your hand with theirs. I loved to feel those warm fingers in mine, the strength of the grasp, the human touch.

Cherish your loved ones. Take care of each other.

Reach out to colleagues and peers. Avoid isolation. Consider the nurses and others in your hospital as colleagues; you are all working together to help patients.

Remember the "second victim." Reach out to colleagues who may have been affected by medical error or death. Don't retreat into a cocoon if you are the one so affected.

Make time for your own spiritual life, whatever that may be. Take time at day's end to make a list, or simply remember, things that you are grateful for. Cultivate compassion, and maintain a sense of humor. Develop resilience, the quality that is often cited as an antidote to burnout.

Take time to teach. When we teach, we nurture our own souls as well as those of our students. The very word "doctor" derived from the Latin word for teacher. If you are in an academic position, then teaching is an integral part of your tripartite mission. One of Dr. Olga Jonasson's many strengths was her infectious enthusiasm and ability as an inspiring teacher.

Teaching is like watering a garden – both the garden and the gardener are nurtured. Even if you do not work in academics, take time to teach. Teach everyone around you. Of course, educate your patients and their families, but also teach the nurses, the aides, the CRNAs. Share your knowledge in little moments of enlightenment. And be prepared to listen and to learn yourself, in those quiet minutes of collegial conversation with physicians in other specialties.

Seek opportunities to educate the lay public. Whether it is through "Stop the Bleed," a few words at half-time during a "think pink" women's basketball game, or a course on surgical anatomy for senior citizens, get the word out.

If you are close to a medical school, volunteer to help in simulation labs, the ATOM (Advanced Trauma Operative Management) course, ATLS or other formal activities. If you are not close to a medical school, you are probably rural, so consider allowing a medical student to shadow you as part of a rural elective.

Consider surgical volunteerism. Learn about the American College of Surgeon's initiative called "Operation Giving Back." Surgeons who have done this state that it gives you a new perspective on the "third world" problems that we face.

Be prepared to periodically reinvent yourself, and to see these reinventions as opportunities to explore new terrain. I tell our trainees and students that you will need to do this about every five or so years. The necessity for reinvention may come from within – as your practice changes, or from technical innovation in your area of practice.

Technical innovation can be explosive and cataclysmic, or it can be evolutionary. I, and most older general surgeons have experienced both. In 1987, the first laparoscopic cholecystectomy was performed. The world of general surgery underwent a seismic change. Until then, laparoscopy had been primarily a gynecologist's tool, used for diagnostic purposes by a small number of visionary surgeons. Cholecystectomy was, and is, one of the most common operations performed by general surgeons. It was done through a big incision. The new operation came into widespread use without the benefit of institutional review boards or randomized clinical trials. We learned a lot from that experience and do things better now, I believe.

How do you learn new skills? You build upon old skills, you fall back upon transferrable skills, you read everything you can, and you take every advantage of training opportunities given through national organizations such as the ACS. You seek mentors and proctors. When I was learning how to do laparoscopic cholecystectomy, my proctor was a supremely skilled gynecological laparoscopist who was facile in performing difficult laparoscopic pelvic dissections for infertility.

Laparoscopic cholecystectomy required acquisition of a completely new skill set. Most changes have not been that cataclysmic, and a more typical example might be the continued evolution of breast surgery. For those of us who trained in the late 1970s, lumpectomy, image-guided biopsy, sentinel lymph node biopsy, and nipple-sparing mastectomy replaced the modified radical mastectomy we were taught to do. But these skills were an extension of those already learned.

General surgeons who have taken trauma call and used ultrasound for FAST (focused abdominal sonography for trauma) exams or to facilitate line placement are well-positioned to add breast ultrasound to their repertoire. A basic ultrasound course, taken online through the ACS, coupled with hands-on courses at the American Society of Breast Surgeons and a case log allows one to attain certification.

My point is this: Just as suturing and knot-tying are transferrable skills, so are facility with ultrasound and other fundamental techniques. This makes accommodating evolutionary change in our practice a bit easier.

Our surgical societies are providing and must continue to provide training opportunities for surgeons whose practice pattern changes, or who wish to bring new techniques to their community. We need to be nimble, to anticipate and produce high quality educational offerings that facilitate skills acquisition by moving, as we do during a difficult dissection, from known to unknown.

Don't forget that part of change requires you as a surgeon to keep current on multidisciplinary management. Neoadjuvant therapy to downstage malignancy and permit less mutilating surgery has drastically changed our approach to cancer at a variety of sites. Accurate risk assessment allows better patient counseling.

Seek additional education in management, leadership, teaching, and other "non-medical" issues. Take advantage of short courses at national meetings – these are typically a day or even just a half-day. Distance learning and on-line courses are available to augment your knowledge in almost any area. Low-residency MBA, MPH, or MHA programs are available at many of the big-name schools. Consider your tuition to be an investment in your own future.

Cherish diversity and each other. View your individual differences as sources of strength, rather than weakness.

Reinvigorate meetings of your county medical society – at the very least, it allows collegial interaction with other specialists, and at the best it provides an avenue, through the state medical society and the American Medical Association (AMA), to advocate for legislative and systemic change. Changes must also occur at the institutional level, and you can be part of that change. Seek leadership opportunities by becoming involved in the various committees of your hospital.

Similarly, participate in the state chapter of the ACS. It can provide a wonderful forum for networking, sharing views, and advocating for change.

The ACS provides ample opportunities at the national level as well. Simply by coming to the Fall Clinical Congress and, more importantly, talking with your peers from other parts of the US and even the rest of the world, you are influencing the future and helping your own career. Keep coming. Take advantage of the postgraduate courses,

I would urge you to say "yes" to every opportunity your professional life offers. The standard advice to young surgeons starting out is, say "no" – or, perhaps more accurately, be careful not to over-extend yourself. Time appears to be a fixed quality – there are only 24 hours in a day – but it is a highly elastic one. The old saying, "work expands to fill the time available" can be turned on its head, and you can find the time to do work that you love. Both the ACS and the AMA have initiatives designed to transform health care. Get involved in these efforts. Volunteer, participate, and reinvigorate yourself.

Don't assume that you are too young, too old, or inherently not qualified. If you are interested, put your name forward or have a colleague do so. If you are turned down, just do it again with another group. Remember that you may be rejected for what seems like a trivial reason – wrong specialty, or wrong region of the country.

I often invoke the "rule of 3s" – one out of three tries will succeed. If you succeed every time, you aren't aiming high enough. If you never succeed, you need to re-examine your goals. But if you can succeed one out of three times, you are doing well. Rejection is part of life, not necessarily something to be feared.

Make time for wellness. Find a way to incorporate stress-relieving physical exercise in your daily routine, even if all you can do is park your car at the far end of the parking lot and walk briskly to and from the hospital. The University of Iowa Hospitals and Clinics, where I practiced until retirement and continue to teach, has miles and miles of corridors and sky walks. I bet your hospital does too. Follow good health habits. Find and use a good primary care physician.

Make room in your life for the humanities and creativity. One of our hospital chaplains (not the one I mentioned previously) always carried small pieces of paper with short poems printed on them. She'd pull one out and hand it to you saying, "Here's a pocket poem." How long does it take to read a pocket poem? Or to write a brief poem yourself, draw a quick sketch, or pull out your smart phone and take a photograph of rabbit tracks in the fresh snow or the sun shining through autumn leaves?

If you are in the latter half of your career, think about and prepare for retirement. Find ways to stay involved. Modify your practice, if necessary, to accommodate the inevitable changes of aging. Cultivate other interests.

If you are just starting out, take charge of your career and shape it to the form you wish it to assume. I've spent my entire life in academics, and it's been a wonderful journey. I've trained surgeons who went on to become academic leaders, and surgeons who went into small rural practices. I'm proud of all of them. Whatever you do, devote yourself to your patients, your family, your job, and your community.

Women who have chosen surgery as their vocation are exceptionally well-qualified to cultivate the sense of joy and to pass it along to students who may be considering a career in medicine in general, or in the surgical specialties. We were drawn to a career in surgery not because it was easy or expected, but because of our passion for the art and science. Let's use that passion as a catalyst to change the system, our institutions, and our lives for the better.

Our interventions as surgeons forever change lives – not just those of our patients, but also their families and sometimes we affect the very fabric of a community. We need to fight back vigorously, both individually and collectively, against the forces that would stifle our sense of wonder and reduce us to mere technicians. We stand, you stand, at the intersection between disease and wellness, offering if not cure, at least significant improvement.

Acknowledgements: I would like to thank Donna Coulombe, Senior Special Projects Manager, American College of Surgeons, who graciously shared material and memories with me. I would also like to thank the ACS Archivist, Meghan Kennedy.

REFERENCES – Note that this is a highly abridged list. For the full lecture, including all references, please see: Scott-Conner CEH, Olga Jonasson MD Lecture: "Recapturing the joy of surgery." Bulletin of the American College of Surgeons volume 105 #2: https://bulletin.facs.org/2020/02/olga-m-jonasson-md-lecture-recapturing-the-joy-of-surgery/

1. Ofri, Danielle. The Business of Health Care Depends on Exploiting Doctors and Nurses. *The New York Times*, June 8, 2019. https://www.nytimes.com/2019/06/08/opinion/sunday/hospitals-doctors-nurses-burnout.html (accessed October 2019).
2. Balch CM, Shanafelt T. Combating Stress and Burnout in Surgical Practice: A Review. *Advances in Surgery* 2010;44:29-47.
3. National Academies of Sciences, Engineering, and Medicine. 2019. Taking Action Against Clinician Burnout: A Systems Approach to Professional Well-Being. Washington DC: The National Academies Press. Downloadable at: https://www.nap.edu/catalog/25521/taking-action-against-clinician-burnout-a-systems-approach-to-professional (accessed October 2019).
4. Dean W, Talbot S, and Dean A. Reframing Clinician Distress: Moral Injury Not Burnout. *Federal Practitioner* 2019; 400-402.

5. Bohnen JD, Lillemoe KD, Mort EA, Kaafarani HMA. When Things Go Wrong: The Surgeon as Second Victim. *Ann Surg* 2019;269(5): 808-9.
6. Charon R, Hermann N, Devlin MJ. Close Reading and Creative Writing in Clinical Education: Teaching Attention, Representation, and Affiliation. *Acad Med* 2016;91: 345-50.
7. Bateman, D. *Berkeley Moynihan, Surgeon.* New York, The Macmillian Company, 1940, 148-149 (available online at: https://catalog.hathitrust.org/Record/001576150 Accessed October 2019).

Writing with Dr. Carol Scott-Conner

KERRI GOERS

Sunlight poured into the atrium of the University of Iowa Medical Education Research Facility. In the center of the atrium, at a round table for four, sat Dr. Carol Scott-Conner with her messenger bag and bike helmet next to her on the floor. She was eating a sandwich and reading *The New York Times* book review of *Heart: A History* by Sandeep Jauhar. She pointed to the screen as I approached and announced that a heart could pump enough blood in one week to fill a swimming pool and then shook her head in amazement. A true anatomist, she appreciates this type of detail, the wonder which is the heart. I sat down, joining Carol at her table for a talk.

The first time I saw Carol, she was part of a panel of editors speaking at The Examined Life Conference. A few years later, as luck would have it, she welcomed me, a virtual stranger, into her medical writing group, and I became acquainted with Carol's literary side. I had no idea how accomplished she was as a physician.

Carol earned a Bachelor of Science in Electrical Engineering at Massachusetts Institute of Technology in 1969, her Medical Degree from New York University School of Medicine in 1976, and was Chief Resident at the New York University Medical Center, where she completed her Surgical Residency. She holds a Ph.D. in Anatomy and Cell Biology from the University of Kentucky and an MBA from the Else School of Management at Millsaps College in Jackson, Mississippi. She served as the Head of the Department of Surgery at The University of Iowa beginning in 1995, one of only two females to have been appointed to a surgical department head nationwide at that time. She has served on numerous committees, including NASA's Committee on Aerospace Medicine and Medicine of Extreme Environment.

Carol is the author or editor of nine surgical textbooks and one collection of short stories: A Few Small Moments (Rachel Lord Press). She has been the author or co-author of over 125 scholarly papers and is the former Editor-In-Chief of *The Examined Life: A Literary Journal of the Carver College of Medicine*. Carol retired four years ago about which she said, "I felt like it was time to let other people do the patient care." She still maintains her certification with the American Board of Surgery, teaches the first-year medical students, and remains the Fiction Editor for *The Examined Life Journal*.

Despite her many credentials, Carol is an unassuming, unpretentious person with a relaxed and self-assured countenance. I asked her about the driving force that has kept her moving forward. "I'll tell you a story that I don't tell everybody," she said. "When I was in college, I married a young man by the name of Chris Scott, he was extraordinarily gifted and brilliant, but he died four years after we were married. So, I felt like somehow, I had to live for both of us, you know what I mean? I had to fulfill *his* promise, and he was a lot brighter than I was. That was a big part of the initial impetus. After that, moving forward became a habit."

However, moving forward wasn't always easy. "When he died," Carol said, "I had been trying to get into medical school, but I couldn't get in because they had quotas for women back in those days. I had pretty much given up. People would actually say in an interview, 'Why should I take you? If I take you, I can't take a man who might get drafted, sent to Vietnam, and come home in a body bag.' How do you argue with that? It was true; it was absolutely true." She shook her head and stared out the window as she spoke. "I was going to take my engineering degree and work in engineering, but Chris had encouraged me to keep trying. I finally got in. In medical school, I remarried. My present husband, my second husband, we've been married for 44 years, so it's almost as if that was a different life, but that was what got me going."

"What made you interested in pursuing medicine?" I asked. She told me her plan had always been to practice medicine. Her father had been supportive of her goal to attend medical school, although he thought doctoring was dirty work. "It *is* messy," she said with a smile. Her dad had told her "that doctors are going to be increasingly dependent on different kinds of equipment, machinery, and electronics, and they don't understand anything about it. So, I did engineering, but I wanted to be a doctor all along." She followed her medical degree with a Ph.D. in Anatomy and Cell Biology. "That helped a lot with my research. And when I decided I wanted to be chair of the department of surgery, I needed the management training, so I went back again to night school and got an MBA. I think going back to school was wonderful; being treated like a student, it's so nice."

In her early days of being a surgeon, there was a lot to learn. She wanted to pursue academic medicine and found that writing was one of the keys to success. Her first mentor told her she needed to write and write she did. When asked about the volume of work she produced, she replied, "Some people will wind up with a whole lot more than I did, but I had a respectable amount. It becomes a habit in terms of thinking whether this is something worth writing about and if I should write about it. I always thought that writing was a way to teach other surgeons, teach them about an unusual complication or a new technique."

Carol's writing has expanded outside of academic papers and textbooks into creative writing. This is the side of Carol Scott-Conner that I know. The intellectual who sits in our medical writing group and encourages those around her with generous support. Despite her skill as a surgeon and her success as a writer, she is always optimistic and able to see the potential in a piece of writing. I asked her when she switched over to creative work. "About 15 years ago. A lot of people kept coming up to me in meetings, you know, senior male surgeons, and they would say, 'I have a daughter who wants to be a surgeon. Is there something I can give her to read?' When I thought about what there was for young surgeons to read, most of the memoirs that are out there that women surgeons have written, tell about how hard it was and how badly they were treated. And I thought I don't want to do that. So, I decided to do stories, set them in the medical environment, and to try to make it seem normal that there was a female surgeon. Just to show that it's normal. To show the joys and the frustrations of life as a surgeon. Hopefully, more joys than frustrations. So that's when I started to write, and then I got hooked."

Carol admits that novel writing was difficult. "I just didn't understand about story arc; it just wasn't any good. So, I cut up pieces of it and made it into short stories. It was kind of an episodic novel anyway. And then I got the bug to get them published. For every acceptance, I probably got twenty or thirty rejections. Later, I started to think, well then, I can put them together. It's like putting them back together in this different shape, and you leave things out, and you put things in." The surgeon in her cut apart her work and stitched it back together, and her book, *A Few Small Moments*, emerged. The preface reads, "My life as a woman in surgery has been a tapestry of many small moments. Each moment, sad or happy, has been fraught with significance." It's divided into "Part I: From the Ivory Tower" and "Part II: From the Heart." Although the stories are fictional, they resonate with wisdom that one associates with experience. Carol's medical writing educates and teaches future surgeons what they need to know. Her creative writing helps us to feel, to know maybe just a bit, what it's like to be a surgeon.

She was once quoted as saying, "Surgery is a wonderful way to help people directly. You have an immediate impact. It combines knowledge of the human body with the art of using your hands and mind to help another person." This generosity of spirit, this willingness to reach out and help others, is characteristic of who Carol is.

As we concluded the interview, I was left with the confirmation that there are some incredible role models in the world around us. People like Dr. Carol Scott-Conner demonstrate resilience and determination. They teach us not to be discouraged when things become challenging. They teach us to be generous and kind towards others.

Carol may be done, in a large part, with her medical work, but she is still writing and is even debating starting her memoirs. She continues to delight in learning something new and views the world with curiosity. I look forward to more meetings with her in our little writers' group.

Cracked, but not Broken

MICHAEL MCGUIRE

Everyone, or almost everyone, knows that the performer, even the soloist, is, at times, elsewhere or, it could be said, is, at such times, nowhere, nowhere at all.

Just as he, or she, is all sexes and none, all races and none, so he or she, young, old and ageless, is a presence and, at the same time, an absence, putting in, at his or her best moments, a nonappearance, at least as long as the pure notes rise.

Though it would be going too far, or not far enough, to consider the performer, the soloist, mere medium, for he must find his instrument, then, as a dedicated parent might note, make the payments, not to mention tune the thing, play it, learn, with the years, what is within it, and what isn't, if only because he doesn't know how to find it.

Yet.

Now, however, the time has come and, maybe, this is the very moment in which our young man must learn that, as he is nowhere, so he is no one and, within limits, everyone and, with his handful of years—for one can hold onto, for an absurdly long time, the hope that he, or she, will, one day, perhaps in keeping with someone else's hopes and desires, be someone with a capital "s" before the word—see where that leaves him.

Yes, possibly, that is what this is all about.

*

Two brothers. Both exceptional. Together, perhaps the *patrimonio* of their not untalented father, they were, very nearly, prodigies if, perhaps, one more than the other.

Xavier, a little less of a prodigy, played, if somewhat systematically, the piano. Ysmael, a little more of a prodigy, played the violin, played it, practically from the womb for, the first time he had picked up his chosen instrument, or, rather, the one that had been chosen for him, he drew a somber melody from it, one that raised, or lowered, all heads within hearing.

For years, the brothers seemed well along their respective paths until, one day, just when Ysmael was about to depart on his first tour, while Xavier plugged away at the regional orchestra, he, Ysmael, disappeared. At first, the family thought he had been kidnapped, for the country was not without its criminal element. His mother called various agencies and had the police on the lookout for him in several states.

To no avail.

Suddenly, however, he showed up, or was found. Nevertheless, whatever had possessed him during those days of absence, had not let go. Ysmael was not Ysmael. He wasn't really anybody else. He seemed, they said, not altogether there, as if he were that which *mamá* would never have wished for either of her boys, nobody.

Nobody at all or, at the most, a somebody with a very small "s," one who refused to speak to anybody, as if silence had, suddenly, become his chosen medium.

Mamá, immediately, for she was not incapable and she loved her sons, both of them, had him put in an institution where they were supposed to know how to deal with these things and she told her other son, Ysmael's brother Xavier, to visit him, to have long talks; to find out, if the experts couldn't, what the matter was.

"No, *mamá,* Ysmael has gone his way, I have gone mine. I'm not going to talk with him. You talk with him. I have other engagements. As you know we, the orchestra, perform every week. Unlike my more talented brother, I cannot be in two places at once...assuming he's anywhere at all. Not, myself, a soloist, I may have a small part in the scheme of things, but it is essential. I cannot let my colleagues down."

Mamá could not believe what she had just heard. They were both her sons. Each, in his way, took after his not untalented father, *en paz descanse*, for the man had drunk himself to death in search of the peace she had not been able to give him. The capable brothers, quick learners both, were not that far apart in years and had, as children, played together at children's games, even before they applied themselves to their respective instruments. What's more, they were friends. But, being, basically, a peaceful, agreeable person, *mamá* did not argue. She did as Xavier suggested. She went to visit Ysmael in the institution to which he had been sent.

The bus rides were bad enough, one following another until, deeper into apprehension, into despair, than she had been when she started out, she found herself in a half-built-up area few visited that the powers that be, in their wisdom, had thought might be just right for the nut cases of this world.

El Hospital Psiquiátrico, when she found it, was worse. Rough gray concrete on the outside, and inside... Unclean. Didn't the—what did they call them: the disturbed?—appreciate and deserve, yes deserve—in fact, need, at least as a kind of starting point—cleanliness?

Within its greasy peeling walls it was no wonder she was soon lost. Faded arrows and indecipherable words pointed down endless halls, up innumerable stairways, in a way that seemed designed to confuse. Perhaps they had been added by the inmates themselves. But the building itself was, apparently, empty. Had they escaped? Had the authorities never really accepted any? Had the loonies been pulled in one door, a word or two, perhaps only a number hung round their necks or stenciled on their foreheads, and shoved out another?

Mamá wondered, if there might be, since the bus rides had been very close to interminable, perhaps a bathroom somewhere, but no.

Passing one room, she heard a kind of moaning within and couldn't resist a peek in a little window that was hanging half open. There—it took her a moment to identify the sex—was a girl with nothing on, squatting, her arms round her knees, rocking, rocking back and forth. It was her tuneless moaning *mamá* had heard. It did not stop. It continued as long as she stood there staring, and something in its rhythm suggested a desperate composition, one the girl might be working on day after day, night after night, until someone, or something, took pity on her and put an end to it.

Here was a young woman, thought *mamá,* not much more than a child, really, who would never know the lightness, the weight, of love, of motherhood, but was already locked in a kind of absence, one in which there was not, and never would be, any role that must be, if only for the sake of someone else, played.

There was no furniture. The walls, the floor, cold damp concrete, gave the feeling of just having been hosed down.

Repressing an impulse to see if the door could be opened, to go in and put her arms around the girl or, at least, talk to her through the little window, to comfort her, *mamá* pulled herself away and continued down a hall relatively free of fading arrows and indecipherable directions.

She took a turn she had to take, for the hall, at the end, went only one way, descended one unavoidable stairway and ascended another until, at last, she found herself in a passageway lined with patients. Every one of them dressed in the same gray, everyone with something like the same look on his face and every one of them male.

Packed on benches they seemed deadened, if not dead, hardly alert to anything at all, though one or two heard the echo of *mamá's* footsteps and, watching all too closely, as if they hadn't seen a female in years, never mind her age, rubbed their crotches as she passed. Hurrying, she asked herself how her more talented, her, if not quite prodigy, of a son could, ever, possibly, have arrived at this dead end. It was not a question that would easily be answered, though her first impulse was to blame not him, nor his long dead father, but herself and to wonder what—what?—she could possibly have done wrong—that wrong—or at least done otherwise.

Eventually, a lone male nurse took her and led her to a desk where they were able, after some mumbling among themselves, to direct *mamá* to her son. More precisely, they directed her to a room where she waited until Ysmael, not unaccompanied, appeared. She stood, he paused. They did not rush into each other's arms. His face, though she was sure hers did, hardly changed. Perhaps he blamed her for his present situation. *Mamá* knew, from experience, how children's minds worked, but Ysmael was no longer a child. He had been out in the big world, made his own way, had a tour coming up, one in which he would play a well known stage or two, perhaps, even, stay at one of the legendary old hotels, that is if he could pull himself together. Suddenly, in spite of his reputed silence, her son was all words.

"I was expecting you, *mamá,* why didn't you come earlier?"

Before she could respond, Ysmael continued. "Not that it would have made any difference. I'm no different now from what I was a couple of days ago, no different from what I will be in a couple more." Here he paused, even took a step closer. "Oh, I know. It was really, all, just beginning. My name in lights, on lips in concert halls around the world. But, a couple of days ago, though, really, it had been building for years, the matter…whatever it was, perhaps no more than a shadow, a shadow of something that wasn't even there…overwhelmed.

"But here I am. I am, aren't I?" he added. "You see me, don't you?"

"I do," managed *mamá,* who was close to urinating where she stood and being led to and sat in the hall she would sit in the rest of her days.

"I know," continued Ysmael, "this shouldn't have happened to me until I had, really, given my all for a few more years. Then, in a couple of decades, it would have been appreciated, perhaps even understood, why I couldn't go on, why I lost it. Why I cracked."

"Are you..." *mamá* could hardly get the word out "…cracked?"

"Cracked, but not broken," said Ysmael.

"Well, that's something," said *mamá* encouragingly. Here she looked at the man, a faceless man, if with an undeniable presence, standing against the wall. "Isn't there somewhere, anywhere, we can sit down?" she asked.

"Not permitted," or something like that, said the man, with the mouth that wasn't there.

"No, they don't want these meetings going on too long," said Ysmael. "Next thing you'll be asking if guests are permitted at our more formal dinners, whether the tablecloths are spotlessly white, the candles lit, if the accommodations are up to snuff. You want to see my room, don't you?"

"No, I..." began *mamá,* picturing the girl in her hosed down cell, but could only get out something quite different. "How, how, do you know all these things?"

"My brother Xavier, your son Xavier—you remember him?"

"I do."

"Yes, my somewhat, my slightly, less talented brother, was here before you. In fact, if I have the century right, he was here yesterday."

"But he..."

"He changed his mind. He knew he'd said some impatient things to you when you asked him to visit me for long talks, to find out what was eating me, but he regretted all that. He came, finally, with open arms, to see how his younger... You remember I'm the younger brother?"

"Yes."

"...was doing...behind bars."

"And how are you doing...behind bars?" asked *mamá,* though the small of her back and the backs of her legs were tightening and she could feel the cold of the concrete and something else, like a great hand, slowly rising, reaching for her heart.

"As well as could be expected," said Ysmael, graciously. "I am, and will always be, grateful for your love. For his too, Xavier's."

"I'm glad you're aware of that. Listen, Ysmael..." said *mamá,* deciding it was time to take control of the situation, at least in so far as it could be taken control of. "Enough of this nonsense. Have they, since we managed to get you in here, figured out what's wrong with you? And what do we have to do to get you out?"

"Cross your fingers, I guess," said Ysmael, and added "if they have figured out what's wrong with me, they've kept it to themselves. No, for the moment, there's nothing...nothing you can do for me. Well, perhaps one."

"Time's up," said the man with his back against the wall, though he hadn't, as far as *mamá* could see from the corner of her eye, even glanced at his watch which, if he had one, was, probably, as faceless as he.

"The time is up when I'm ready to go," said mamá to the man. "Tell me, Ysmael," she asked, taking a step toward her more talented son, "what I can do for you. There is, as you were saying, perhaps one thing I…"

"Bring me my violin."

"Bring you your… But, will it be safe here? It wasn't cheap, you know."

"Oh, I know. I know. You never let us forget the price of our respective instruments, did you?"

Mamá ignored, as usual, all references to her…well, yes, of necessity… her perfectionism. How else was she supposed to serve her sons' talents if not with the best, the best? But she couldn't help asking…

"And what business has my more talented son, my, yes, my prodigy, got playing in a madhouse? This isn't Carnegie Hall."

"It isn't even *el Teatro Degollado.* I just want to play. *Mamá,* please..!"

*

And so *mamá,* promising to bring Ysmael's violin, backed out of the room, not wanting to lose sight of him until, he supposed, he really was 'gone.'

And, a few days later, there he was, very nearly a kind of trustee, if a relatively young one—not considered a danger to himself or others—wandering the halls, the stairwells—a little too much reverberation there—as well as the yard out back, wall to wall—and he was beginning to learn what wall to wall meant—concrete, where his associates seemed quite pleased to listen to him play. In any case, they didn't mind. Nor did they, in the one gray room that had one, turn up the television. Perhaps they were…it certainly appeared to be the case…reflecting upon the music they had never in their lives, however much time they had on their hands, had a chance to listen to.

True, it was not the tour he had lined up, not that many days ago, but it was better than nothing. And playing, whether there were handshakes, deep bows (his hand on his heart) and encores or not, gave Ysmael time to think.

Where, so soon—and so young—had he gone wrong? Where had he, so to speak, taken a wrong turn? It couldn't have been somewhere between the wrong hallway and the wrong stairwell, for he had been speeding down the wrong road before they put him here. Surely *mamá,* he reflected, for he knew how his mother's mind worked, had asked herself, essentially, the same question, but it had now, obviously, fallen to him to figure this one out for himself.

Let's see now, thought Ysmael...

One day, one eye on some of his awards, his citations, that nearly covered one wall, and the other on the calendar, he was practicing. The next... Well, the next, he was walking out the door. Then, somehow, he was on the back road to the coast, the one where the police had been ambushed not that long ago and, as they say, "disappeared." He might as well, he concluded, when consciousness returned, continue on the road he found himself on. Persevere. That was what he had always done, wasn't it? And it had gotten him quite far, hadn't it? On his way, as it were.

At least until he lost it.

So Ysmael found himself a cheap hotel, one in which you wouldn't know the continent ended in half a block, that, if he walked that way—he knew this, somehow, even before he did it—the unfathomable ocean would rise like a backdrop, only coming out at you in some variation on reverse perspective and, just the way Orozco would have done it, reaching, reaching just for you. For him. He avoided the bars where lost souls sipped tropical cocktails, the beaches where beauties covered little more than a tuft of hair.

Ysmael walked, instead, the loneliest of seashores. He listened to the surf at its most mournful, in the late, or early, hours, when only a determined strip of white could be seen cracking the darkness, rushing landwards, fingering the sand at his feet, emitting a low rumble that merged, imperceptibly, into an intimate whisper, as if confiding to him, Ysmael, the fact that it, the sea, would, in the end, prevail. If he'd had his violin he would have played it, improvising in response to the weight of water slamming into the sand, precipitating a shudder he felt as if it were his own.

What would it be like, he asked himself, to feel the darkness of the sea close overhead? There was no way to know, of course, without trying it. It couldn't be, simply, nothingness, for there was, also, something there. Yes, if not quite a personality, an undeniable presence. Something in it, in the sea, comparable to music. The sea, he noted, was never silent, well, almost never.

As a musician, Ysmael appreciated silence. It was more than golden. It wasn't only there just before and, again, just at the end of the piece he would offer to it. It was there between each and every note. There was more, or less, of it, that was all. For a moment, Ysmael envied Xavier, his slightly less talented brother, his instrument, for surely the piano was better equipped to value silence than the violin.

But what if, he, Ysmael, were to put down his instrument, to never play again? Would a sea of silence rush in to finger the earth he stood on? Or... Would it slam itself into the continent as a shiver rose to, and from, the pit of his stomach? No, a bus would screech, a woman would laugh, some poor bastard, spending yet another night in the street, would moan, the bad, bad music of mankind would rise above it all and, so to speak, drown it.

But who was he, Ysmael, still thinking for himself, wondered, even to raise such questions? He was no philosopher. But...

If, one night, he took a step into the surf, and another, and felt the cold, cold fingers rise about his ankles, his shins, just as he had already felt them... rise and let go...

What then?

Cold at the surface, yet colder still, and the impulse, the instinct, to inhale ever greater, though he would have to exhale first that from which, he supposed, he had taken all there was to take, and darker, ever darker, a darkness that light itself could only penetrate so far and, strangely, in motion, in motion with a force of its own and who was he to say that that motion, that which, if it had not always had, now had him in its grip, was not, in its way, life itself?

But, there is motion, too, Ysmael reflected, in the hand that slides the bow or fingers the keys, and the night in which he couldn't close his ears, or wish them closed, passed, as well as the next night and the next, nights in which he stood there, beyond self, looking at the selfless sea with its undeniable presence. Looking at and listening to.

But, having turned his back upon its siren call—for the silence that follows that is all too easily found—Ysmael found himself or, more to the point, his mother and those she had marshaled in his search, found him, and he was spirited—yes, that was the word, spirited—to *El Hospital Psiquiátri*co, though, more likely, it was titled after one of the pioneers of mental health, whatever that is, a someone with a capital letter.

No doubt, there it was, etched in stone over the door...Ysmael just hadn't noticed as they led him in...the man's name on an institution he would never, were he not safely dead, have approved of.

Now Ysmael was in his room, behind a barred window, which had nothing to do with the bars—a way of marking time, of course—of the music he still considered to be the language of life, life itself, if life could speak. *Mamá* had come again and gone again—she wasn't coming back, he knew it, she couldn't stand it there—and Xavier, his somewhat less talented brother, hadn't time.

Considering, once more, time—for calendars, apparently, were no more allowed than clocks in a building which was, like the sea, not without its distinctive sounds, its smells; a building in which your peace with the world must be, if slightly delayed, imminent—Ysmael knew...in his hands, in his fingers...that the time for his tour had come and gone and...in the pit of his stomach, if not deeper...that it didn't really matter.

It was, there it was, once more, or soon would be, time to begin again. From the beginning. Perchance, as the moment in which the world would come to a stop, the moment in which he would release his spellbinding, his unforgettable, solo, had come and gone, the time had come, at last, for the duet he had always been telling himself that he must, with his brother, one day play.

'You mustn't think of it, Xavier, as accompaniment, the pianist accompanying the real soloist who is playing the violin but, as in a trio, or a quartet, the instruments being equal, equal...'

'Then I must not be,' Xavier most graciously responds, 'the less talented brother, at least for this one night, the night of our duet.'

'I'll be the first to admit *mamá* never got exactly what she wanted out of either of us, when we were young, younger,' Ysmael is about to observe, but Xavier is going on...

'Yes, it will be as a twosome we will wow the world and *mamá* will be forced to consider us—and our instruments—an investment well made and, finally, for she will still be alive, a timely one.'

Here, the silence which, even in the moment before an imagined concert, the silence that is very nearly always waiting in the wings, very nearly falls.

But Xavier, showing his teeth, as he is prone to do when he is about to play his piano and Ysmael is about to play his violin, continues his monologue, his solo, 'yes, a certain opportunity—for you anyway—having come and gone, perhaps forever, it will be in our middle age, we shall do—together—that which prodigies so rarely do.'

Here Ysmael opens his mouth to continue the wordplay, the banter, the jousting that is always there, between brothers, but Xavier, not yet finished, presses on 'and then, arrangements made, the impresario tempted or, at a minimum, the deposit on the hall made, the flyers out, word-of-mouth doing its thing, we, you and I, shall, at the end of our days and better late than never...'

But here, the Xavier of the mind, of the imagination, falls silent, as Ysmael wonders if the time has come to cling to the bars of time and scream, but no, that moment, he realizes, has also come and gone. Now it is time, at last, for the silence, however short-lived, that comes before the gathering of forces that heralds every effort, every note about to be played, in the world out there, as in the world within.

Though perhaps Ysmael, having concluded his fanciful dialogue with his brother is, in his mind, which is, after all, beginning to recover, to, without that much help from those who were supposed to be of help, heal itself, is still going over that last night on the beach, one in which he, with the help of natural sounds, natural silences, began, for himself only, of course, to straighten it all out; to see, clearly enough, the difference between the spotlight others wish for us, that which we have taken in, in some cases, with our mothers' milk, and the relative obscurity demanded by the daily labor, if not by the instrument itself, that which waits, within, for one who, if not entirely selflessly, is ready to find it.

No, there is nothing really remarkable about taking leave of this earth. Everybody does it. What matters, what is important, is to distinguish that silence from the silence that every performer, every soloist, in that moment, whether he is someone, his name in lights, or no one at all, will, instrument, hopefully, at hand, one day step into...

The silence that precedes, the notes that, only now, at last, are ready to be played.

*

Yes, *mamá* made it out that time. She found the bathroom, a different arrangement of buses, somewhat less twisted and, the next day, returning with Ysmael's violin, an even better lineup of cold corners and half empty wrecks. Only the future—*mamá* had always considered the future, if not her own—would tell if she had done something right this time. They certainly didn't look as if they knew what they were doing in *El Hospital Psiquiátrico*...though the doctor she had run into in one of the halls (perhaps, as she, looking for the way out) had assured her to the contrary...but, who knows?

And Xavier, when she corners him between obligations on his all-too-predictable rounds, will assure her...

"Just keep your hands off him, *mamá,* don't say a thing, let my somewhat more talented brother find his way. Let him, since, as he may have told you, as he has told me, that he is cracked, not broken, somehow, pull, at least hold, himself together, for I have a feeling that the stage he is about to step onto is the one in which he plays, not, however dutifully, for you or, however childishly, against me, but, well, just the next stage, the one onto which I would follow him, if I could; will follow him, if I can."

And *mamá,* waiting as, it is supposed, or used to be, as women must, not for the husband who will never return, not for the weekly visit of the son who has found steady employment with the regional orchestra, not even for the release of her more talented boy, the one who was supposed to come home, one day, trailing glory, from the madhouse, though *mamá* herself may well have decided that the time has come to stop waiting, as it has to stop pushing, to follow no one, not even of the same blood, with that follow spot that is always heating in the hands of a determined parent, perhaps, even, as her less talented son, the one she never expected very much of, has, in his wisdom, suggested, to not say a thing.

This Is a Fine Place We've Come To

MAUREEN NEAL

I know for sure that things are going downhill for my mother when I find the blue flyswatter in the freezer. Please note that my mother is not senile or demented; she does have severe macular degeneration and serious hearing loss, not surprising in a person who is 92 years old. She also has a stenotic heart valve that she has chosen not to repair. One last important fact: she has chosen to live alone, maybe because of, maybe in spite of, these things. When she was relatively well, she made me promise to support this choice, along with the DNR order taped to the refrigerator. Which I did.

But now the chickens are coming home to roost.

The flyswatter in the freezer is important because when I visit, food—planning (or lack thereof), procurement, preparation, eating, storage of leftovers—has become an important consideration and part of her ongoing care. When I am able to visit, which never seems to be often enough or long enough for either one of us, I sometimes try to cook something up from scratch in her kitchen. I make a weird fried chicken wrap with ranch dressing and iceberg lettuce and store-bought tomatoes one night, which is a total disaster; then I try store-bought chicken salad and English muffins, then scrambled eggs with Velveeta cheese and red salsa, then reheated Meals on Wheels Mexican meat loaf. One night, our most scrumptious dish turns out to be canned pineapple slices with a dollop of mayonnaise and topped with grated cheese. All these things my mother eats, but she isn't really interested in food. On the other hand, I eat everything in sight, including the pineapple, an entire bag of Stacy's Pita Chips, and five chocolate macadamia nut cookies that my mother baked herself, with no help from anybody.

We are fond of picnics, too, or we used to be. But then there is the moment when we are sitting at a table in the park by the river, trying to eat the sandwiches I have brought from the deli case at the grocery store, and my mother asks, very loudly, because she does not have her hearing aids in, *Is that a big dog?* This is in reference to a woman in gray tights who is lying on the grass, stretching after a run along the riverfront trail.

No, I whisper, right into her ear. *That's a person,* and she nods, her mouth full of ham and cheese, and says, Oh. Then she goes back to eating the sandwich, her eyes fixed on the picnic table graffiti, which she cannot read and which says, in faded black Sharpie, *Angie loves me only me.* For some reason, this breaks my heart six ways from Sunday. The woman gets up and stares at us, rather loudly I think, before she moves off to a safer place.

Food, for me, is an unwelcome marker of decline, because my mother used to be a great cook. I love the story she tells about not knowing how to make anything at all when she was first married, and trying to work her way through the 1945 *Better Homes and Gardens Cookbook* from one end to the other in two years. When my father said that the ham sandwiches she made for his office lunches were dry, she sent him to work one day with a sandwich filled with shredded newspaper and yellow mustard, and he stopped complaining. In her best cooking years, though, she never used recipes. The way she cooked involved ingredients like a handful of flour here and there, a pinch of salt in the coffee, a splash of coffee in the meat loaf, leftover meat loaf in the stuffed cabbage, shredded cabbage in the roast pork, then dry ranch dressing mix and Campell's condensed tomato soup poured over all.

One Sunday morning before I start my four-hour drive home, my mother wants to make me breakfast. Food for the journey. She whisks together eggs and her special secret ingredients, slices cranberry bread, sets out oranges and grapes. I worry when I see her trying to light a burner on the stove and I smell gas. But she succeeds in getting the back burner to ignite, and then she holds up a small plastic spice bottle labeled Salad Supreme® and asks me what it says. I say Salad Supreme, but it doesn't look like the Salad Supreme I remember, with paprika and onion powder and sesame seeds. She sprinkles it over the scrambled eggs in the pan nonetheless.

We say a heartfelt prayer about how grateful we are for our time together and for each other, and she squeezes my hand so hard it hurts. But after the first big forkful of egg, I know something is not quite right. I plunge on, smaller bite by smaller bite. Pretty soon I am asking myself if it will be worth it to have food poisoning on top of Red Mountain Pass rather than say something—I don't know exactly what—about the eggs, which have an unfamiliar crunch and a dusty, greenish aftertaste. Before I take another bite, my mother stops eating, too, and we check the Salad Supreme bottle, which has toasted garlic bits in it instead of Salad Supreme, and I look more carefully at the expiration date on the cheese, which turns out to be three months past its use-by date, the plastic bag caked with mold. Oh, honey, she says, by way of apology. *No harm, no foul,* I say, and try to laugh. She almost cries, but not quite. Then she swears never to cook again.

The food is just the opening salvo in another kind of battle.

Just before my mother and my stepfather, Mike, were married, Mike had let it be known that he was not exactly fond of cats. He told my mother that her house smelled terrible and that they would not be entertaining any cats in their house—not while he was alive, anyway. That was that, for over 35 years. Three days after my stepfather died of cancer, my mother went down to the Humane Society and picked out two kittens, eight weeks old. She put their litter box under the desk in Mike's office and fed them wet food on the kitchen counter, and neither Mike or anyone else had anything to say about it.

A few months later, while I'm talking to her, my mother says, between little puffs of breath, *I've had a little mishap here, and I need to get off the phone. But don't worry,* she says. *I've got it under control.* Turns out that no one is actually in control, including one of the cats, who has caught his head between the slats of the miniblinds in the bathroom and who is howling and struggling to extricate himself. She tries to pry him loose, which she succeeds in doing, but not without a fight that involves biting her to the bone and lots of old-fashioned kicking and scratching. The mishap turns into tremendous staph infection, major debridement surgery, and an intense three-month home health recovery. The cat ran away or was eaten by coyotes. From a distance, I learn to translate the words *a little mishap* into *a serious accident often requiring stitches.*

There are lots of little mishaps to come. One day when I am visiting for the weekend, we find a dead mouse, still warm, on the carpet of the living room floor, where the surviving cat has thoughtfully placed it for our inspection. My mother can't see, so she asks me, *What is that? Is that a pillow from the couch or is that what I think it is?* I tell her it's a mouse, and I wrap it up in a plastic bag and throw it away in the trash can in the garage. But then we find another body on the back porch, this one in several chewed-up pieces, with the teeth and ears and a few whiskers still intact. My mother says she'll dispose of this one, so I let her. But when I ask what she's done with it, she says she has thrown it out under the hollyhocks, because it will smell bad if we put it in the trash can. *Oh, crap,* I think. *There are bears in this neighborhood, and raccoons too.* After my mother has gone to bed, I take the flashlight out to the hollyhocks and root around in the dark for the body parts. The cat sits on the sidewalk, watching.

Another day: One of my mother's friends calls and says to us, *You need to come down here. Your mom's had a little mishap and is in the hospital. She's fine, but she's in a lot of pain. I don't think they'll want to do surgery this time.* She has fallen over backwards, or maybe forwards, in the garage, she honestly can't remember which, and has dislocated her right shoulder. Under duress from the hospital social worker, she agrees to go to rehab at a nursing care facility, but she doesn't plan to stay there long. And sure enough, she doesn't. After three weeks, she comes home, risen from the living dead.

Another day: My sister starts her email from the emergency room: *Don't worry, she's fine. She had a little mishap with the bookcase last night, but we don't think there's anything broken and the doc doesn't see any evidence of a concussion.*

Another day: A home health aide answers the phone instead of my mother and says, *We've had a little mishap over here, but your mom is all cleaned up now and we've gotten all of the blood out of the carpet.* This time, they don't sew her up with needle and thread but with Super Glue. The ER doctor then carefully braids a little strip of my mother's hair away from the four-inch slice in the back of her head, where she hit the corner of the bathroom counter on her way down.

I ask myself why I feel I need to tell this story.

At first, I think that I am writing this about my mother for my mother, to honor her and her choices, to come to terms with her desire to be left alone and to not ask for help, for tea and sympathy (which would be more dangerous by far than another fall in the garage). Then I imagine reading this out loud to her, in the same way I have read countless newspaper obituaries and *Reader's Digest* profiles, and I think she might be hurt that I have broken our bond, our secret pact, that I would be so willing to share these pieces of her with the outside world. *Oh, honey,* she might say, shaking her head. *This is a fine place we've come to.*

So I sidestep the issue of breaking her heart for a little while by thinking, well, no, maybe this is for me—it's a warning, a lesson, a taste of things to come: surely I need to know (though I cannot imagine it right now) that my mother's falls in the garage will become my falls, her wobbling legs my legs, the cut and clot of braided hair my hair, the blue flyswatter placed for safekeeping in the freezer my flyswatter. And then I come back again to thinking, no, this is about my mother. No one else. And that's the truth.

1918

ANN HOWELLS

Our country is at war.
Few believe a soldier's letter
can cause burning in bones and joints,
vomiting, diarrhea, rib-cracking cough,
drown victims in their own fluids.
Blued skin provides a name: *blue death.*

Honey with milk toast comforts,
as does ginger tea, but sweating fever
kills. Ida ties onion on Buck's feet,
come morning offers blackened slices
as proof it draws the poison.
Aggie dies, aspirin overdose --
if one is good, twenty must be better.
Ruth scrubs with carbolic soap
and lye water, doses with coal oil,
turpentine, and mercury.

B&O doesn't stop where flu is present,
but porters toss infected mailbags.
Stores and post offices close,
church service, and public gatherings.
Red Cross feeds the sick,
paints red X on door, wraps dead,
lines them up in front rooms.
Morticians refuse to embalm flu dead.
Grave diggers, masked and gloved,
drop bodies into graves with hasty prayers.
Belief in science vanishes.

* * *

Fifty-three thousand Americans die
fighting a World War;
six hundred thousand die of flu.

The Statistics and the Silence

LINNET DRURY

The statistics grew exponentially like
everyone's uncut hair or the hedges
forsaken by the council or the strangling
queues round shops. The statistics

couldn't understand why no one appreciated
their magnitude, why no one was proud of them.
They couldn't be kept quiet; too young to realise,
too old to be expected to find out for themselves.

Silence became chewy. Politicians
began to speak about science and scientists
began to speak about people, which confused
the statistics, slowing them down.

But they had already grown too far
to be reclaimed, like how
when I next see you you'll be a head taller,
and I'd have missed it, my cousin

will have learnt to talk without me, my granny
will have shrunk, and the silence
will have begun to take root,
having taken our friends since the first day.

You and Me (and Our LLC)

ERIN FITZGERALD

I know You. I've seen You before. I've palpated your edges, swept my heart over your rough surface. I watched daughters reach their hands out, calling back father from You to this very room, this very bed. Of course he was already gone. You had taken him. I saw a family of farmers permit their son to submit to You, recognizing his work here was done. I've seen You take so many of them. I've even witnessed You trading babies for mothers, your own fucked up mortal bartering system.

I know You. I've seen You so many times that You should be an old friend, old news, so familiar that your presence is background noise, a hum-drum humming of filler flowers. God damned carnations and baby's breath. I can even predict your arrival most times right down to the hour. I'm onto your itinerary. As if we're in business together. Me as your sidekick. Your minion. With my pocketful of morphine to ease the drowning and charcoal for the stench of You. You and me in our LLC of Death.

You drop me little hints every now and then. First You make them tired, shackling them to their beds first 25 then 50 then 75% of the day. Then You take away their hunger—first for solids then liquids, hot foods then colds, savories then sweets. Then You begin to decay them from the inside out. Distal to proximal. You waste away their face flesh, creating animated skeletons here on Mother Earth. Then the mottling, the decreased urine output, the rotting of guts. You even allow them little glimpses to their Beyond, teasing with tastes of Pasts and Futures all at once, dropping little film shorts of the Journey featuring those that have gone before them. Then You snatch their very breaths. First You take away its innateness, its involuntariness. Then You steal breaths' ease, the soft rises and falls. Then one by one, You force frequency to decrease, then amplitude, until 14 glorious full soft rises and falls a minute becomes 10. Becomes 4.

So I get it. I know You. We've met before.

Another Country

DINA ELENBOGEN

The country where I don't want to live or die is not the kind of place you get to by plane or by train. It is a state of mind you enter into, when you discover that the strange feeling of your breast filling, almost a decade after you've stopped nursing your youngest child, is not mother's milk but a malignant tumor. This is not a place you enter at your own will. It is a place you are dragged into by an image on a screen, shadows.

In this new country, at first there is nothing but shadows, a cloud darkening the sky.

The sky begins to open a little as you learn the language of this place: Invasive carcinoma, DCIS, lumpectomy, margins, chemo, cold caps, mastectomy, tram flap reconstruction. Those words would eventually become a daily part of my vocabulary as the months spun and then dragged by, doctors disagreed about treatment, made mistakes and then finally came to a conclusion about what my course of treatment should be.

Just as I fought against being in the country of breast cancer and breast cancer treatment, I wrestle against revisiting the gory details that were part of that existence. I fight against writing it the same way that I fought against fully inhabiting it. I kept it in another place, next to me, so I could tend to it but not become it. I did not feel an affinity with other breast cancer patients the way I did with with other mothers as soon as I became pregnant with my first child. I did not want to watch my hair fall out, embrace baldness or write slogans on my skull.

I did not want to follow the dress code for this new country: a bald head, a wig, a hat or a scarf. People stop me regularly on the street to ask if my curls are real, natural, my own. When I was younger and still trying to live up to other people's standards, I tried to make them straight. When I was a child my mother cut them short. That is why from the time I hit 28 until I entered this country, my hair has fallen down my back.

So even before I know for sure that I'll need chemo, I talk to my cousin's ex-wife Gail, the only woman I know who went through chemo and didn't lose her curls. On the phone, after I tell her the grim news, she tells me about Penguin Cold Caps, and I read everything I can about them. They are frozen caps that you place on your head before, during and after chemo;

they help you save most of your hair. In this way and this way only, I am prepared. Then I wait and I pray.

During the Days of Awe between the Jewish holidays of Rosh Hashanah and Yom Kippur I began my first waiting and praying period. This was before the biopsy results confirmed cancer but after the mammography doctor stared at the image and remained silent. After I told him I could no longer endure the unknowing, he said that yes -- he was pretty sure that it was cancer but a possibility still remained that it was benign. I prayed for that possibility, and I prayed to have my life back in all of its imperfection. I prayed and prayed and thought about the week before, serendipitously running into my friend, Nathaniel, on the train on my way to teach, and how we took the 22-minute ride to talk about what we'd do with our lives if we could change them. He was applying for a new job where he'd get to do more writing and less editing. I was burnt out from teaching the same classes to the same kinds of people at the same place for over a decade. I missed teaching younger people upon whose lives I might have more of an impact than on adults who were often stiff-necked and married to their habits. We spoke about our concerns for our children, wondering if they were at the right schools, with the most compatible friends. I don't know if it was my awareness of the lump -- although it was still weeks before anyone used the "C" word, but I was feeling lethargy rather than excitement about the coming year. As if my body already knew for certain. I remember the way Nathaniel looked at me with affection as we said goodbye. I took the Water Taxi along the Chicago River to Gleacher Center on Michigan Avenue to teach my class, thinking about what I'd do if I had to lose my hair. My breasts. If men would stop looking at me.

After the train ride and before The Day of Atonement, I prayed even more fervently and read the world for signs, as if someone was giving me another chance to do everything right. If I passed this test I suddenly believed, the lump would be benign. I ran into an acquaintance in the hospital parking lot, whose wife had been fighting colon cancer for a decade, and I offered to bring her food. I rushed to do other good deeds I had put off because I thought I was too busy.

All I wanted was my life as I knew it. I wanted everything that I already had; I just wanted to touch it, to feel it more deeply, to do it better, to not be so afraid. If the week before on the train I craved change, suddenly I didn't want anything to change. Not my family, my work, my body or my hair. I wanted my ten-year-old son to pounce on me with his typical ferocity, my 14-year-old daughter to argue and then hug me with delight after I braided her long wavy hair. I wanted my husband's humor, passion and warmth. I wanted to stay in the Garden of Before.

After the pathology report removed any doubt and led to my first lumpectomy, the praying died down. The next pathology report showed microscopic levels of cancer in one out of three sentinel nodes. I was told by my oncologist that I would indeed need chemo. This is when he told me about Cold Caps, but in this one instance, I was a step ahead. After my oncologist gave me his blessing, I ordered the caps.

A week later, on our way to a teaching session about chemotherapy, my husband, Steve, and I were told at the check-in desk that my surgeon wanted to see me first. If so far, between tears and praying, I had numbed myself from the harsh reality of this new country, this moment did me in. We were told that Beth, my nurse coordinator, would lead me back up to the cavernous offices of my surgeon for a talk, before I began chemo lessons. Steve and I sat in the lobby of the Kellogg cancer center waiting, rushing to the nearest chair as my legs started giving out. I felt my face drain of color and saw my terrified expression in Steve's eyes. We knew that for my over-scheduled, disorganized surgeon to want to see me, there must be more bad news. If prior to this moment I just wanted to return to the Country of Before, now I just wanted to stay where I was, for things not to get any worse than they already were. Beth walked us back to my surgeon's office where we were told that the second lumpectomy I'd had the week before did not get all of the non-invasive ductal carcinoma (DCIS) that sat next to my tumor. My surgeon suggested casually that I should strongly consider a mastectomy, or at least another lumpectomy to see if they could get clear margins before beginning chemo. His words sounded like babble, offering what felt like two impossible options. He had told me many times, that I would not need a mastectomy, so I had ruled that out and had not done much research on the subject. I stared blankly at him who just a month before had said my situation was the best case scenario, a small tumor, early stage, estrogen positive and that a lumpectomy and radiation should do the trick.

I just wanted to begin chemo so I could finish it, put it behind me, find my way back to the world before this nightmare. While my surgeon said I had two days to make that decision, doctor friends reminded me that I really had the four months of chemo to make a decision about the future of my breasts.

I rescheduled my chemo prep session for the next day, received the caps in the mail, and prepared. Actually, it wasn't that simple. In fact, it was so complex that I hardly thought about chemo. I was getting ready to begin Cold Caps.

When friends called and asked what they could do: bring food, drive me places, drive my children places, I put them on my new committee which at first I called "The Committee for the Preservation of Dina's hair. " I knew that sounded too vain so I soon changed it to "Cold Cap Committee." I had a long list of women to whom I sent an email with times and dates of teaching sessions led by Cold Cap veterans, along with my chemo schedule from November through March. Maybe I'd be able to keep my hair, but I could already see that I wasn't able to look at my friends in the same way. There were those who dragged their feet, partook in the proper gestures and asked, "What do you need," and there were those, like my rabbi, one of the busiest women I know, who said, "Just put me down for whenever you need me and I'll be there." That was the only response that spoke to me.

Whether I wanted to be or not, I was in new terrain.

I had whittled the list down to a few people: My high school friend Iris, with whom I'd recently become close again and my newish next door neighbor, Lexa, who I thought might help during the four hours after chemo when I'd be sitting at home on my couch, still changing caps every twenty minutes. The obvious people, some of my closest friends, were not on this list. Although many offered to be there, I continued to see people with new eyes. Anyone who was the least bit unreliable, tardy, squeamish or judgmental, was instantly crossed off my list.

At the teaching session my erstwhile cousin, Gail, and her sister, Nadine, who had been her Cold Cap partner, shared with us the nitty gritty details and the necessary precision involved with this task. "Your hair will thin out a lot but no one but you will know," they assured me. "There are strict rules about what shampoo you can and cannot use, but mostly no one notices your loss," they repeated. The rituals surrounding these caps include making sure they stay at 34 degrees below zero, changing them every twenty minutes, keeping them on dry ice, warming the ice with your thick-stockinged feet. And then the process of securing these caps, that look like ancient football helmets, to your head. This means one person standing behind you, holding the remaining hair while the other places the cap on your head, securing it with several bands so it is tight enough to do the work of preventing the chemo from getting to your roots.

At the end of this session, Gail said I needed to have the same people with me each time, that there is a learning curve, and rotating helpers would be like starting from scratch.

When all of these lovely women left, and I was alone with Steve packing up Cold Cap paraphernalia, I tried to choose the two people who I'd want with me for the six sessions of Cold Caps. I asked questions like, who do I trust the most in this universe? Who would never be late or never cancel, who is meticulous, who loves me the most? Who would I be okay sitting with all those hours? The names I came up with had not even been on the list: Steve and my 87-year-old, biochemist father, Gil.

During practice I had a sense of how complicated, cumbersome and painful Cold Caps would be, but I couldn't imagine going into chemo bareheaded. It gave us something to think about (where to get ice, how to make sure caps stay at the right temperature, how to coordinate the nurses and doctors' work of taking blood and examining me first while timing the caps). Most of this responsibility fell to my husband. I was still trying to keep it in another country, and now the Cold Caps were my accomplices.

In the country of breast cancer there were survivors with opinions about everything from which doctors to avoid, what herbs to take and if green tea is good or bad for cancer. There were support groups and yoga classes, mindful meditation circles, pink t-shirts, and wig salons. I still didn't want to join this club. I put a cap on my head and began chemo.

The first infusion, which later morphed into the other five infusions, remains hazy in my memory. The night before we took our children to sleep at my sister Beryl's house in Skokie, not too far from their school at the time, so they wouldn't have to be a part of our early morning anxiety of packing up Cold Caps, getting to the the Kellogg Cancer Center on time, taking all the drugs I'd need to prevent side effects and so on. I wanted my kids to get to school without the hard evidence that their mom was about to begin chemo. I wanted their lives to remain untouched.

I arrived for my first chemo session in a daze, armed with the steroid, Decadron, which made me manic, irritable, and spaced-out, as well as other pre-chemo drugs. Steve and Gil dragged in the two large blue coolers filled with dry ice and Cold Caps, and in the pack that usually attaches to my bicycle, I carried bottles of water and books. We were not brought into the large, communal infusion room, but after blood draws and a brief visit with my oncologist, we were taken to a private room where there was space for our ammunition. I was the first patient to use Cold Caps at Evanston Hospital; doctors and nurses watched wide-eyed, some skeptical and others respectful that I was trying to hold onto my hair and the essence of who I was.

My father held my hair up while Steve tightly secured the cap to my head.

It was on so tight that the ice burned my forehead. I got up every few minutes with my IV to urinate and stared at my reflection in the mirror: a Martian from outer space.

We did this again and again and again. The three of us sitting together, not speaking much, hardly looking at the poison dripping into my veins but at the timer that told us when to switch caps and the thermometer that told us if they were cold enough to freeze my skull.

All autumn I had tried hard to keep my diagnosis and procedures separate from my teaching. Yet I felt I had to let my students know in case I had to cancel class, and because so much of what we were discussing in the memoir and creative nonfiction writing classes I was teaching, was about speaking the truth. I did keep it out of the room by emailing them about it and then being available after class for anyone who wanted to talk about it. One student, a retired physician, brought me The Emperor of All Maladies by Siddhartha Mukerjee, the best book, she said, written on the subject.

It is the book a dutiful cancer patient should have been reading during chemo, but I brought James Atlas' biography of Saul Bellow which, by the second infusion three weeks later, I discussed with my father, while he read Dickens' Bleak House. My father grew up in the same neighborhood as Bellow, about a decade behind him. "I am an American, Chicago born," begins one of his great novels. Bellow was saving me as I became captivated by the ups and downs of his life as a writer, his loves and infidelities, his passions, how he put his discoveries into his fictional prose, and how, although he travelled constantly and frequently lived away from Chicago, he is steeped in a Chicago and Jewish sensibility that is inseparable from his art.

It was Steve who read the big cancer book. I never got to read much during chemo, anyway, because my face was smooshed from the caps and I couldn't get my reading glasses on.

Afterwards, we drove the ten minutes home with a cap still on my head, finishing the last one by the time my sister and children arrived for dinner. My sister, Beryl, who has been an incredible support since my daughter was born, and shortly after my mother died of Scleroderma, had again become the person without whom I can't imagine having survived this. Along with caring for my children whenever care was needed, she organized food so that each infusion day a friend would bring a meal. Love loomed large, as James Kugel described in his cancer memoir, In the Valley of the Shadow. My father and I loved through books, with others it was through food, and with a few through silence.

The days after infusion I'd still be high on Decadron, productive, and amorous.

I would plan huge parties, the guest list comprised of everyone who helped in some way, propose new courses (which now I have to teach) and run along the early-winter lake. I finished teaching my fall classes and then collapsed on a couch, with my winter running clothes next to me. Even during the most exhausted days after the Decadron wore off and the chemo was still in my system, at my doctor's urging, I managed to roll into my winter running clothes and run the exhaustion and the drugs out of my body.

I decided to take winter quarter off of teaching to focus on what I needed most: to do enough research to make an informed decision about the next step in my treatment. My surgeon was pushing the surgical option, but my oncologist, the one doctor I trusted from the beginning, disagreed.

I wanted to continue to write and prepare for a panel at a large writing conference that would take place in Chicago in March. When I realized my presentation day coincided with my crash day from chemo, I moved my final infusion back a week. This panel, and my intensive reading of Saul Bellow, Gwendolyn Brooks and Carl Sandburg, got me through the most difficult winter months.

It trumped finishing chemo a week earlier.

As I walked Chicago streets, sometimes still high on Decadron, I fell more deeply in love with my city and with these three souls who thrived on Chicago, spoke for the people and for whom social justice was inseparable from their art. I began to identify with these poets and prophets who came from such different worlds: Black, Jewish, socialist, but who put all of their sweat and blood into everything they wrote.

If during the days leading up to chemo I didn't want anything to change, now I was fighting to keep the essence of who I was. I did this through writing with whatever energy I had left, long walks with friends, and running almost everyday along the now frozen Lake Michigan. I should have been calling doctors, reading up on options for reconstruction and visiting surgeons, but first I needed to immerse myself in what I loved. All that stuff, along with a visit to another surgeon for a second opinion, would come in time.

When I picked up my kids from school or when I went to Whole Foods for groceries, most people I ran into did not see a change in me or maybe thought that I was having a season of bad hair days. To the outside world, the illness did not show up. Whenever I saw those with whom I was closer and who knew of my secret country, I was greeted with expressions of utter surprise and comments like, "You look so good? Beautiful," as if chemo somehow suited me.

But I saw the subtle and less subtle changes. My hair was thinning. There were darker rings under my eyes. Sometimes I was so tired I couldn't get my kids from school; they learned to make their own lunches. I would stare at my reflection in the mirror remembering an image of myself from Before. Often critical of my extra weight, sometimes unruly hair and not being twenty-five anymore, the mirror and I were often at odds. But on an August morning I had looked at my naked reflection and was thankful for the golden tint of my hair, the shape of my breasts, my leaner body from a summer of running and going on several fifty-mile bike rides. I had felt beautiful, grateful and at the height of my powers. Now I felt altered, unbeautiful, scarred.

During the worst days of my suffering from breast cancer treatment, people brought gifts. I treasured these tokens of recognition, because they were evidence that friends remembered who I was. They understood that I had not become my erstwhile disease and that the treatment for the disease was an inconvenience I was dealing with, a calamity if you will, but I was still me. So the woven, brown, turquoise and amber Indian scarf left on the porch by Susan and Jonathan, delicate silver earrings with blue stones delivered from Char, a friend since second grade, the glimmering pair brought back from Israel by Iris, recording of Mary Oliver reading her poems and photo of Carl Sandburg from Amy, a newer, treasured writer friend, pumpkin muffins, stuffed animals and green teas, brought me back to those parts of myself that others still remembered. They said: Here you are.

By the time I reached my last infusion, I learned how to say that to myself.

I learned how important it was to remember who I was before I entered the cancer center, that was, despite the caring doctors and nurses, often dehumanizing.

I got up an hour earlier, wrote and quietly drank coffee before entering the place where I became a band around my wrist, a number, a series of stats. Where I became my name and birthdate that I had to repeat each time a new person entered the room. Where I looked odd with hair still hanging down my back.

Session six was as uneventful as the others: I still barely noticed the poison dripping in my arm, but each time a cap was removed even for a minute, to be replaced by the next one, I breathed a deep sigh of relief. But not the kind of relief I felt hours later, at home, taking off the final cap and letting the ice dissolve.

"Change. Don't change," is the advice that the Israeli poet Yehuda Amichai gave to a young Jonathan Safran Foer when they met in Jerusalem. Foer had been with his youth group and had asked the bard for words of wisdom about his life. When he recounted this at a recent lecture in Chicago, I thought it perfectly summed up this year. He was telling the young Jonathan to hold onto the vigor and questing of youth. And he was reminding him that change is essential and inevitable.

As I take those words into my year, I think about all that I was able to keep. My hair. My strength. My spirit. My vigor. My love. My health. My scholarship. All of those experiences were also changed, deepened in the most unexpected ways. I could dig deep inside myself and find strength even when I was spent. Most of the new ways that I looked at the people in my life were positive. Even in my darkest moments when I tried to push people away, my oldest friends said things like "I'm not letting you do this without me" and "you are still so much yourself." My newer friends showed their love in ways they were unable to before.

By June, when it had been one hundred degrees for days on end, our house was filled with people whom I was finally able to thank properly. We had the lovefest I'd been imagining all winter. By this time I had also lost my breasts, but opted for tram flap reconstruction so that my new breasts were made of my own flesh. The surgery and recovery were much more difficult than all of the months of chemo, but I did what had to be done. My oncologist, armed finally with enough information, had come to agree that this was the safest option. Although my body was now altered to the extreme by my new surgeon, I never felt more myself. My daughter sat with her first love on the porch swing and my son led a pack of kids through the house and garden. My father sat on the porch steps in the intense heat with his oldest friend and people who I knew would never let me do it alone crowded every room.

Later that evening, when my husband suffered from heat exhaustion and was taken to the ER by his close friend Sam, who over the course of the year had become even more dear to me than he had been before, I knew he was in good hands. Stunned that something like this could happen to Steve, who had been strong and solid most of the year, I didn't know what to do. The same people who took care of me all year were now in the kitchen drying dishes and putting away food, something I never would have allowed in the country of Before.

Change I did, in wonderful ways. My heart opened wider with the ability to let people in, to be vulnerable, the way it had opened 14 years before with the birth of my first child. I now know how to help others who are going through trauma, to understand more profoundly, what they may or may not need.

And in spite of the caps my hair has changed. I shed even more as a result of the general anesthesia during surgery. The caps protected me from baldness, but my hair thinned enough that I had to keep cutting it shorter and shorter.

Almost a year after chemo I spend time in the same old places, the classroom, train and Water Taxi. I run along the lake during every season. There are new places where I find myself as well: yoga studios, mindful meditation circles, and tea shops. I do these things with all kinds of people, not just those who have survived breast cancer, but with anyone and everyone who gracefully endures the large and small traumas of being alive. I did not join the club. And I did.

This Morning Two Police Officers

KATY GIEBENHAIN

This morning two police officers
elbow the counter of a bookstore café
in a mid-sized city on the edge
of bankruptcy.

This morning the bookstore
is a battleship,
engines opening up, the crew
at their tasks
amongst used books, new books,
the clunk of the espresso machine
the steam wand's scream,
ceiling fans accelerating in the rafters,
sale carts jostling
onto the sidewalk
under a freezing, wooly sky.

This morning, like any
used bookstore this one's filled with hurts
with publisher copies bumped,
smudged, injured
in one way or another.
Rooms smell
of tangled narratives, cookies, dust.
Hurts on the shelves, hurts outside,
hurts of bodies
moving up the back stairs
with a barrel of coldbrew.

This morning, let the officers drink
with the Golden Retriever

warming the tiles at their feet,
big as a pony, calm as a lake.
Good cops? Bad cops?
At the moment, who can say?
Downtown is the book
that opens them. Downtown is the book
they open every day.

stroke

SLAVENA SALVE NISSAN

before we meet you
we meet your stroke
on the CT

we all look at the screen silently
the hyperdensity
impossible to ignore

in your room
we hear about
your wonderful life
and that terrible day

i keep it together
until your tough guy husband says
i miss her
and strokes your cheek
while wiping away
the tears from his own

My Bird Bill

PHILIP DIGIACOMO

I was always an oddball, or so I've been told, first by my widely respected doctor father, and by various other persons of authority over the years. When I was a child of eight, my father was gone for a year, attempting to cure some disease in Africa. Not a letter, not a telegram, not a phone call to his young son Chris. Upon his return I received a pat on the head and a huge, live African Gray parrot that my mother donated to the Hartford zoo the minute my father left for Patagonia a week later. I had named him Bill, and when my fifth grade class took a field trip a year later, I saw him perched on a high bamboo pole in the aviary. I don't think he saw me, but I knew it was him.

* * * * *

Miss Collins, our teacher, arranged us in two rows, boy, girl, boy, girl and even made us hold hands as if we were little kids. When I saw who my partner was I panicked. Debbie Zelf stared at me with clear blue eyes from behind her thick glasses, smiled sweetly and held out her hand. But it wasn't a real hand. It was a contraption that started at her elbow and ended in two curved metal pincers that opened up to accept my hand. I gingerly hooked one finger around them and tried to smile as we ambled along the zoo path. I stared at the ground unable to escape the revulsion I felt at the touch of her cold metal hook. Hours spent pouring over the pictures in my father's medical books had produced in me a fear of human deformity of any kind. When we arrived at the vast aviary, we broke rank and crowded around the high wire enclosure. I tugged at Miss Collin's coat sleeve.

"Miss Collins, that's my parrot way up at the top, his name is Bill!

Most of the kids laughed and someone called me an asshole. Miss Collins clapped her hands loudly.

"Alright class, settle down, lets keep quiet and respect all the animals. Line up please and we'll go to the reptile house. Come on, find your partners!"

Miss Collins looked at me like I was out of my nut, making me feel worse than I already did, but then Debbie did something so sweet and kind I remember it still.

"Let's switch, Chris, and walk on the other side, okay?"

The hot blush I felt was part shame and part relief and as I took her real hand in mine, she whispered to me –

"Bill is very beautiful, Chris."

Here Be Sisters

JOY CUTLER

It's Thanksgiving morning, and when I wake up my first thought is, *Thank god I don't have to cook today.* My older sister, Lynne, is coming up to New York, and it's the first time we're having a Thanksgiving dinner in a restaurant. It's just the two of us and it's a little weird. Our mom went to Arizona earlier than usual this winter, our brother Norman stayed in Chicago, Lynne's daughters are at their dad's house, and for the past six years our father's soul has been gallivanting across the Universe so won't be making an appearance. We feel like orphans.

Our holiday meal is a little strange too. Lynne and I are on restricted diets because of a genetic illness we both share, so we choose mostly protein and sugar from the menu. It still surprises me what we can and can't eat. Turkey sausage and a couple decadent desserts seem like a safe bet, but it's tough to keep away from the forbidden roasted potatoes and beautifully arranged dark green vegetables beckoning from the sides of our plates. "Eat me!" they cry. Even our water glasses are trying to entice us – the ice tinkles seductively, beads of water collect on the sides of our glasses reflecting our yearning faces. But the doctors say it's important to restrict fluid intake, so we take careful sips instead of gulping and refilling like we both desperately want to do. We should have known the sausage would be too salty.

Thanksgiving is not the only reason Lynne and I are together. Our mother is sending us on a mission to attend a cousin's son's bar mitzvah. From the Arizona desert she gives the commandment to go forth unto Connecticut, mingle with the *mishpucha* and watch a Jewish boy become a man. I'm not thrilled about this *mitzvah,* the good deed we'll be performing by attending the bar mitzvah, but, am resigned to following her plan. But as the Yiddish saying goes, people make plans and God laughs.

The next day while God's warming up for a few good guffaws, Lynne and I take a train to Wilton, Connecticut and register at a hotel just down the street from the synagogue. I can't argue with the convenience of the location, but there are no sidewalks, and the streetlights are so dim everything outside their pale glow is lost in blackness. I don't like the suburbs. At night I get the unsettling feeling trees are creeping closer to the windows to spy on me, like arboreal peeping Toms. I feel safer in the city. That evening we trek in the dark across the frozen grass, our boots making an ominous crackling sound as we sneak by tall, malevolent pine trees to the synagogue for the Friday evening service. The main event, the bar mitzvah itself, isn't until the next morning. This is just the warm up. After our brief but daunting journey in the dark, I'm relieved to get inside this refuge, but as we enter the sanctuary a pine branch knocks loudly against a windowpane, and I quickly steer Lynne towards the back row away from the windows. But Lynne doesn't want to be steered.

"We shouldn't sit back there. We'll look like we're hiding."

"That's where I want to sit."

"You really should make an effort to be friendlier. Everyone thinks you're aloof."

Everyone does not think I'm aloof. Only some do.

"I just don't want to sit over there."

The service is about to start, and Lynne can either sit near the relatives we barely know or follow me to the back row.

She whispers what she has told me on many occasions, "You're so weird."

But she joins me anyway. We sisters need to stick together.

The seats are just uncomfortable enough to keep us from nodding off while the bar mitzvah boy performs a small role in the service. Even from the back row I can tell how seriously he takes his duties, and he's darn adorable in his blue and white crocheted yarmulke, but the service drones on and we're tired. When the service is over, we "Shabbat Shalom" everyone and make it safely back to our hotel room without getting smacked by swinging branches or tripping over pinecones. We kick off our boots, collapse on the king size bed and do what sisters do together – we yak. We talk about how her girls are doing in school, how my young dog likes to carry a bagel in her mouth on our walks, how odd, but devoted our brother's boyfriend is and how our mom drove the car onto the lawn of her retirement community again.

"It was the strangest thing. The curb just leapt out at me," she told me later.

And Lynne and I kvetch about being on dialysis. No one likes dialysis; dialysis sucks. Like a blood-starved vampire the dialysis machine chugs rhythmically from a vein in my arm, the tubing connecting my vein to the machine hiccups with excitement with every pull on my blood. It gives me the willies. I come to the clinic three times a week, and, I'm stuck in that recliner for four hours with nothing to do except watch lousy daytime TV or try to read. My heroic attempts to tackle Dostoyevsky's *The Idiot* are doomed and soon my eyes stop tracking the words and I flip the book over on my lap. It's impossible to concentrate. The machine beeps constantly, a loud alarm blares if I move my arm even slightly on the recliner, or I might have a sudden excruciating attack of leg cramps from excess fluid being removed by the dialysis machine too quickly, or I itch so badly I'm begging the nurses to save me with a shot of Benadryl and immediately fall in love with whichever nurse gives me that shot, or maybe an impatient patient yanks out a dialysis needle from her arm while the machine is still cleaning her blood and suddenly her blood is arcing overhead like it just catapulted over a prison wall to freedom. There are easily forty patients in here, all with alarms and beeps and itching and leg cramps. Who could read a book through all *that*? The only thing I enjoy is that rare shot of Benadryl, because it leads me straight to the escape hatch and right out of this place. My head snaps back against the headrest of my recliner, my mind turns to pink smoke, and I drift and curl along the ceiling. Such bliss. I also like it when the patient I call Dr. Candy hands out sweets like the Good Fairy of Dialysis, and if he has my favorites, Peanut Chews and SweeTarts, I'm actually happy and the clinic doesn't seem quite so bad. But the rest of the time... it sucks.

I know dialysis treatments are a better alternative to being dead, but I wouldn't wish it on anyone, especially a family member. Lynne and I and our brother, Norman, inherited a rare disease called Alport Syndrome that causes kidney failure and hearing loss. Losing kidney function is bad enough, but having hearing loss on top of a potentially fatal disease is downright insulting. I've discovered there are people in this world who have no patience when I mishear them. Once a woman stopped me on the street to ask where she could find a decent wine store. Under normal circumstances that would have been a simple exchange, but not when my damaged hearing can't help but twist words into confounding new meanings. Instead of a "decent wine store" I thought she asked where she could find a "peace of mind" store. Since this interaction took place in San Francisco her question seemed plausible to me. She shouted, "I said a DECENT WINE STORE!" and stomped off down Mission Street in her Doc Marten boots with her thick, blond dreadlocks thumping against her back. But when Norman, Lynne and I are together our misheard words can cause a lot of laughter.

"What were they doing with manikins and elephants?"

"Not manikins and elephants. *Man Against the Elements*!"

There's an explosion of laughter from Norman and me. Lynne chimes in, "I really liked that movie."

"What movie?"

"The Elephant Man."

More laughter.

Here's an interesting fact about Alport Syndrome—it's one of fifty-seven diseases on the Ashkenazi genetic disease list that also includes cystic fibrosis, Tay-Sachs and the weirdly named, Maple Syrup Urine Disease. L'chaim to that, I guess.

As sisters Lynne and I have more in common than just kidney failure and dialysis. In fact, we both had the chance to get brand new kidneys. I mean new to us; obviously the kidneys were secondhand—one from a living donor and the other from a non-living or cadaver donor.

In May, seven months before our Thanksgiving bar mitzvah weekend, I got a phone call there was a kidney in Chicago with my name on it.

"You better catch a flight out here as soon as possible. This kidney can't wait forever."

Oh my god!

I feel like my water just broke.

I'm about to have a kidney!

I'm already planning our future together. When we return home from the hospital my new kidney and I will have lots of time to bond. I hope this kidney will like me. I'm already crazy about her.

When I finally arrive at the hospital and after several anxious hours waiting to be wheeled into the OR, a surgical resident suddenly materializes in my room. I perk up and grin at her.

This is it!

"Hi! I've been waiting so long I thought you guys forgot about me up here! Haha! So do I get my kidney now?"

She looks embarrassed and has a hard time making eye contact. And that's when she explains the kidney that was meant for me was too damaged and the surgery was cancelled.

NO! We had plans!

"I flew all the way out here in a thunderstorm so bad we almost couldn't land, and now you're telling me: Never mind??"

"I'm very sorry."

So ends my plan to get a new kidney and renew my life.

I bet God's laughing so hard He peed in his pants.

On the flight back to New York, I stare out the window while my mind caves in on itself like a collapsible drinking cup. For such a long time I had fantasies of showing off my new adopted kidney.

See that incision? My new kidney lives under there and she's gorgeous!

Instead, I drag myself back to the dialysis clinic.

A month after the fiasco in Chicago a friend of Lynne's offered to donate a kidney to her. Lynne is crazy thrilled and I am crazy jealous. No one ever offered to give up one of their kidneys for me. I'm like the kid at school who always receives the least number of cards from her classmates on Valentine's Day.

It's not fair.

I had just missed a chance to get my life back, and now Lynne's going to get her very own kidney and from a friend! I'm pissed that my sister, who hasn't been on dialysis nearly as long as I have or had nearly as many life-threatening infections, is getting her transplant before me! I know it's not supposed to be a competition, but right now it sure feels like one, and I can't let on how upset I am. I'm supposed to be happy for her and a part of me is, but resentment and envy are sloshing around in there, and I hate that she's leaving me behind to wade through the muck of dialysis on my own.

Now Lynne's calling to talk about the medical tests her friend, I'll call her Jan, is undergoing to get approved for the transplant.

"She's got great kidney function and she's a really good match!"

"Uhh... cool."

"I don't even know her that well. What an incredible person, right?"

"Yeah. Incredible." I let out a sigh.

Annoyed because I don't sound very excited, "What's the matter with you?"

"Nothing! It's great news, Lynne."

It's not easy to keep up my murmurs of enthusiasm. Then it gets worse. In June Lynne decides to throw a gratitude ceremony for her donor friend, and I know she'll kill me if I don't go. My sister can get very guilt-trippy when she wants something. Our brother's off the hook, because he's a professor and he's busy, but she knows damn well I have no such excuse. So I'll be there to participate in her happiness, but how do I fight off the cacophony of mental bullies attacking me?

It's not fair she's getting a kidney first. She doesn't deserve it.

Stop it.

You were in the hospital with that insane fungal peritonitis for two months, and she never came to New York to see you. You nearly died.

She was just starting dialysis then.

She's got better friends than you do. Your cool artist friends are selfish and don't give a shit about you.

SHUT UP!

They don't shut up.

In the Virginia countryside where Jan lives, Lynne's daughters, her friends and I stand in a field in a big circle and one by one we walk into the center to declare what we're most grateful for. The guilty feelings that rise inside me collide with the underside of my skull making my scalp prickle. My sister's celebration has turned my bad thoughts into a torturous itch. I'm nervous and embarrassed and have no idea what I'm going to say. I don't think I can get through this, and it's nearly my turn in the circle. Just then three cows from a nearby pasture lumber up to us and studiously observe our ritual.

Cows!

Lynne planned out every aspect of this ceremony – from the sage-burning, to the poetry readings, to presenting Jan with a gold bangle engraved with these words, *To Jan - Oneness is Truth. With Love and Gratitude, Lynne.* But there's no way my sister could have planned these cows. It's so absurd and right up my alley. I love it! I laugh, and my laughter begins to unravel the tangled ball of emotions I've been trying to keep hidden. My laughter keeps bubbling up as the ball rolls out my head and onto the grass where, to my surprise, it quickly fades away. The voices have gone mute.

Bye-bye, brats.

It's my turn in the circle. I smile at the cows, silently thanking them and then smile at my sister. I'm ready.

"Lynne, I'm grateful for all the people in your life who are here for you, who enjoy the richness you contribute to their lives, love you for who you are and support you no matter what." I stop. One of the cows nods her head urging me to continue. I go on.

"Umm, and even though over the years, sometimes we felt the other sister was being favored by Mom or Dad or had more advantages because of our position in the sibling order or sometimes I think you give me too much advice I didn't ask for and sometimes you think I get belligerent and stubborn, it just doesn't matter. I'm happy for you. Congratulations!"

I walk out of the circle feeling pretty good, but then a very familiar emotion slowly slithers back in. Goddammit, I still feel abandoned. Lynne won the jackpot and will soon join the winner's circle, and I won't have anyone to commiserate with anymore. It'll be lonely.

The surgery is scheduled for September 10th. Lynne's in a state of high-octane ecstasy and God begins to chuckle. Two weeks before her transplant, Jan loses her nerve and backs out, and my sister has a breakdown. She can't sleep for days, and she can't stop ranting how her so-called friend screwed up her life. Not surprisingly, she insists Jan return the gold bangle and now keeps it in a black velvet pouch at the bottom of her jewelry box. Finally I get it—the refuge we're so sure is saving us can collapse at any time. One night a branch bangs on a window, the glass shatters and the night trees get in.

Back at our hotel room it's very late and we finally go to sleep in the hotel's enormous bed. There's a bar mitzvah in nine hours.

Very early in the morning a crow begins to scream.

I mutter, "Shut up, you stupid crow. It's Shabbat."

The screaming continues relentlessly. Even though it looks like a Hasidic old man with its feathered long black coat and ponderous walk, evidently this crow is not Jewish.

As I struggle out of my dream the screaming turns to the sound of a ringing phone. Lynne doesn't wake up; she probably can't even hear it. The ringing makes even less sense than my dream.

Who even knows to call us here?

I look at the hotel's clock radio.

And at five in the morning!

I grab the receiver. A light blinks. I push a button and listen to the voice of my friend Victoria who's staying with my dog while I'm away. I forgot Lynne gave her the hotel phone number before we left. I never would have thought of that. Victoria sounds half-asleep, but her words are clear.

"Hey, call the hospital. They've got a kidney for you."

Holy crap! I write down the number, but my hand's shaking so badly it takes me four tries before I push the right buttons and reach my transplant coordinator.

"Roxanne, I'm not in town, I'm in Connecticut for a goddamn bar mitzvah! I can't miss this kidney!"

"Just get here as soon as you can. Sooner!"

Trying to wake Lynne I'm so agitated I squeak like a chipmunk.

"Kidney! Train! Hospital! Oh my god! Stop staring at me and get up!!" But Lynne's in a daze and takes forever to get ready. The more I push her to hurry, the more she dawdles. At last, she's packed and leaving the room, but now she's making a beeline towards the dining room.

"We don't have time for breakfast."

"I have to eat something before we go. Want some of my bagel?"

"I can't eat or drink before surgery! You know that."

"Oh… that's right."

She takes a sip of her tea.

I'm pacing between the dining room and the lobby checking if our taxi has shown up yet.

What if he drives off if we're not out front when he gets here?

I'm hyperventilating.

I'm going to kill her. If we miss our train and I miss my kidney transplant I'll have to kill her. Please, God. I really, really, really want this transplant, but my sloth of a sister is going to fuck it UP!

Suddenly a calmer voice speaks above the mental static.

Don't worry. This time will be different. You've got this.

Are you kidding me? Look at her! She's eating a freaking bagel and cream cheese! She doesn't want me to get this kidney. I know it. She's jealous I'm the one in the winner's circle now and she isn't because Jan ruined it. I get it, I really do, but she has no right to sabotage my chance!

The calm voice loses patience, *Stop with the shpilkes already!*

I don't even know what that means!

I'm a watered-down Jew with a lousy Yiddish vocabulary.

Stop fretting. This kidney is meant for you. It's your beshert.

My what?

Your DESTINY!

Lynne is almost through her bagel.

"What time is the train again?" I'm trying really hard not to blow up in her face.

"6...18. And there's not another train for three more hours. Three. Ow-wars." She stands and reaches for the handle on her suitcase. *She's finally moving. Maybe I won't have to kill her.*

"Oh, wait. I have to pay the waitress." *Oh no.* A horn honks. I run into the lobby.

"Come on, come on! Our taxi's here. He can't sit there forever!"

"Be right there. Leaving a tip."

"LYNNE!" We catch our train just in time.

The train is full to overflowing and hot and it smells of sweat and turkey leftovers and Lynne's face turns the color of a funeral lily.

"What's the matter with you?"

"I think I'm going to pass out." *Noooo! Please don't do that!* A man gives up his seat. She puts her head between her knees taking deep breaths until the color comes back to her face, but she looks exhausted.

We make it to the hospital through my sheer determination and bossiness, "Keep moving! We have to catch the A train. Hurry up!" We're escorted to a hospital room, and Lynne heads straight for the bed, immediately falling asleep. When a nurse enters to get blood samples, she isn't sure which one of us is the patient.

"It's me!"

"Who's in the bed?"

"My sister." The nurse's eyes move back and forth between the two of us.

"You two sure look a lot alike." That's true. But *I'm* the one getting the kidney.

In the operating room the anesthesiologist injects a syringe into my IV line. I count backwards—100, 99, 98... I taste metal in the back of my throat. Total nothingness lowers itself on top of me.

Time slows.

Time stands still.

I move into the night darkness where the trees are waiting. I stare up at their outstretched arms hovering above me. I take a breath. The trees step aside, their leaves applauding as I walk past to meet my *beshert*, my destiny.

Several hours later when I return to consciousness in post-op, Lynne is standing by the bed waiting. She waves.

"Hi. Welcome back. How do you feel?" I'm mad. I have searing pain where my original right kidney sits inert as an extinct volcano. This makes no sense. I know the surgeons didn't put my transplant kidney there.

"It really hurts! Why does it hurt so bad? Do something!" I glare at her as best I can through an anesthesia haze.

"Where does it hurt?" What does she mean, 'Where does it hurt?' She's my big sister and should instinctively know where. "In my back!" Now I'm moaning.

"Stop holding your breath. Breathe into the pain." *Ugh, more big sister advice. But I try to do what she says.* She slips her hand under my back and massages it. It still hurts, but it's so good feeling her skillful fingers touching me. It's a nice perk having a massage therapist for a sister. I'm so grateful she's here with me, caring for me, being a perfect sister, but I hurt too much to tell her so.

Two years later Lynne got her transplant from a friend more reliable than Jan. There was no gratitude ceremony, no gold bangle, just an understanding that her friend was totally committed to giving Lynne one of her kidneys. Two months after her transplant, my sister died in her sleep from a heart condition her doctors didn't detect on the MRI before her transplant surgery.

I regret I never had the nerve to tell her how jealous I was when we thought Jan would be her donor. I regret I never asked if she was jealous the morning I got the call in our hotel room. Maybe then we could have released the little envies and tugging resentments we both carried inside. I miss looking at Lynne and recognizing myself in her laugh, the way she walked, her facial expressions. I miss the advice only a big sister can give, even if I didn't ask for any. When I was with her, I knew I was home.

Here be sisters.

Living Fictions

LEE COOPER

Nearly eight months into my wife's pregnancy, 23 months after experiencing cardiac arrest in my sleep, I had a dream that challenged my sanity. It eroded the line between wakefulness and dream-state.

At 2:30 am on a Sunday, I am working as a senior commanding officer in an enormous underwater fortress. This is no mere submarine. It is a full-sized battleship two dozen stories high, cruising through ocean trenches. Looking back, it was probably modelled on Captain Nemo's Nautilus, from the 1954 cinematic version of 20,000 Leagues Under the Sea, which I watched on VHS in my grandfather's living room, beside the dry warmth of wood-burning stove.

Below a white-capped sea, I request an intelligence briefing from a junior officer, who happens to be one of my cousins (as dreams go), and then we part ways. My cousin-slash-colleague walks up a staircase and I walk deeper into this maze of a vessel. Three or four flights down, I reached my destination, the bridge of the ship. Unlike the rest of the ship, which is comprised of narrow steel hallways and staircases, the bridge has floor-to-ceiling windows of thick glass that can withstand the pressure of the deep sea. It is exposed to the ocean like a vast underwater aquarium, looking out into cold darkness.

As I swing around the last railing to the cockpit-aquarium, red warning lights and alarms begin flashing ominously. Something is threatening the ship. Is it an incoming missile? A compromised airlock? An internal fire? I have no idea, but the deep-sea base is growing suffocatingly louder, redder, chaotic. And then…

BOOM!!!

The glass walls explode around me with a hot, deafening sonic boom that cuts through my chest, blowing me backward off my feet. It is the type of explosion that would surely kill me, ending this nightmare, because getting killed in a dream means you wake up into the real world. But not this time. The explosion doesn't disappear. If anything, the sensation intensifies, and my perceptions of time and place entangle. I wake up feeling as though I am getting punched in my chest, along with a glowing afterburn up my sternum.

I gain a bit more consciousness and ask myself, "Am I dying? Is this explosion real?"

A bit more consciousness, and I think, "Am I suffering a cardiac arrest in bed, again? Am I feeling my body give out in real-time, before I say goodbye to this life?"

A bit more, and, "Holy shit, my defibrillator must have gone off."

I am terrified, and suddenly gain clarity. I remember that Caitlin is in bed on my right-hand side and she has been through this trauma one too many times already. Except now she is pregnant. Our next trip to the hospital was supposed to be for the birth of our baby boy. I want Caitlin to be stress-free, which I know is now impossible.

"Caitlin," I try to say calmly, as I reach out my right arm to nudge her and ensure she is also awake. "Caitlin, I think my defibrillator went off. Don't panic, I think I am okay, but my defibrillator just went off. I need you to call 911."

I am trying to remain calm, for me and for Caitlin, but my mind is becoming a scramble. Less out of fear for my own physical health than out of immediate concern for my mental health: Did I really just feel that bang, or did I imagine it? Are the wire leads from my defibrillator actually warm? Is everything psychosomatic? Did the shock insert itself into the flow of my dream, or was the whole dream a prelude to the shock? Will I ever be able to navigate the line between my fears and my reality? Are they one and the same?

No, it was real. It had to be real. I feel for the rigid electrodes that run from my device under the skin of my sternum, and they feel a bit warm. Or do they? Yes, they do.

Caitlin calls 911 from her cell phone. She tells the operator that my defibrillator has gone off for the first time and we need an ambulance to go to Tufts Medical Center. My electrophysiologist is at Tufts and we know the value of his care.

When Caitlin hangs up, I do my best to tell her that I feel okay, physically and cognitively. I need her to stay as calm as possible, because I don't want her to fall into a vicious feedback loop of stress. If she fears for my health it might cause a bit of stress, which feeds her guilt for what that stress might do to the health of the fetus growing inside of her, which in turn amplifies her stress. And so on.

I am scared, and shocked. But I am also immediately grateful, noting to Caitlin, "At least we know the defibrillator works, and I feel surprisingly good."

If my heart had been doing something wrong, the device shocked it back into rhythm. My mind begins to feel adrenaline-induced acuity

We try to maintain some normalcy. I am sitting up in bed as Caitlin packs a few items into a grey duffel. We may end up in the hospital for many hours, or possibly days. I don't get out of bed entirely for fear of fainting or triggering another event. We have no idea what is going on with my heart except that I feel okay, which is a blessing.

We see the flashing red and white of our local fire department stop in front of our home within three or four minutes. The firefighters are compassionate and ready to help as needed. A few minutes later, the ambulance arrives with two EMTs. The first man is around 40 and the second is a younger man around 30. Both of the men balance professionalism and good humor to maintain calm. They take control of the scene and the firefighters head out, back to their station a few blocks away.

The EMTs ask me some questions to understand the situation, and slap on some stickers with wires that run to a mobile device for taking a field-based electrocardiograph. They tell me that my heart rhythm appears normal, and they kindly give me the printout of the reading for my personal records. Caitlin sits up front with the driver, the older of the two. Then we are off to the hospital, cruising 50 miles per hour down the main artery from our home to Tufts Medical Center, in the heart of Boston's Chinatown. I am on the stretcher in the back with the younger man, who inserts an IV port into my left forearm.

There's a hard-to-describe moment when a dream becomes lucid. We can observe our own dreaming and let it unfold, witnessing the story. Sometimes we even actively allow ourselves to stay in it, avoiding waking up and breaking the spell, shaping it for a few more moments, which might be hours or days of dream-time adventure. Lucid dreaming can reveal the impermanence of our lived experience.

For many months after my defibrillator went off, as soon as a dream would become lucid, I would wake up with intense anxiety. I could not let myself return to a place where my consciousness perceived that I was being threatened. What if a dream could trigger adrenaline or other stimuli that might cause my defibrillator to go off?

I'd lie in bed restless, thinking about the suffering I might cause my wife if I slipped into the wrong dream ending. I didn't want to relive that intense trauma, for me or for her. I'd wonder, "Am I really so psychologically broken that I can't accept sleeping, dreaming?"

In moments of trauma-induced anxiety, I could sense different parts of my psyche fighting for primacy. The truth-seeking part of my brain recognized that these dreams are unlikely to cause physical harm. My *20,000*

Leagues Under the Sea nightmare almost certainly emerged out of a sudden physiological change in my body, not the other way around.

The answer-seeking part of my brain preferred to cling to small fictions that cohered a narrative, even if an irrational one. Sleepless in the comfort of my safe home, I grew frustrated because sleep is supposed to be a time for processing and integrating, not for fearing.

Reflecting now on the power of such dreams, I am reminded of a short story by Argentinian writer Jorge Luis Borges. In *The Circular Ruins*, Borges describes a nameless protagonist who aims to "dream a man…in minute entirety and impose him on reality." He pursues his singular goal with ferocity, expending all his energies on this god-like task that is "not impossible, though supernatural." He eventually achieves it, dreaming a son out into the world. As soon as he does, he is consumed by flames, but he feels no heat or physical harm. As the fire roars, the protagonist sees the truth of his own existence: "With relief, with humiliation, with terror, he understood that he also was an illusion, that someone else was dreaming him."

Borges' story gives me the chills each time I read it. We are all the realization of the dreams of others, and we, in turn, have the creative power to enact the same. Poetry, film, quantum equations, drug patents, software, legal codes. We can imagine lives and entire realities, but we are also indebted to and dependent on those who imagined ours.

There is also another, more subversive element to Borges' story, about the psychological uncertainty of drawing a clean distinction between objective and subjective reality. In a sense, we are all living fictions, weaving personal narratives, and following those of others.

When I was sitting in that Emergency Department waiting for the electrophysiologist to clarify whether my shock was real or psychosomatic, I wasn't sure which outcome I wanted to be the truth. If the defibrillator had not gone off, it would mean that my emotional recovery from the original cardiac arrest was far less advanced than I had hoped, with a night terror waking me at three in the morning on a Sunday. If it had gone off, I needed to know what was going on with my heart. Did I want to be physically stable but emotional shattered, or did I prefer to be on the path to psychological recovery, but with a heart that had lost its rhythm twice in less than two years?

The more time passes, the stronger my preference to be certain of my grasp of reality, even if it means physical weakness. There is, however, a real cost from a medical intervention such as a defibrillator. Every morning when I brush my teeth, I see the scars on my chest and the bulge of the hockey puck-sized device under my left armpit. Then I see it again at night. And sometimes once or twice in between. I feel it externally where my left arm rubs against my ribcage on a jog or in a yoga class, or when I am raking leaves. I go to annual electrophysiology checkups to check in on the device, including its battery life, which is supposed to last five to ten years. The check ins are effectively a countdown to invasive, heart-stopping surgery.

The defibrillator is a reminder of a genetic disease that I can never outgrow because it is written into me. And yet, I wouldn't dream of trading back my defibrillator for the illusion of normalcy. When I go to bed each night, I am almost certain that I will wake up in the morning to be there for my wife and son. Not perfectly certain, but far more certain than I'd be without it.

Sometimes, when I hold my young son, I can feel his little heart beating so quickly. It's normal for a toddler, and yet it's jarring for me. As his father, part of me wants to imagine our hearts pulsing in unison. But if my heart were to match his pace, beat for beat, I'd probably be on the receiving end of an electric defibrillator punch. And so, I let go of that story and keep holding him, quieting my mind. There's no need for the elusive pleasure of that daydream when instead I can listen for the eternal lucidity in each beat.

Mothering: *From Grief to Gratitude*

KRISTINE CRANE

I'm trying on a butterfly-print skirt at a store in downtown Iowa City, my hometown, when I realize that I am pregnant. It's the beginning of July, and I've been home for six weeks without having a period, but until that day, it doesn't occur to me that I could be pregnant. I've just turned 43, and there was only one time that my partner David and I hadn't been careful. Sometimes I'd felt a little queasy, but I figured it was the strong smell of manure on the farm outside of town where I was staying.

But as I glance sideways at myself in the dressing room mirror, I notice extra weight around my belly—not a bulge, more like a half-moon arc that's beginning to fill out. I try to suck it in, but it doesn't budge or wiggle, as if it's part of me. The dressing room curtain is slightly open, and I catch the store owner staring at me. Embarrassed, I tell her how pretty the skirt is and ask if it's one-size-fits-all. After I buy it, she gives me a sweet Indian drink made with rose water and Sprite. She tells me to stay safe in the heat.

• • • • •

That night, I go to dinner with my dad and step-mother and my one-year-old daughter, Julia, at the Bluebird Diner. I pick it because I like the 'blue' in its name. I'm convinced my baby is a boy, because I barely feel nauseous, supposedly a sign of carrying a boy. I feel like I'm sitting on a big secret, but I don't say anything. Part of me wants to take the test; finding out I'm pregnant in my beloved hometown would be grounding. But I'm scared. A second child isn't in my plans. I know Alex will freak out. He is ten years older than me, and already has two teenaged children from a previous marriage. He doesn't want a fourth.

Julia and I leave for Florida the next day, and the day after we get back, I take the test.

"It's negative," I shout to Alex from the bathroom, both surprised and relieved. It's the Fourth of July, so not being pregnant seems like an appropriate way to celebrate the holiday, but I'm a little disappointed. And worried.

If I'm not pregnant, then what's wrong with me? I wonder. I've been a health reporter for many years and a life-long hypochondriac. Those two influences lead me to the worst possibility: ovarian cancer. Considered "the silent killer," when symptoms emerge—such as missed periods, hormonal fluctuations and bloating—the disease is often too advanced to treat. "You don't have cancer," Alex says. He comes from a medical family, so I trust his insight. And I don't feel sick. Just strange.

Unsettled, I buy another pregnancy test to take the next morning, the recommended time to take it. We eat a healthy dinner of salmon, kale and sweet potatoes, unwittingly pro-pregnancy foods.

I wake up at 6 the next morning to pee. I'd placed the test on the counter the night before, so all I have to do is grab it and go. It's a generic pregnancy test—the same kind I'd taken when I found out I was pregnant with Julia. I remember the positive sign staring up at me like a miniature flag of Finland.

I'm both shocked and relieved to see that same little sign staring up at me—except one line is very faint. "Hey, can you come here?" I whisper to Alex. He gets up and looks at it, squinting as if he's examining something microscopic. We look at it together, as if in deep study, but there's no denying it. "It's positive," he finally says. "You're pregnant."

I slide back into bed next to Julia, careful not to wake her. But I can't resist holding her. I like being a mother. It's tested my patience, but opened me up. *I get to be a mother again,* I think, thankful that it's not cancer.

• • • • •

"Well, you're definitely pregnant," my doctor tells me the next day. We are staring at an ultrasound image of the fetus moving in my womb. Not only am I pregnant. *Eleven weeks pregnant.* Embarrassed that I'd missed the cues, I tell the doctor that I had thought that the odds of another pregnancy were simply too low. "I was home writing this summer," I explain. "I thought I was pregnant with the book I've been working on."

Bemused, the doctor points out the fetus' head, chest, heart, legs, arms, hands. "Look, he's waving at you. 'Hi, Mom,'" he says. I've been tense for the whole appointment, but I finally break into a smile. "I think it's a boy," I say confidently. "Well, I know it's a boy," the doctor says. "Or a girl. And I know it has a heartbeat. And it can dance."

"Congratulations, Mom," he says.

It's the end of the day, and although dusk is beginning to settle, the Florida sun is still bright, a nice backdrop to what I find by my car: three white ducks nibbling at food. I take a picture, as if for posterity. *You're a Mother Hen,* I tell myself, enjoying what I sense is a singular moment of private joy.

• • • • •

"I mean, at least it's not ovarian cancer," I tell Alex, who cups his face in his hands when I tell him how far along I am. I don't show him the ultrasound images: the hands, the feet, the heart. The spectral of dancing light that is our child.

"Did you ask the doctor anything?" he says.

"Well, I didn't ask him about an abortion," I say, reading his mind. "I think it's a felony for a physician in Florida to perform an elective abortion at eleven weeks. But anyway, I don't want to get an abortion," I say flatly. Although I hadn't wanted a second child, once I know that I have one in me, I want to keep it.

"If you don't want to be a part of it, fine, I'll manage," I tell him, wondering if I'm looking for a ticket out of a relationship that's fraught with tension. I'm also trying to avenge, with my second pregnancy, what still pained me about my first.

When I got unexpectedly pregnant with Julia I was at a crossroads. I'd just been accepted to a two-year writing program in Vermont, and I had reservations about my relationship with Alex. Plus, the circumstances of my pregnancy were challenging. His previous marriage had ended badly, and his ex-wife's animosity had found the perfect target in me and my pregnant self. She worked this hostility through their children, who glared at my growing belly and treated my pregnancy like a scandal. I couldn't help but feel a little resentful, and robbed of some joy.

All this weighed on me, especially during my first trimester. I spent that summer in Iowa City, and a few times, when my nausea spiked, I'd call the abortion clinic to ask about getting an abortion. But I pushed through. I was taking a poetry workshop, and I think that poetry saved the baby's life. It got me through my nausea, and mostly, my self-doubts. It reminded me of who I was inside, and how, regardless of anyone else, my own dreams and sorrows had prepared me for the miracle that was in me.

My mother had died a decade before. A nurse and a devout Catholic, she was also pro-life. I'd found a pro-life pamphlet of hers that summer, in her desk. I'd always been pro-choice, and my mother knew this, and didn't contest it.

As the pregnancy progressed, however, it was Julia herself who insisted on life. She moved all the time, punching her legs out, growing a full head of hair that didn't give me indigestion. I felt so connected to her that I remember telling Alex that if I ever got pregnant again, I would carry the child—unless there was a medical problem.

• • • • •

The week after I find out about the second pregnancy, I am heading to another appointment with the nurse when I see a missed call from the office. When I call back, I'm put on a long hold in which unnerving Muzak plays over and over again. The nurse finally gets on the phone. My doctor isn't in today, she tells me, but he wanted to let me know my blood work came back abnormal.

"Oh?" I say, surprised, relieved and concerned at the same time. The bloodwork detects fetal abnormalities, and gender. She tells me to come in so the doctor on call can explain more.

That doctor is the same one who delivered Julia. I remember him telling me what a great job I was doing as I pushed; when she came out, he announced, in a way that I found both clinical and tender, "Well, it's definitely a girl. Congratulations."

When he comes into the exam room to explain my bloodwork, he is kind but quiet. He explains that the fetus has one of the "trisomy" conditions. Trisomy means three of something; in this case, three chromosomes instead of the normal two. The most common condition is Trisomy 21, or Down syndrome, when the fetus has an extra chromosome 21. The other two –13 and 18—are more severe, he explains, calling them "incompatible with life." About half of the fetuses don't make it to term, and those that do typically die within a week. I won't find out until later that day, at my radiology appointment, which condition affects mine.

"I'm sorry," the doctor says. "I wish we had better news."

I ask about termination, and he explains that they do medical terminations at the hospital on fetuses with trisomy 13 and trisomy 18, but that scheduling terminations of Down babies is more complicated because not all nurses will take care of you.

Stunned, I can't help but think of my own mother, who thought Down babies were beautiful and special in their own right. *Would she have taken care of me if I abort?* I wonder.

As soon as I'm outside, I call Alex, who had since come around, tepidly, to the idea of another child. He'd hoped for a girl. "Well," I say, drawing in a deep breath, as if trying to suck the emotion out of myself. "As I suspected, the pregnancy is abnormal."

Walking as I talk, I reach the hospital's duck pond, where a little duck family gathers at my feet. The identical brown ducklings, all with the same yellow stripe down their backs, seem to want something from me, but I have nothing to give them. Suddenly, the reality of my pregnancy sinks in. I have to go, I tell Alex, adding, "It's a girl."

• • • • •

The ultrasound technician silently takes several snapshots of the fetus. Then she asks me to go empty my bladder so she can get a better view. But when I get back from the bathroom, the radiologist is ready to see me. She's seen enough images. They all confirm trisomy 13, also known as Patau syndrome.

I ask to "see" what is wrong, and she shows me an image of the fetus' thick neck—the recognizable trait of a Down child as well. Then she shows me the brain, pointing out that it hasn't divided properly into two hemispheres—that all the tissue is stuffed into one. This causes a number of developmental problems.

"It's a miracle that there are more than seven billion of us on the planet," the doctor says, flinging her head back dramatically. "So much can go wrong."

The radiologist remembers me from when I was pregnant with Julia. Remarkably, she remembers Julia, who looked so perfect *in utero* that the radiologist had said she could be a GE model.

As she continues to point out anatomical abnormalities on this fetus, she tells me it's nothing we did wrong, adding, "It always happens to the nicest people, too."

"Oh," I say, a bit embarrassed. "I mean, the pregnancy was unplanned. And I froze my eggs so if I want another..."

"So smart of you to have done that," she cuts in.

When she asks me what I want to do, I don't hesitate to say terminate. I'm relieved that the decision seems so straight-forward. It would have been a much harder decision had the baby had Down syndrome.

The radiologist quickly agrees that I should terminate, and before I leave, she slips the business card of an abortion clinic into my hand.

• • • • •

The abortion clinic is in a windowless tan brick office building in a gentrifying neighborhood with Gainesville's oldest grocery store, and my favorite coffee shop called Curia on the Drag, inspired by the Latin word 'curia,' for community. There is also a commercial strip mall, a Goodwill, and random objects on the sidewalk, like broken strollers and shopping carts. I remember watching a dead possum on the curbside grass ossify into the ground, its body eventually forming a faint outline.

I call the clinic, and a woman with a throaty, smoker's voice answers. She explains that abortion is a day-long process, starting with medications to slowly dilate the cervix. "Will it hurt?" I ask. And, "Will I get nauseous?" I have a fear of nausea and vomiting from childhood. My older brother regularly got the intestinal flu, and the sound of his retching, and my imaginings of his body convulsing in pain, have made me cover my ears and shut my eyes whenever someone is sick. I myself get so tense if I'm nauseous that I'm barely able to bring up anything.

"Well, it just depends," the receptionist says. "One woman the other day got sick over everything. But the woman next to her didn't get sick at all. You won't know until you take the medications."

I change the subject and ask about cost and insurance. It's a $650 out-of-pocket fee, she says, and insurance almost never covers the procedure, even for medical conditions like mine. "Really?!" I gasp. The health reporter in me feels tipped off to a potential story, especially when she continues to explain that insurance would cover the labor and delivery of a baby with trisomy 13—even though many don't make it to term, and those that do often die soon thereafter. If I was living in New York and on Medicaid, she adds, my abortion would be paid for.

Although Gainesville is a progressive college town—which gained a certain notoriety for its activism in the 1990s to support the Morning-After pill—it is rimmed by the Bible belt and ruled by a conservative state legislature. Later that day, I will drive by a half dozen anti-abortion protesters outside a Catholic center. They are mostly women, wearing floppy sun hats and long skirts. They hold signs that say, "There is another way. Let us help you find it."

• • • • •

In the week between my diagnosis and the termination, I read about Patau syndrome with a certain morbid curiosity about disease that I've had since childhood. Perhaps it was having a mother who was a nurse, but diseases and hospitals frightened me more than anything. My mother embraced the world of the sick with such ease and strength that perhaps in that way that daughters pass through a stage of never wanting to be like their mothers, made me shy away from medicine altogether. At the same time, her world drew me in, perhaps because she embodied it so fully.

She had euphemisms for throwing up that sounded even scarier than 'throwing up,' like 'vomiting,' the clinical term, or 'up-chuck,' the colloquial one. Since I feared vomiting but loved words, I feasted on these new terms with a push-pull that characterized my whole relationship to medicine.

I had the same relationship to books about sickness. The book that struck me most was *Fireflies* by Alex Morell, who lived in Iowa City and was most well-known for his series of Rambo books that then became a movie. "Fireflies," was a quieter, more dramatic account of losing his teenaged son to cancer. My mother read it first and passed it on to me. Morrell's son was sick in the eighties, before less harsh chemotherapy existed. The scenes about his son getting violently sick in the hospital, to the backdrop of falling snow outside, terrified me, even though I couldn't stop reading.

My mother's diagnosis with metastatic breast cancer, when I was in my twenties, marked a turning point in my hypochondria. I was a reporter in Rome, and I had just finished covering the death of Pope Paul II. "They can't cure me," she'd told me, by phone. "But they can manage the disease."

I didn't trust the word 'manage,' but when we got off the phone, I went straight to my computer and put my hypochondria to work, researching her illness, and finding out about trials and treatments. I became my mother's personal cancer reporter then, which would later inspire me to become a health reporter.

I apply the same intensity with which I'd learned about my mother's illness to learning about Trisomy 13. I learn that Danish scientist Thomas Bartholin, in the 1600s, was the first to describe the condition. Some three-hundred years later, in 1960, a geneticist at the University of Wisconsin, Klaus Patau, for whom the disease is named, discovered that its cause was a chromosomal defect. Chromosome 13 makes up about four percent of our genetic material, or 300 to 400 genes that tell proteins to perform various functions throughout the body. Deletions of parts of chromosome 13 can cause certain genetic defects, and cancers, but an entire extra copy of the chromosome, which every fetal cell contains, wreaks the physiological havoc that is Patau syndrome.

This manifests in abnormalities ranging from appearance (small head and eyes and ears, extra fingers and toes, cleft lips and palates, a big forehead) to functional (heart and kidney defects, sleep apnea, seizures, deafness, and feeding difficulties).

I obsess over whether the sperm or the egg is at fault. Most likely it's the egg, my doctor later tells me. Eggs are mostly responsible for the trisomy conditions because of the simple fact that they age. Women are born with all the eggs they will ever have, so their eggs age with them, losing procreative function. Sperm, on the other hand, is made fresh. My doctor explains that there are many genetic conditions that afflict eggs, causing them to die on the spot, without ever forming an embryo. But the trisomy conditions—though "incompatible with life" –are compatible enough to fertilize. So, afflicted eggs survive, but the fetuses they give rise to generally don't.

"I can guarantee you that if the baby hadn't died during pregnancy, she would have right after birth," my doctor tells me. "She just didn't have a chance."

Still, about one in 5,000-12,000 annual births in the U.S. are born with trisomy 13. I wonder about the parents who actually proceed with the pregnancy knowing the diagnosis.

I also wonder how their babies' lives unfold. I read about a study of 69 living children and their parents. The average age of the children is eight years old, and parents report some developmental milestones. Most children don't develop cognitive abilities beyond those of a six-month-old, but they do develop socially: They share, imitate, show affection. According to the study, "A child who cannot name relatives may show clear concern when someone is sad, taking a hand or gently touching a face."

• • • • •

I can't get that sentence out of my mind. One day especially, its gravitas hits me. I'm sitting at a table outside the grocery store, drinking fresh-squeezed orange juice and eating a cappuccino muffin. I am waiting for the sugar to pick me up, but instead, it clots in my throat, which is sore. I've caught a cold from Julia. We share everything, me and Julia: a bed, my breasts, germs. We've passed minor infections back and forth during her first year-and-a-half of life. Alex washes his hands religiously when she's sick, but I'm not as careful, or just more porous.

As the cold orange juice coats my throat, I'm reminded of something I once learned about the chakra in our body: that both grief and gratitude gather in the throat. I'm trying to fight the lump in my throat, as I think about how children with trisomy 13 will rub your cheek or take your hand if they sense you're sad.

Suddenly I feel connected to the creature that's in my body. I think about my own journey into adulthood, and how I've struggled to move from head to heart, journalist to writer—a coming-of-age back to the poem I wrote when I was eleven years old and first surrendering to feelings. I think about my own vulnerabilities: the stress of my pregnancy with Julia that I'd never dealt with; the deep wound of missing my mother, especially at a time like this.

I also think about all the cruel abnormalities that would assail this baby in life, and my inability to protect her from any of them. Tears run down my cheeks. I can imagine committing my life to hers, and how chaotic, yet life-affirming that would be. I feel, perhaps more than ever before, like a mother: fiercely protective of a child whom I will never meet.

• • • • •

Still sitting there, sipping my juice, I also ponder my childhood fear of children with disabilities, perhaps an extension of my hypochondria. I remember in sixth grade, my first at public school, that there was an entire class for children with disabilities, who shuffled instead of walked, and moaned instead of talked. Watching them was another kind of breaking in I experienced that year, like writing my first poem, and envying popular girls with Guess zipper jeans.

Our science teacher also had a disability, a metal arm. When he turned his back to write on the board, some kids made fun of him. That never occurred to me, but I did wonder what it was like to be like him, and the disabled children. I feared the human condition at its extremes, or the terror that "that can happen."

If I was deeply curious, I was also empathetic. I shunned cliques and defended the underdog. Once when a girl fell down at dance practice, I went to the bench where she sat in tears with her mother. "It's okay, we all fall down sometimes," I'd told her. The girl continued to cry, but her mother thanked my mother.

As a young adult, I carved out a space to combine my curiosity and empathy when I interviewed refugees in Italy under the tutelage of a literature professor, Armando Gnisci, who was also an advocate for immigrant rights and the author of books with titles such as *The Poetics of Diversity*. He was also deeply critical of America. He was the first person who made me cry about my country. He made me see America in a new light—one that still casts a long shadow on the shortcomings of American capitalism in human terms. I was more than just ashamed of America. I felt sorry for it.

I sought out Gnisci's ideas shortly after Donald Trump was elected president, when I became homesick for Italy. "The bullies have won," I remember saying to myself. And, "Vulnerability itself is under attack."

I think about Gnisci as the sun beats down on me. He died just a few months earlier, and it feels like a luminary in my life is gone. I miss his idealism about a world based on empathy, connection, and compassion. His ideas had felt wonderfully other-worldly when I'd first encountered them, yet deeply familiar.

Gnisci fought for the Other—mostly immigrants, but also the vulnerable—and it occurs to me that I now embody the Other, literally. I carry a profoundly vulnerable child within me. And I live in a world where the Other is at risk.

I begin to think that perhaps I should carry my disabled child. I don't want to politicize my body or my child, but a voice inside me wonders: *Have I missed my calling to mother the Other?*

• • • • •

At my pre-op visit the next day, I nibble on graham crackers in the waiting room, and drink water from a Styrofoam cup. A Western movie is on the television. The movie is replete with stereotypes: there's a fight between a white man with guns, and an Indian with a bow and arrow. A sensual American Indian woman with long braids stands by. I watch the people who are watching it and wonder what they're here for. Although no one is notably obese, some women have wrinkly facial skin, and deep coughs. From my health reporting days, I know rural North Central Florida to be a disenfranchised part of the country, with chronic health problems. Some adults in their fifties and sixties have never been to the dentist. I again feel sorrow for America, and how it doesn't work for everyone. I'm not even sure it works for me.

I'm called back to a room where a pleasant woman will flip through my paperwork. "Well, I just can't find a thing wrong with you," she says, cheerfully. I hate to tell her the reason I'm here. When I explain that the fetus has trisomy 13, her tone shifts to somber and apologetic. I suddenly feel cold in the overpowering AC, and notice how clean her office is, how tidy her desk. *But grief is messy*, I think to myself.

Afterwards, I meet with the doctor who will perform the termination. It's the same doctor who delivered Julia; the same one who gave me the news that the fetus had an abnormality. When he tells me again that he's sorry, I try to brush it off by saying that the pregnancy was unexpected—that I was writing in my hometown most of the summer. "Where's your hometown?" he asks, smiling. I notice he has dentures. It occurs to me that he's probably the oldest doctor in the clinic. He wears sporty Nike-framed-glasses, and his hair is brownish-grey, but his back is stooped, and his aspect is gentle.

I tell him I'm worried about nausea related to the anesthesia, and he says they'll take care of that. Then I venture, "So, have you ever delivered a baby afflicted with Trisomy 13?"

"No," he says. "But I've delivered a Down baby that was undiagnosed." He doesn't say anything more. Instead, he walks me to check-out. It's the first time a doctor has ever done that for me. He shakes my hand. He is more compassionate with me than I am with myself.

• • • • •

The day of the termination, I wake up early to prepare Julia's food for the day with unusual fastidiousness. I cut up her berries, shred her chicken, peel her grapes.

We leave her with the sitter and head to the hospital, where I have a medical abortion that is entirely covered by my insurance. Without insurance, it would have cost more than $10,000. I'm given an olive-green hospital gown that looks exactly like the one I wore during labor. When the nurse asks how I am, I tell her I have a cold, and she covers me in warm blankets. My procedure is delayed nearly an hour and a half, so I have a lot of time to reflect on what is about to happen. I try to meditate, and pray, but I'm restless. The Italian phrase *una parte di me se ne va* goes through my mind. A part of me is leaving.

Since the procedure is brief, they don't give me the drug that knocks you out before the actual anesthesia, so I take in the full theatrics of the operating room. It's cold, music is playing, and people are doing things purposefully. Someone shifts my body to the operating table, and I stare up at the bright lights. I think about all the times I've been "on the other side," watching surgical procedures as a health reporter, at this very hospital. A nurse gives me a breathing mask and tells me to think about a place I love. Just when I'm debating between a beach somewhere in Italy, or the Java House in Iowa City, a nurse tells me that I will feel a spicy tingling in my throat.

That sensation is the last I remember before waking up in the recovery room, where another nurse asks me how I feel and offers me water and pretzels. The doctor comes in to tell me that everything went well. He says it took thirteen minutes to remove the fetus from my body and clear out the fetal tissue. I'm startled by this detail. I'm in my thirteenth week of pregnancy when the termination takes place. The baby has "Trisomy 13." *Maybe thirteen really is an unlucky number,* I tell myself..

That night, I request Italian comfort food for dinner: risotto with egg. For dessert, we eat Alex's birthday cake from a few days before. It also happens to be Julia's eighteenth-month birthday. I feel fragile, but calm and grateful. I recall the day Julia was born. As I feed her cake, and watch her frolic around, I am perhaps more than ever stunned by the miracle that she is.

I recall the day she was born. She had a full head of dark hair, dark eyes, and a serious expression, all of which reminded me of my mother. When they placed her in my arms, she felt as familiar as she was foreign.

As I feed her bites of cake and watch her frolic around, I am perhaps more than ever stunned by the miracle that she is.

Big Pharma and the Barkeep

KATY GIEBENHAIN

Excerpted notes for cocktail recipes

Lobbyist Lemon Drop

Tart. In taste and character.
Sunny –
by all appearances safe and refreshing.
This cocktail
has something slipped into it.
This one takes you
from Kansas to Oz and back.
You just don't know it.

The Good Journalist

A call drink with your favorite brand
of gin, Diet Coke, lime,
is on the house, every time.
We need Clark Kent more than Superman.
Listen.
We need reporters who know
the way to save the world
is to inform it.

F.T.C. Fizz

This one takes a swizzle stick
with a tiny plastic crane.
Use cracked ice
before the grapefruit juice, before

the Prosecco.
The Federal Trade Commission prevents
anticompetitive or
deceptive business practices.
Except when they don't.
Except when they won't.
This one has a lonnnng aftertaste.

The Formulary

A daily special,
its price changes any time.
Its availability changes
any time.
The barkeep gets a phone call
and goes back
to erasing and hand-lettering
the chalkboard.
This drink is named
for contemporary
Pharmacy Benefit Managers,
the post-merger Goliaths.
You must repeatedly show ID to prove
you deserve
the chance to be served.

The Prayer

Serve The Prayer in ceramic steins
hand-thrown
by Benedictine monks.
Serve it hot
like Glühwein.
Spicy, comforting, sharp.
Drink it with your eyes closed
(obviously).

Front Porch on a Rainy Afternoon

TAMARA NICHOLL-SMITH

When it all becomes too much
I just need to sit and stare
at the gray wall of rain,
curtain of soft hyphens,
and listen to the mild motor sound
of town pigeons,
dressed down doves,
in their come-as-you-are
          feathers.

Sometimes;
I need the wind's help
to cut the power,
to shush the wires, cease the clocks
so that silence can express its thingness
and sit in slow breath at my feet,
like a retired sheep dog.

I would like
to invite you
          here into my room of rain,
where we will set aside
our petulant
ping-ding-buzz boxes.
          (For what have they to say
          that cannot wait?)

I could have lost you last year.

What could be more
important than sitting here
in our great relief
the air hung
with the deep scent
of hydrangeas?

You'll Cut Your Teeth on Duty and Dismay

CORINNE CARLAND

In every coming of age story, there is a moment where circumstances push the main character out of the metaphorical nest. This descent from safety represents a psychological loss of innocence. We point to these moments, crystallized in retrospect, where everything changed.

The surgeon was too large for the walls of the hospital. He barreled down the halls leaving in his wake scurrying techs and medical students, flurries of nurses, flickering computer screens. I am sure paper didn't actually flutter to the floor in his eddies, but when I picture the scene in my mind, that's what I see. Our patient was a middle-aged woman with a mass in her descending colon. She was as small as he was large. Cancer, muttered the surgeon. Cancer, the nurses said conspiratorially. Cancer, I echoed, to fit in. We took her to the OR. After the case, the surgeon tasks me to get the pathology report.

In her cozy office, the pathologist shows me jeweled cells splayed on glass. I stay with her for hours studying slides from dozens of patients. I marvel at the order she imposed upon the bloody, sinuous mess we cut from the patient's body. Cancer, she confirms what we all knew. Specifically, Stage IIC, with no nodal involvement and no evidence of metastasis. I look again at the bright menacing cells splashed under the microscope, subjected to the indignities of formaldehyde and dye, rendered impotent. Surgery was curative.

The rest of the afternoon passes in a flurry of patients and pathology. The surgeon finds me and asks about our patient. I cast my mind back and report that surgery was curative. He stands immediately: let's go tell her. I follow him, breathless excitement fracturing under doubt as we approach the patient's room. He confidentially shares the good news. The patient's eyes brighten with tears. Uncertainty was now a torrent in my mind. What if I got it wrong? What if I mixed up the patients? What if I misunderstood the staging?

We left the room and, as if he could read my mind, the surgeon says: I hope you were right about the pathology. I was fatally uncertain. Why hadn't he double checked? Why had he trusted me? Where were the checks and references--why now was the safety net ripped away? I wasn't ready, I would fall, I'd bring us all down with me. I had a job and I didn't treat it with the reverence and meticulousness it deserved. To my shame, I wondered if this could be the pathologist's fault – maybe she misunderstood me.

Back in his office, we pull up the patient's record. It didn't matter if the pathologist didn't understand me, it didn't matter if someone had deliberately handed me the wrong report. It was always ultimately my responsibility to get it right. My heart hurt as I prepared to rip away the immense relief we had only just given. I practiced my speech. It was all my fault, I messed up the pathology results. I am so sorry; I am so sorry.

Good job, the surgeon says, stage IIC. We have cured her. I sagged against the wall. I might cry. Somehow in this process, that patient became my patient. My first patient for whom decisions were made based on my word and assessment. The memory of this fear will be a lens through which I see the rest of my medical career. The weight of responsibility was heavier and more precious than I had ever imagined.

Protective Measures

EILEEN MCGORRY

In the early days of COVID-19, even before the stay at home mandates, I tell my husband that when he goes out in public, assume everyone has the virus. Also, around others, protect them by acting like you are infectious. It makes it easier. Don't think, is this person safe, is that person infected? Assume none of us are safe. There may be degrees of risk, but there is no safety. It makes me more comfortable to think that way, I tell him.

His face is strained when he says, I don't find that comforting at all.

It is among the differences between us. Especially when it comes to illness and health issues. When he gets sick, I corner him and say, do this, this and this. He barely listens and instead calls his doctor who usually gives him the same advice. When the news began to tell people to act as if everyone has the virus, he accepts this as if it is a new idea. I turn away to avoid saying I said that weeks ago. But I fail and the words tumble out anyway.

My husband has lived a rich life. His experience is broad and varied. But he has never wrapped himself in protective gear and walked into a hospital room to care for a patient with an infectious disease. A disease that, if you make a mistake, might kill you even if it doesn't kill the patient. I was nineteen and in my second year of nursing school when I first walked into one of those rooms. Fifty years later, some of the procedures I learned then have changed; others have not. The changes come with the emergence of new bugs and from improvements in protective devices. But the principles remain the same. As does the fear. Which is most always rational.

In nursing school, no one says outright that going to work will, at times, put your life at risk. Instead, they teach you isolation techniques, give you radiation badges, test you for things like tuberculosis, offer vaccinations for hepatitis and instruct you in the pathology of infectious diseases. They imply that proper interventions will keep you safe. Then a patient walks in with suspicious symptoms. No one knows exactly what is causing the symptoms, but the presentation suggests an infectious disease. You trust that conventional protective mechanisms will keep you safe as you care for your patient.

Until the last decades, nurses didn't label themselves essential. They simply showed up. The first time I remember being tested on the essential nature of nursing, I walked a mile in three feet of flood waters to get to work. I was in my twenties and living on Galveston Island. Overnight torrential rains left neighborhood streets flooded with water the city advised was likely contaminated. Cars were useless, so I pulled on a pair of shorts, stuck long pants and shoes into a plastic bag and dug out a pair of plastic sandals. Walking through the muck I tried not to think about snakes.

As a young nurse tuberculous was the infectious disease we feared. Back then we were tested every year to see if we had been exposed. It was all very routine until someone tested positive and had to have a lung x-ray. Many positive tests were the result of exposure without illness. But if your x-ray showed active disease, even if you were symptom free, you were required to swallow a year-long course of difficult-to-tolerate medicine.

Then HIV appeared. I was living in San Francisco in the early days of that epidemic. I was in graduate school during the day and working in the city's public hospital in the evening. Before HIV had a name, or was even identified as an infectious disease, when it was still just a cluster of symptoms, people were dying.

A 1995 paper published by the Institute of Medicine reports that as early as 1980 doctors began identifying small cohorts of gay males with infections that generally appeared only in individuals that were immunocompromised. Because these symptoms were initially limited to the gay male population, it was labeled GRID (gay-related immunodeficiency disease). Then, in 1982 the symptoms appeared in three patients with hemophilia, all of them heterosexual males. By that time experts were tracking what was called GRID and were noting reports of similar cases in people who used intravenous drugs and, in smaller numbers, in heterosexual partners of HIV positive males. Clearly whatever this new disease was, it was caused by an infectious agent;one that was likely carried in the blood and passed on through intimate sexual contact or contact with the blood of another person, such as in the practice of needle sharing by drug users.

A chronology of the spread of HIV in the same report, states that by late 1982, there were 593 cases of what was eventually labeled Acquired Immunodeficiency Syndrome (AIDS). And these numbers were limited to the United States. Forty percent of the 593 cases had already died. It was not until 1984 that the HIV virus was identified as the causative agent.

Even as we waited for the virus to be identified, health care workers were treating patients infected with HIV. Some presented with symptoms of immune suppression. Others, not knowing they were infected with a new virus, were simply arriving for routine medical care. Hospitals, acting on newly emerging information, initiated protective measures toward targeted populations, gay males, intravenous drug users and hemophiliacs. Questions about sexual practices and the use of intravenous drugs, now standard, were added to the initial medical assessment. We asked these questions knowing that people were not always forthcoming in reporting sexual practices or drug use. That knowledge soon prompted the introduction of universal precautions with all patients; a standard that has continued to this day. Over thirty years later, when I told my husband to assume everyone had COVID-19, I thought I was thinking intuitively. But it was not intuition, it was experience.

In San Francisco we watched a lot of people die. Initial treatments like AZT, seemed to slow the progression of the disease but everyone who had the drug knew, that even with AZT, AIDS was going to kill them. As the deaths rose, there were those who, while in the minority, loudly claimed that by engaging in homosexual acts or intravenous drug use, the people dying had brought this scourge upon themselves. The real victims, they said, were people who became infected through blood transfusions, or inadvertent contamination of medical equipment or health professionals providing medical care.

Most people in the medical community disregarded the noise of the moralists and went on treating any patients who were sick with HIV. The public hospital where I was working became one of the primary centers in the country for the treatment of AIDS. They were at the forefront for emerging treatments and in the development of effective protective measures for health care workers. For me, the implementation of universal precautions, brought comfort. But being comforted is not the same as being unafraid. I was still nervous giving an injection or drawing blood. Accidental needle sticks, always an occupational hazard, became a potentially lethal error. Changing bloody dressings was no longer a routine procedure. I noticed every skin crack on my over washed hands. Gloves were not accident proof and each opening was an invitation for the virus to enter my body.

That's why I tell my husband that assuming everyone is infected with COVID-19 is not meant to relieve his fears. Having no fear then or in our current situation would be irrational. But practicing self-protective behaviors gives you a way of being in a pandemic.

The epidemics I faced in my career were bad, but COVID-19 is worse. It combines a highly infectious agent, an often scarce supply of protective devices, limited testing capacity and care that demands continuous close contact with patients who are infected. It is a recipe to be afraid. When I was working with HIV, I would wake from dreams of my scratched hands soaking in infected blood. I wonder about the dreams of these frontline warriors. Their dreams must make their hearts pound.

I worked decades beyond HIV, and now I know that being essential is not limited to epidemics. It is not even always the stuff of national news. Sometimes it is just a matter of getting to work in adverse situations. In my late thirties I was working in Houston when, in the midst of our usual temperate winter, ice began falling a little past midnight. I was working in a psychiatric outpatient clinic that was on the grounds of a large university medical complex. I knew the hospitals around us would remain open, but outpatient services would likely close. But I ran our small methadone program. We administered daily doses of methadone to heroin addicts. I knew our clients would slide on ice for miles to get their medication.

In the early morning, layered in the warmest clothes I owned and wearing my running shoes, I stepped onto a sidewalk slick with ice. Before I had driven a mile, I slid into the curb three times. The only thing that saved me was the lack of any other traffic. My hands shaking and my breath quickening, I slowed even further. I watched the needle fall below ten miles an hour and crept along. By the time I eased into an empty parking lot, my breathing was shallow, and my hands were moist. A campus that was usually bustling was still.

From my car I saw eight of our thirty clients huddled around the clinic door. I knew more would arrive within the next hour. Those waiting were all males, big guys, sturdy guys. Guys who could easily overpower me to get more of the medication they craved. Since we opened earlier than the rest of the building, procedure demanded that a security guard be present when we opened the clinic. Due to the conditions in the city, I was not surprised that the usual uniformed security staff was not standing near the clients.

I could have made them wait. It was the rule. But a lot of our clients had jobs. The kind of jobs where a late arrival, even in an ice storm, was a firing offense. I moved slowly over the slick parking lot. The clients moved back from the door to let me near. As I turned off the alarm, I told them, maybe someone else will show up, but right now it's just me. I'm not supposed to open the clinic alone. But the ice is bad, and everyone is probably late. I need your help, I said. You have to make sure we all stay safe in there.

Once inside they quietly lined up to get their dose. Each of them thanked me. Most of them quickly left. Two of them lingered. "We're going to sit around here for a while," they told me. "Just to make sure there's no trouble."

All nurses and doctors have these stories. Most of them have more stories than I do. So do cops and firemen and EMTs. They are all used to running toward an emergency rather than running away. In hurricanes and floods, they send their families out of town and stay behind to work. And while we praise them, we expect nothing less.

When I retired, I feared I might miss the satisfaction of showing up when others stayed home. I craved the freedom of retirement, but I feared not being needed in the world. And I guess I did miss it because a few years after I retired, I began volunteering at an agency that helped homeless individuals find housing. I had been doing that homeless work for three years when the COVID-19 crisis arose. In the early days of COVID-19, despite recommendations that older adults stay home, I continued to show up. It was different than healthcare, but the need to show up felt the same to me.

Besides, the work was good for me. I was always amazed at how much we could do with so little money. With just a few paid staff to supervise a contingent of mostly older volunteers, the agency worked relentlessly to assist people who had been living for months in shelters or on the streets. Some of them had been homeless for years. The clients did all the work, hunting for weeks for some small place, sometimes just a room that they could afford. But without deposit money, no matter how cheap the place, they couldn't get in.

Often, our depleted budget and rising rental costs meant we couldn't give them all the money they needed. I would tell them what we could do, sometimes short of what they needed. "I am sorry we can't do more," I would say. "It is something," they would say back. The next day they would return saying, "the landlord says he'll work with me for the rest," or "the church on the corner can give me some money," or, "I finally got a hold of my brother and he is going to give me the rest." It was always their veracity, not our money, that got them housed.

The work was challenging but, hard as it was, it was easier than nursing. I was happy to be doing it.

But with constant reports that the virus was spreading, I became nervous. People came to our community center not only for housing assistance, but to hang out in a warm and dry space, to get access to showers and laundry services and to see a variety of medical providers. It was a crowded place and social distancing with continuous sanitation of surfaces was impossible. I worried about getting the virus, and I worried more about bringing it home to my husband. I finally decided to follow the recommended guidelines for my age. For the first time in my long career, I stayed home.

Two days after my decision, the local hospital that ran the community center, closed it down. A few days after that the governor closed the restaurants and bars. A week later, he mandated all nonessential business close. After the community center closed, the homeless agency, deemed essential by the state, set up shop in a small house outside of downtown. The house is owned by a church, and in the past, before the large downtown community center opened, we did our work in that neighborhood house. The agency encouraged all at-risk volunteers to stay home as the few paid staff, assisted by one or two volunteers who were young and less at risk, continued the work.

Weeks passed, and as predicted, things got worse. I soon stopped watching the news because it felt pounding, relentlessly repetitious and tirelessly dramatic. I started limiting myself to online news checks twice a day. On my iPad I bookmarked the public health sites of several states. I studied the numbers of my state and several other states. I was looking for that tiny light that suggests the numbers were slowing, knowing it was too early to see a change. I cleaned, I did yard work, I walked, I read, and I wrote. Somedays, I watched too much Netflix. Normally admitting binging on Netflix would embarrass me. Now I didn't care.

None of my immediate family live near me, so my emails to them have gone from occasional to weekly or even daily. I am on the west coast which has been hit, but I fear more for many family members who live near New York city.

My sister, who is 69 years old and has three serious chronic illnesses, two of which compromise her lungs, tells me her biggest problem is fighting the desire to get out there and help. She is a longtime intensive care nurse. When she says this, I realize my urge to help is not as strong as hers. But I don't tell her that. I want to feel the way she feels. I don't want to say that I am relieved not to be in the midst of this emergency.

"I thought you let your license go," I say to her. She tells me they are letting us come out of retirement if you want to help. "You know that the virus will kill you," I say to her. "I know," she says. The next week she doesn't talk about going back to work and tells me she is no longer going to the grocery store. "I'll get delivery," she says. In the beginning of the outbreak she continued to visit once a week with my brother and his wife. She has stopped this as well. I am thankful she has decided on these restrictions.

After a few weeks, the homeless agency activates a plan for volunteers to work remotely. If volunteers have computer access and are willing, they can return to work. They hope the quarantine will soon end, but they are acting as if it won't. I have a new computer with a camera and a microphone, so I sign up for a shift. I attend a few video meetings that help me set up my computer to access the files I will need to work. The first day I sign on to my work remotely. I am nervous. I always worry about being competent in new work settings. And I think about how old I look on video websites. Then I am talking to a client and forgetting those fears. I fall back into the work and the satisfaction of doing something to try to help someone else. After my first shift, I tell my husband that once I'm used to this whole remote thing, I might increase the number of shifts I work each week.

We have now been quarantined for eight weeks and face at least another month. The days are aggressively the same. But some things have changed. The walkers I pass in my neighborhood no longer pass me with their eyes down. Instead they smile and speak, as we keep our distance. And suddenly I am looking forward to going to the grocery store once a week. I park far from other cars, I wear gloves, and later, when the recommendations change, I wear a mask. I keep my distance. I am purposeful and do not linger in any aisle. On my way out, I buy a coffee from the grab-and-go Starbucks. I enjoy sitting in my car, drinking coffee and watching people go in and out.

The tedium of the confinement overwhelms me. Then, because this is our life right now, I adapt. I hear my husband, who has amazingly even moods, tell a friend on the phone that he finds himself getting irritable. I haven't noticed that he is irritable, and I'm surprised to hear him say this. I am happy he is not commenting on my irritability, which is common in normal times, and certainly a behavior I strain to manage now. We are lucky that we and our families are among the healthy and this helps us persist. There is too much suffering to do otherwise. We know our situation might change at any moment.

I have begun to think that going to work may not be the only way to be essential. Doing the things that keep me well, restricting social activities, getting exercise, eating properly, means that I am less likely to become infected or to spread the virus. They are all protective measures.

I may not be able to help, but I can focus on not adding to the problem. Returning to volunteer work, albeit remotely, has helped me. And I know that staying home is a responsible behavior. It demonstrates the respect and gratefulness I feel to those who are brave enough to remain on the front lines: the doctors, the nurses, the dieticians, the housekeepers, and the aides. Staying home is the only way I can help the healthcare workers who will help us if we get sick. That is the least I can do for them.

Pandemic Blues

ROBIN PERLS-SHULTIS

My tipoff to my own fear was the edgy and judgmental thoughts I had while watching TV. I was watching the news on MSNBC and instead of being grateful for the brave reporting, I was mentally criticizing the hair and outfits of the women on the broadcast. "Her hair is too poofy. Look at that pink jacket. It's glaring. That lipstick isn't the right tone for her complexion."

I looked down at myself slumped on the couch between our dachshund Toby and our black cat Lucky. My exercise pants were covered in dog hair, my short grey curls hadn't been trimmed since I started growing hair a few months ago, and my black thermal shirt had a wet spot from my eternal and ever present cup of tea. "Hey, beauty queen," I thought to myself, "maybe you're not exactly in a position to judge too harshly right now."

Our high school shut down seven weeks ago—seven weeks in dog years. Time has become an invisible field of molasses that we move through each day, slowly and constantly, step by step. We teach five hours of classes online, once a week per class. I spend three to four hours a week in meetings with staff that usually end up with a round of this:

"Anyone hear anything from Rachelle? She fell off my radar, stopped coming to Global."

"Yeah, I texted with her last week around 10 p.m. She's ok. We are going to touch base to get work done this week."

Or no one has heard from a kid and we send an email to our head counselor who notifies our principal, who sends our School Related Officer out to the poor kid's house so that we all know the kid's okay. Every week, every student is accounted for. Teaching has been whittled down to love. No one pretends to care too much about anything other than that our kids are okay.

I spend the rest of each day preparing assignments, grading papers, and working one-on-one with kids and their parents. Over the phone or through our computer screens, I try and calm down the parents and ask the kids and their parents to reach out to teachers instead of fighting with each other over the work. Students and I work on their assignments while they watch siblings, eat, or bicker with their parents. It can take an hour to get one short assignment done. I get texts at 6:26 in the morning and 10:15 at night from kids with questions about their work. Sometimes they just need to connect. I wait to write back or, if I'm up anyway, we text back and forth. I hold my own Google Meet classes and co-teach a few others. We teach kids at desks, and their kitchen tables, and in their beds. I am relieved to see their young, open faces. I try not to stare, and I never let myself tear up.

The day can be so constant that at first, like all of my colleagues, I worked straight through and forgot to eat or exercise. Ten hours whooshed by. Our principal asked us all to do less, teach less – to take weekends off. I learned to get up early and ride my exercise bike, and eat breakfast, and schedule a lunch. I dance between everything – classes, grading papers, snacks. I pick a specific Just Dance video to practice until I learn it. It's so ridiculous that I have to laugh. Fifty-seven-year-old grey-haired me dancing to Bruno Mars songs. It helps.

I was at real school for six weeks before we closed. I had just come back from my medical leave when the coronavirus pandemic broke out across the world, and made its way to us.

Next week I have my second three-month check to see if I am still free from ovarian cancer and in total remission. Dean is going to be home with me while we have our virtual doctor visit. No bloodwork, exam, or CAT scan. Dr. Pothuri will meet with us over my cell phone. Through our conversation she will determine if I am still in remission. This seems flimsy to me, as if my life is resting on gossamer wings, but I am in no position to catch the coronavirus. My doctor is doing the very best she can, given all the factors. I am not sure if we will know my status in a tangible way after this check. I am taking a sick day from work. Dean and I are going for a walk after the virtual doctor visit. We have the day figured out. It's under control.

Damn, but I like to be alive. I spent so many years dreading my own life; dreading seeing people I couldn't get to like me; dreading the feeling of not keeping pace with my responsibilities; dreading my childhood memories seeping into my dreams; dreading the sympathy of people who knew how to be happier than me. In the interminable irony of life – now I'm happier. Even in my semi-quarantine – I am mostly filled with gratitude. Seeing my daughter's face fill my phone on Facetime; getting a text from her best friend Rose; laying my head on Dean's lap while he watches TV; getting a call back from my stepson; listening to the wonder in my student's voice; taking a masked walk with Robby or Karen; hearing our great godchildren's laughter; watching Toby frolic in the grass – it overwhelms my heart. I can be mesmerized by the way the sun lights up the leaves on our Magnolia tree and lose track of time. In the new world of surviving the coronavirus while surviving cancer – I am bowled over by my blessings – a roof over my head and food to eat, my husband and family, friends I adore, teaching, dancing, and writing.

I understand much more fully that I die at the end of my life – that there is an end – not to my soul, but to this incarnation. If it's my time, it's my time. I think the whole world understands at a new level that physical life is finite on earth.

Is that what makes it enthralling? Is the beauty of life based on its definitive ending? It'll be a mess if the cancer comes back, but having had excruciating pain from chemo – I'm not afraid of pain. I know the people in my life love me, or most days, I know it. I am starting, slowly, quietly, to develop a kind of appreciation for myself. It's not outright self-love, but I'd say I'm becoming slightly more than casual friends with myself – like I'm glad to see my own face in the mirror in the morning. It doesn't seem like the end of this story yet. I'm still in rising action.

But hey, I'm not G-d. So. Great Unknowable Bigger Than I Can Ever Understand Universal Force That Connects Us All To Everything – I am going to hand my life to You – over and over – as best I can, and focus instead on my dance moves.

Is it Too Soon for Meaning?

ANDREA L. LINGLE

Last November, Jane E. Brody wrote an article for the *New York Times* about grief. It was honest and articulate. She was responding to David Kessler's new book, *Finding Meaning*, which outlines a sixth stage in the grieving process: meaning. Kessler, as one of the foremost grief researchers, probably knows best. But my gut clenched up. Meaning is what I have been trying to resist. Six years ago, on a beautiful October day, my husband and I, thirty-eight weeks pregnant, drove to the hospital for a quick check. Our fourth child, due in two weeks, hadn't moved all day. I had been through pregnancy three times already, so I wasn't a particularly nervy mom, but I just wanted to be sure she was ok. Then I would have a good laugh at myself for being so worried, regret the cost of the hospital visit, finish putting the kids to bed, and have a warm cup of tea.

Turns out, we didn't come home that night, or the next. For unknown reasons, our baby had died, full term. Named. Loved. Stillborn.

My first child and my third child are thirty-seven months apart. This fourth baby would complete the set in sixty-one months. Four kids all in a row. Boy, girl, boy, girl. Just like I planned. But this was unplanned. This was a rupture. Death came silently, unbeknownst to me. An unwelcome, unwelcomed guest. Now, seventy-eight months later, I am sitting in my office, typing away on my computer, wondering about meaning. Have I found meaning in a stillbirth? Should I? Should I hope to?

When I first encountered grief, lots of people tried to inject meaning into my broken life. People, most of them kind and well-meaning, needed me to be better. Needed me to be less raw, less broken. So there was the promise of good things, lessons learned, strength gathered. All these platitudes felt like applying fine-grain sandpaper to a sunburn. I would hug my tender arms to myself and run from "heaven needing another angel." I would sit behind the walls of my house shielding myself from the horror of the strength I was developing from "what didn't kill me." What wouldn't kill me. I was devastated by the fact that broken hearts keep beating, but I needed to be where I was. Meaning was the last thing I wanted.

In her article Brody quotes an idea of Kessler's: finding meaning in grief brings healing. Can I tell you a secret? Healing was one of the things that

I most feared. If I healed from the grief of losing an unborn child, would I lose her? Grief was my only experience of her. To even admit a possibility of meaning, and, by extension, healing was terrifying. Still is. But, it turns out, sorrow didn't stop time. I couldn't hold on to her. To tell you the truth, there are moments that go by that I don't think about being a grieving parent. There are moments when I don't remember her weight in my arms. This is a whole different bucket of grief. But, it leads me to ask: Is it too soon for meaning?

I suppose the whole problem could be what is meant by meaning. Perhaps this is a vocabulary problem. If meaning equals purpose, then, I have to say, I have not found meaning in the stillbirth of my daughter. Grief has a lot of results. Grief grows you up. It launches you straight out of young adulthood into something else—judging by the etching of my face, something akin to exhaustion. Within the space of a moment, I found myself disjunct from "before." I was entirely altered. She, the woman I was, is like an image deeply recessed in a mirror. I see her. I even recognize her, but there is no way, no dimension, no pathway—even if I press my naked body to the mirror—that I can touch her. She might still *be* in some space-time continuum way, but she is no longer me. Grief certainly has results, but purpose? Purpose implies intention, and that is a road I cannot choose.

If meaning means something good, then I reject even wanting to apply such an idea to grief. Please do not make me find good in this situation. Not now. Not ever. Sure, some good things have happened through my baby's death. I have discovered some strengths, found some wisdom, developed some skills. I would trade them all for her. Every. Last. One.

If meaning means finding value in who I have become, I can give a weak huzzah. Why not? I can't get out of it, so it makes sense to embrace this person, on this side of the mirror, and move forward.

But, what if meaning is a bit deeper? What if meaning lies beneath the sod, beneath the bedrock, nearer the bubbling magma. What if meaning is not something to be made of grief, but is something that can be discovered through grief? Through cognitive science we know that *homo sapiens* are meaning making primates. Humans are deeply intuitive and desire, fundamentally, to make sense of their lives and actions. This could be taken two ways. Meaning could be a bit of evolutionary nonsense that developed as a byproduct to staying alive within the chaos of the natural world. If the grass moves and it has meaning for you (there's a hungry tiger in there) and you hoof it out of there, you get to live (whether or not there was a tiger in the grass). If you assign no meaning to the grass moving, sometimes you're dinner. But, as I sit here, I am wondering, could meaning be a capacity that humans have? Our senses, sight, smell, hearing, taste, touch, and proprioception, tell us about the world we inhabit. Is meaning a sense that makes it possible to perceive something in the fabric of our world that lies beyond the grasp of our other senses? Is there something about grief that can help creatures be more sensitive to whatever meaning senses?

Writing questions is lazy. It is easier to pose a question, appear pithy and mysterious, and walk away quickly, than to think through your questions, take a stand, and risk being wrong.

But, then, life is risky. There is a woman across the way from my home-office window. We are both currently living through the COVID-19 pandemic and resultant quarantine. We have been at home for five weeks and a little change. She in hers, and I in mine.

We have never met. We are contiguous strangers.

Her yard is due east of mine and looks like an adolescent beard. Patchy at best. Mine is weedy but thick. We have both taken time, while sheltering at our respective homes, to tend to these neglected spaces. She has been seeding and fertilizing, I have been trimming bushes and spreading mulch. We have both been attending to what had not been done in the hustle of life before the trauma of global pandemic. Seed and nitrogen, shears and shredded bark. These things seemed un-get-to-able before. There were meetings and birthday parties and two different swim teams. Unnegotiable doing. But here, watching her walk behind her standard green seed spreader, I am overwhelmed by the thickness of life. Back and forth she walks. Is the seed getting in her shoes? After a few passes, she rocks the spreader back and forth—rearing and bucking to get the last of the seed out, then she walks, slowly, back up the hill to her garage to refill the bucket. There is no hurry. Even the grey-brown rabbit crossing her driveway in her absence isn't hurrying. Life is thick and slow today.

While she walks, I write, thinking. This is another moment of before and after. Global shut down, deaths, fear, mistrust; these are the words of this moment. There are more words, words like family dinner, mop headed brothers chatting on swings. Nowhere to go. Nothing to do. Happy words. Even so, there is grief here. There are broken lives. So many lives and dreams lost. There is no way around it. There will be trouble after this. There will be hesitation before a hug. There will be avoidance of the crowded aisle. There will be nagging fear. We have been encased by quarantine. The seeds my neighbor scatters plink to the ground, sprayed in a horizontal arch. What do they meet on the ground that convinces them to burst out of their shells? Forgive me for a metaphysical flight of fancy! Do they encounter meaning, and find the courage to forsake their safe shells to sink their roots down toward some risky, vital force?

These seeds must have been collected from an expanse of perfect sod. A uniformity of genetic material. One seed exactly like the next. The collection is sewn into a plastic burlap bag, and each bag, a little lighter than it looks, is taken via truck or plane or boat from one place to another. Unintentionally. No one thinks about where that one seed will go. It's journey is meaningless. The bag is selected, placed in a cart, a trunk, a garage. When it is opened an oblong of sky appears above. It might be overcast or clear. It might be cool or warm.

Seeds are tiny promises. This one promises green, traffic-resistant ground cover and reduced erosion. Does it anticipate the mower? Does it hope for the day it will feel the gentle buffeting of wind? Does it brace itself for pets? Does it long for gentle dawn showers? Why does it try? Why does it forsake its hard casing for the terror of growth?

She, my unknown across-the-way neighbor, is gone now. She has finished her task of spreading potential life, and left my line of sight. She has left it for the sun and meaning to do the rest. Will she come back to check on her seeds? Will she worry about birds or heavy rain picking or washing her work away?

The questions. The questions! I am too nervous for statements. They are so definite, so misunderstandable, so refutable! But questions are more slippery. More forgiving? They are a side door.

Meaning is. Noun verb. A property and existence. Meaning is nested deep in mundane life—depth that is there regardless of your attention (I am actively resisting typing a question mark). It is hard to make a statement and risk being wrong, risk being laughed at. Depth is not equal to happiness or joy. It is vitality. Could meaning be that which allows a person to sense the depth of life?

Finding meaning in grief does not mean making grief meaningful. Meaning and meaningful are vastly different. Meaningful is a forced smile. Meaningful is good for you. Meaningful is well produced and tidy. Meaning is raw. Meaning is a child's wail over a frustrated hope. Meaning is laughing until you cry playing charades with your kids in the middle of a world-wide melt down.

Grief is a process by which one discovers meaning. And sometimes meaning hurts.

My neighbor hasn't started watering her seeds yet. I wonder if she will. I wonder if she will feel any remorse if she does. Watering a seed is a bit like grief. Water softens the indifferent shell and cracks the seed's protection. Will it be too much? Will it overwhelm the seed, rotting it before it can grow? Will the seed refuse to crack, and, instead, be washed away? Grief cracked me open. At times it felt like it pulverized me—bits and pieces blew away, unusable, unsalvageable. I have lain under the steady drizzle of grief for six years. Is it time for me to admit the possibility of meaning? If meaning is a deep vitality that inhabits all of life, then the rupture of grief could make space for meaning to seep through.

Grief is not safe. It might be riddled with questions, but it is most assuredly not ambiguous about its arrival. Grief is choke-slam level definite. Ignore it at your own risk. I have never been as aware of my edges as when I have been confronted by grief in the middle of a group of people. Here I am. Right here. I am not over there. I do not have that point of view. I can't even pretend to have that point of view. I don't even remember what it would be like.

So, why can't I talk about grief without equivocating? Why must I leave myself an exit?

Pandemic has made me aware of edges again: turning my face away from another shopper in the grocery store to keep my breath in my space, covering my hands and face with personal protective gear before turning over the tomatoes. I watched a man introduce himself to my husband today, and we all tensed up when he automatically raised his hand. We are all learning to stay an average-man's-length away from our neighbors. We are all cartoons now, drawn in thick, dark lines. Lines we shouldn't color outside of.

I do not have any full-length mirrors in my house. I didn't notice this until I went to the home of someone with, what I would consider, a lot of full-length mirrors. It seemed that everywhere I would go, there I was, from head to toe. Standing, dislocated from myself, presented in full. I am average height, average weight, average build, average shoe size. I am physically unremarkable. If I want to, I can walk through a crowded room without being seen by anyone. It's my superpower. I can recall walking around the corner in this be-mirrored house and seeing myself all at once. There I was. Surprisingly. I don't always feel somewhere. I can get caught up in my thoughts and feel disembodied: a-carnate, but there I stood: enfleshed. Grief does that too. Grips you in definite corporeality. You can feel tears that drip into the collar of your shirt. Sobbing makes your head throb.

I've been watching my neighbor's yard for a week. These words have taken a while to form. They have built up in tentative piles, allowing me time to be sure of them. I love that about words. They are so patient. The grass doesn't seem much greener in my neighbor's yard. I don't blame her or her seeds.

It has been chilly. The rain yesterday filled my dogs' outside water bowl to overflowing. That isn't ideal for seeds. Too much too quickly. This weekend is supposed to be warm and gentle. Maybe that will embolden the seeds. Maybe we will venture into the sunlight. Maybe I will whisper to them. Be brave little seeds. Let's be brave. You and I. Let's let the sun and the rain and the tears do their job.

Titch by Titch

GAIL GOEPFERT

FOR DEB BEYER

Scoot over just a titch, she says—
eyeing the space on her table.
Titch? I question.
I have a quirky affection for words.

It's a word. A small amount.

It is a word! She was right—
my physical therapist
with hands and eyes that seem to hear
what rattles wrong in the body.

It's been months, no years now.
And still there's no end to her repertoire.
Each visit, first I walk,
and she observes my motion.
We talk about my body's pain and performance—
like an engine diagnostic.
And her repairs are rarely the same.

In-between I text with questions.
Always a response about what to try.
My tush is on fire—
Place one hand on the base of the skull.
The other hand on the chest spanning
each side of the sternum.
Gently rock the chest hand
side to side (a small amount).

I do. And it's better.
Titch by titch.

The ankle's tight, doesn't flex—
If you have Kinesio tape,
tape back the distal lateral ankle bone
and try walking. Then try taping the talar dome,
the tape pulled open maximally.
Like a Band-Aid.

Her knowledge. Wisdom—a Band-Aid.
Salve for the wounded. The hurting.

I've spent years looking for fixers.
Self-fixing. Learning names of the anatomy
because I needed to. Tunnel-visioned
in desperation.

Go easy along the line from the ischial
tuberosity to the sacrum.
That's the route of the sacrotuberous ligament.
Titch by titch.

At times I fret the fixers will give up.
That she will. That I will.

I think you need to get your diaphragm
on board—breathing is a must.

The pain subsides. She gives me tools.
Body-mechanic tools.
Yoga Nidra to muffle the nerves, modify the cells.
NFP, neural fascial processing—
a tune-up. Blueprints for redesigning
the body without new parts—

all repairs I can do
to bring back the body's humming
when the pain ratchets up.

Titch by titch.

I need to clone you, I say.
No cloning, she texts,
adding the scared paled-blue-head
screaming in fear emoji.

And once when I'm afraid, I write—
I hope you don't ever give up on me.

Never giving up!

What You Missed that Day You Were Absent from Medical School

ERIK CARLSON

A medical student's version of *What You Missed That Day You Were Absent from Fourth Grade* by Dr. Brad Aaron Modlin

Dr. Nelson explained how to use a stethoscope to listen
to your own heart, how to find meaning in charting,

how the physical exam can be a form of prayer. She took questions
on how not to feel lost during a code.

After morning rounds she distributed worksheets
that covered ways to remember your very first patient's

voice. Then the team discussed falling asleep
without feeling you had forgotten to check on your patient's —

something important — and how to believe
that the name on the white coat is your own. This prompted

Dr. Nelson to draw a chalkboard diagram detailing
how to console one another during coffee breaks,

and how not to squirm for sound when your self-doubt
is all you hear; also, that you are enough.

The grand rounds lesson was that *I don't know*
is an acceptable answer.

And just before sign-out, she made the diagnosis
look easy. The one that proves that hundreds of questions,

and feeling frightened, and all those sleepless nights spent looking
for whatever it was you lost along the way, and each beat of our hearts

adds up to something.

Dr. Brad Aaron Modlin's poem "What You Missed that Day You Were Absent from Fourth Grade" is beloved by many and originally appears in his book *Everyone at This Party Has Two Names.* This adaption of his original work was written with the express permission of the author.

Costco and the Apocalypse: (a letter to my friends and neighbors)

SHERI REDA

I apologize, in advance,
    for being the one
who dropped from my sleeve
    the viral speck
that lodged in the throat
    of the stud at the gym
who showered and shopped
    and brought his own bag
that was touched by the clerk
    with the purple hair
that brushed the shelf
    that was cleared of goods
in the Costco
    where you prepared to survive
the Apocalypse.

The World of Sickness

PAUL ROUSSEAU

A guttural sound rises from my belly. My head pitches forward. A slurry of pancakes and coffee spew from my mouth. I race to the bathroom and slam the door. A soft knock. *"Are you okay? Can I get you anything?" "Jesus Dad, give me some time, my guts are hurling. And no, I'm not okay."*

Cancer, at thirty-five years of age.

Mom died ten years ago, same cancer, breast. Genetic roulette; I lost. Then, six months ago, after my diagnosis, I moved back home, to survive; I'm too sick to live alone. It's just me and Dad.

"This will all be worth it one day, just you wait and see. It's tough now, but..." "Just shut the fuck up Dad."

He's a doting father, but he smothers with concern. He gets up when I get up; he sits down when I sit down; He laughs when I laugh, he cries when I cry. And, most annoyingly, he questions my every need, continuously: am I hungry, do I have pain, am I nauseous, am I taking my medications, have I peed or pooped, am I comfortable on the couch, do I want to watch television, do I need anything from the grocery, can he do my laundry? He did the same with Mom. He's a kind man, and he means well, but he's healthy, he has his hair, his eyelashes, and his appetite. He doesn't understand the world of sickness. He's a bystander, unsure and afraid. He's a father caring for a very sick, and possibly dying, daughter. *"Are you okay?" "Dad, for chrissakes, give me a few minutes."*

I rest my hands on the sink. I stare in the mirror. My body looks light, but I can feel the weight of cancer. I turn my head side to side, as if to be sure I'm still alive. My hair is gone, my brow furrowed, my eyes sunken and surrendered. *"Well, let me know if I can help." "Just leave me alone Dad."* I clench my hands and pound my narrow thighs, my muscles mere fibrils. Fat tears fill my eyes. My fingers and toes tingle and burn from nerves singed by chemotherapy. My skin hangs from bones rising like periscopes. My mouth tastes like stale metal. My body has been taken from me.

~

It's chemotherapy day. I'm in the infusion room. My nurse is dressed in a protective gown with a face mask and gloves. A quasi-Hazmat suit. All to protect her from the drug she's spilling into my veins that will seep into every crevice of my body like spilt mercury. It's a frightening thought. It will kill, hopefully, cancerous cells, but there will be collateral damage—the death of non-cancerous cells. Collateral damage, soldierly patois implying a war. Or maybe it's all just learning to die.

I sit in a reclining chair amongst the many others wagering their lives on poisons and potions. We, the sick and unwell, glance at each other, frequently. The glances are hurried, as if unintentional, but they aren't. *What does that person have? Will they be alive this Christmas? Who's the sickest? Do I look as bad as her?* And when someone suddenly disappears, there's a buzz of whispers. *Are they hospitalized? Are they on hospice? Did they die?* I want to know, but I don't.

My Dad steps into the room. *"Can I get you anything?"* I shush him away with the flick of my fingers. The nurses frown at my dismissal. They adore him; he brings them pastries. But they don't live with him. *"I need to run home for a bit, but I'll be right back. Don't you leave without me."* His lips twist into a half-smile; then, as he turns to leave, a soft snort. I look away.

I wish I could go back to my apartment, sleep in my own bed, sit on my own sofa, eat in my own kitchen, use my own bathroom. Have my old life. Be alone, without Dad. But I can't.

The IV bag empties. *"All done."* The nurse is too cheerful. But that's her job, cheer and hope. I stand and topple to the side. She hurries a wheelchair under my crumpling body and pushes me to the waiting room. *"Your father should be here soon. You wait for him. I'll see you in three weeks."* I look around the room. The sick are everywhere. One sits with a vomit basin to catch her insides. Three sit with face masks, all one breath from pneumonia. Five wear bandanas covering hairless heads. Seven drink oxygen from nasal prongs. One rests on a gurney, unmoving, eyes closed. He may be dead.

I touch my head, my face, my arms, my legs. I'm no longer whole. I feel as if parts of me have died, I'm just not sure it's the cancerous parts.

~

I fling the door open. Dad is sitting on the couch, his back toward me. I slam my purse to the floor. *"Dad, why didn't you answer your cell phone? I had to get my old girlfriend to bring me home. The lesbian you hate. Her car doesn't have air conditioning. And it's July. You know what that's like after chemotherapy?"* I collapse on the chair by the door, my blouse heavy in sweat. *"Dammit, Dad, answer me."* I reach for my purse and throw it toward the couch. *"Dad, put your fucking hearing aids in."* I stand and feel a swirl of nausea. I stumble and follow the wall like a blind man follows braille. I grab the arm of the couch and plop down. Dad's body bounces once and falls to the side. A sliver of sunlight catches his face. It's pale, his eyes open. I can feel my heart in my temples.

it b like that

DESIREE SCHIPPERS

In the phase of my life affectionately referred to as "The Big Fat of 2018," I had been taking prednisone for so long that my face became a round dough ball, my hair fled my scalp, and between excruciating bowel movements and steroid induced insomnia, I was averaging about 4 hours of sleep per night. Ulcerative colitis ravaged my poor, unsuspecting large intestine, creating a wound gnarly enough that the bleeding made it so I couldn't leave my house or walk up a staircase without getting dizzy.

One morning in the spring, I called my gastroenterologist's office when the inflammation began attacking my joints. I told the nurse that my knees were filled with knives and broken glass and bees covered in sulfuric acid; that I had converted my bathroom into a small studio apartment and conducted all of my personal business from the toilet.

"You know," she said. "That's just the nature of the disease. I'll let Dr. Brown know how you're feeling."

I continued living my life like the dog in that meme where his house is on fire, but he sits calmly with his suave little dog hat and a cup of coffee. He's a cartoon, but somehow his eyes reveal that he's seen some shit. His speech bubble reads: "This is fine."

That June I had to start being driven to my summer Spanish class, because I couldn't walk from my car to the classroom without starting to black out. After being dropped off at the front door, I would take two breaks inside the building to catch my breath and lower my heart rate before reaching the room. I couldn't figure out how to say,"I think my inevitable march towards death is proceeding far too quickly" in Spanish, so I settled for "estoy muy cansado."

When my mom figured this out, she summoned the wrath and spiritual power of every one of our ancestors to express her fury at my inaction and demanded that I see my primary care physician immediately. Because I knew literally everything there was to know about life—"you don't even live with me anymore, Mom, your 19 extra years of life experience mean nothing" --I resisted going to the doctor, reminding her of the nature of my disease. She brought in my childhood doctor for backup, who called with the polite equivalent to a listen-here-you-little-shit speech, telling me that

I was going to be seen. I heard the Pope, Obama, and Jesus Christ himself were next on the line if that hadn't worked.

I made an appointment for noon and promised myself I could get Sonic when it was over. It was 99-Cent Mozzarella Stick day after all.

*

Edna was the neediest, most frustrating resident I had ever worked with.

When I would come on to my shift, the CNA giving report would always tell me how many times Edna rang her call bell that day, which was usually an astronomical number compared to other residents.

"34."

"Bullshit."

"I'm serious," she would tell me. "I reached 20,000 steps today by noon. If they don't start her on Xanax or something, I am switching halls. No joke. I can't do this shit anymore."

I would begrudgingly relieve her of her pager and begin my 8 hours sprinting between Edna's room and carrying on with my regular duties.

When she wasn't freaking out, she was a really pleasant woman. She had a faded tattoo of a butterfly on her foot and would remind us that men are trash and that we don't need one to be happy. But most of the time, she was inconsolably panicking.

I would come into her room and hear her hyperventilating before I would even see her. She was skin and bones, only about 95 pounds, and almost disappeared when she sunk into her bed. She would throw her covers off and sit up in bed, desperately clinging to her oxygen tubing.

"I think it's kinked somewhere," she would say. "I can't breathe. I. Can't. Breathe. I'm going to. Die. I'm going to die."

Knowing damn well the oxygen was working perfectly, I would check the tubing anyway.

I held her hand. "Breathe with me. In for three, out for three. In, 1, 2, 3, out, 1, 2, 3."

It didn't help much, but she was just relieved to have somebody there. Though this happened at least five times a shift, there was genuine fear in her face every time. But then another call bell would ring, and I would be off to the next task. I didn't have time to sit in her room and hold her hand all day.

I would report the happenings to the nurses, who would remind me that she had an anxiety disorder and that it was all in her mind. I asked if she could see the doctors about it.

"She does. Pretty much every week."

*

I had a friend, Sam, who used to be a hippie in high school, with bare feet, long hair, and round glasses. I never kept in touch with him, but my boyfriend, Cheyne, did.

"So I think Sam is kind of a neo-Nazi now." He told me one day.

"A what now?" I couldn't picture it. Sam had been one of the most liberal people I'd ever known.

"I think he's spent a little too much time in some bad subreddits and 4chan forums," Cheyne said. "He was saying some white-supremacist shit in our group chat. I thought he was joking, but I don't think he is."

I read through some of his messages.

"Why are any of you still talking to him?" I sure the hell wouldn't be.

"Nobody really is anymore. Everyone made a separate group chat without him. They even kicked him off the Minecraft server."

"Good," I said. "You guys shouldn't condone that. It's disgusting."

A few months later Cheyne showed me another message chain with Sam, this time with Sam displaying incel behaviors, telling Cheyne that women are all sluts and gold-diggers, only chasing after Chads instead of guys like him. He spewed misogyny and resentment toward women and his entitlement to sex.

This was the last straw for me.

"Jesus Christ, quit talking to him. You are virtually supporting him!"

I told Cheyne that people like that don't deserve attention or friendship. That in my eyes, not vehemently denouncing him was about the same as saying his behavior was acceptable. I didn't want people to think Cheyne was like him or supported him. I wanted Sam to end up sad and alone. He deserved it. I reminded Cheyne that incels and neo-Nazis were often mass murders and shooters, who deserved the hate they received.

"He's my friend," Cheyne said. "I'm just trying to be here for him. Nobody else is."

"Because they have backbones and morals."

We didn't discuss Sam much after that. I did my best to keep my mouth shut when I saw notifications from him on Cheyne's phone.

*

After seeing my heart rate, temperature, and blood pressure, my primary care doctor sent me to the hospital to get blood tests and receive fluids. After being sat in an IV therapy room with four other people and poked three times by nurses and phlebotomists, I finally saw a concerned nurse. She told me that my hemoglobin was at 6.3 and said she was going to call my doctor. I didn't know the implications of this statement, so I sat uncomfortably as the man across from me stared in my direction. I figured he was blind, seeing his white cane and blank stare, but he was sure focusing in on me. Given the area's complete lack of acoustic privacy the man, who introduced himself as Dave, had interpreted my results.

"Did you walk in here by yourself?" Dave asked.

"Yes." I said.

"She said 6.3, right?" He raised his eyebrows.

"Yeah," I said. "Is that bad?"

"Is it! It's supposed to be above 12. I bet they give you a transfusion."

Dave wished me good luck.

Shortly after, the nurse came in and carted me to the ER, where they ineffectively tried to start another IV five times before finally hitting a vein. I received one unit of blood and was shipped two hours away to the nearest university hospital under strict orders not to eat or drink. It was 1:00 a.m. when I reached the hospital and realized that I would not be able to observe Mozzarella Stick Day, which fell just after Christmas and Halloween on my list of important religious holidays.

I was stabbed three more times upon arrival and carted to what felt like eight different radiology tests. It was just about 4:00 a.m. when the sweet relief of sleep was finally within my reach; I snuggled my halter monitor and IV tubes and dreamed of stringy cheese for a whole five minutes before another phlebotomist came to take more blood.

"You need to drink more water," she told me, annoyed.

"I have 23 bowel movements per day and can't put a drop of anything in my mouth without immediately having to run to the bathroom, bitch," is what I wanted to say. But at that time I was still pretending to have a shred of dignity, despite being balding, moonfaced, and practically incontinent. I was tired of being a lab rat.

I thought hospitals were supposed to be places of healing.

*

Edna's daughter was supposed to pick her up for a haircut, but Edna was having her second panic attack of the day.

I sat on the edge of her bed and let her squeeze my hand. She asked me to please do something. I reminded her that I'd told the nurse, but I couldn't diagnose or dispense medication since I was only a CNA. I waited impatiently for her panic to pass so that I could get her dressed and get on with my shift—I was already an hour behind. After 10 minutes of coaxing, she decided she couldn't go, which was fine by me, so I left and scrambled to get the rest of the hall to breakfast.

I knew I was in for a treat when her daughter power-walked toward me in a huff about 20 minutes later.

"Mom was supposed to be dressed and ready to go!" She tapped her wrist and looked me up and down. She wore cheap costume jewelry and looked like she would try to sell me weight-loss shakes or essential oils on Facebook.

"She was having trouble breathing and didn't want to leave. She told me she would call you. I'm sorry."

She rolled her eyes and walked down the hall toward the door, without going back to say goodbye to her mother, which I thought was shitty for two reasons: one, because she had already blocked off this time to spend with her, so why not just hang out in her room for a while anyway? And two, because I knew it would be me running to her room every ten minutes to remind her to take deep breaths and assure her that she isn't going to die.

*

Cheyne would visit me in the hospital and sleep on the tiny couch by the window so I didn't have to be there alone. He looked a lot like George Harrison during his long-hair-and-beard period in late sixties and early seventies. He was much cuter than George Harrison, though.

Cheyne and my parents would walk down to a cafeteria for lunch while I rested. Cheyne often trailed behind my parents. I liked how he walked, with his feet pointed out slightly. He didn't like pickles, but would order them on his sandwich, wrap them in a napkin, and put them in his pocket.

My mom said she looked at him funny one day and he noticed.

"Desi likes pickles," he told her, as if it were obvious.

Sometimes love is a warm dill pickle.

*

I came in for my shift a few days after Edna's daughter had walked out and noticed that her room was empty during rounds.

"Where did they move Edna?" I asked the aide giving report.

"She died like, two nights ago," the girl said. I stared at her in shock.

"Yeah," she continued, reading my face. "Turned out she had congestive heart failure, but nobody'd figured it out. The family is pissed."

She continued walking forward, but I stayed behind, staring into her room. My mind flashed through all of the times she told me she couldn't breathe and that she was afraid to die. I remembered every time I had been annoyed with her call bell, not wanting to take the time to listen to her complaints another time. They had told us it was in her head.

She was afraid and actually dying. All she wanted was for someone to hold her hand.

But we were too busy to be inconvenienced.

*

On my third day at the hospital one of the top gastroenterologists came to evaluate me. I told him that I had been suffering for months, unable to leave my house without crippling fear of incontinence. I described my pain and blood loss, how the steroids and immunosuppressants weren't working. I told him that I didn't feel like a human being and that I was getting depressed. That I would spend days in my basement only leaving my bed to go to the toilet.

"Well at least you don't have cancer," he said.

*

Cheyne is a physicist, and while he is by no means a Sheldon Cooper, he still wasn't the most emotionally intelligent person I ever met. I was the empath in the relationship and probably a self-righteous one at that. I felt physical pain when I saw others get hurt, I was gentle with my residents, I made sure nobody was ever left out of a conversation. Cheyne didn't remember other people's names and would often forget to say thank you to workers at restaurants. He would argue with anyone for the sake of it and could never really validate my feelings, but he taught me a lot about loving others.

"I got Sam to see a therapist," he told me one day. "I think it's really helping."

A few weeks later he told me that Sam made a female friend. That he seems a little bit happier.

I asked Cheyne how he influenced him.

"Gently," he said.

He showed me love is something you practice. That it's something you've got to actively cultivate and pull out of yourself, rather than feel. And it's fucking hard work.

Several months later I was listening to *On Being* with Krista Tippet. She was interviewing physicians who worked with anti-vax parents. One of them explained their strategy: "We don't argue or try to be right. We know their fears are irrational. But rather than honor the irrationalities, we honor their fear. That's what helps us get through to them."

*

After I was dismissed from the hospital things didn't get better. I had an allergic reaction to the medication that was supposed to heal me and had to go back for two more units of blood. I dropped out of my Spanish class and spent most of my days in my basement.

Cheyne and my roommates would take me on little walks up and down the driveway. They would fiercely deny that my bald spots were getting bigger or that my face was getting puffier. They let me join their D&D games and sit in their rooms as they studied Feynman lectures and looked at girls' profiles on Tinder. One of them suggested I make a reddit account and join the Ulcerative Colitis Support Group.

The first post I read was someone similar to me, venting about being in the hospital on IV steroids. The top two comments were:

"that's really fuckin shitty man." and "it b like that sometimes."

I realized that I didn't want someone to comfort me or try to help me look on the bright side. I didn't need someone to try to solve my problems by telling me to eat more fruit or to do yoga.

I wanted someone to sit next to me in my dank basement and acknowledge that my situation sucked. That it was really fuckin' shitty.

That it do be like that sometimes.

Explosion at takeoff or landing

ELIZABETH LANPHIER

...is the trouble with being an astronaut
The night I dyed
my hair purple Eric and I talked
about dead mothers while I got drunk
from one glass of red wine
and not sleeping, not eating,
he and I were only children
of lawnmower fathers, milk carton
mothers in boxes on the shelf.
I have always dreaded
unpacking. The night
Eric's mother died we might have been
having sex. If she died
at night, or in the morning.
Or maybe while she was dying
we were finishing dinner
off each other's plates or
earlier still, watching the sun
set into Manhattan from a fire
escape at a party, hands
covering other people's bodies
so skin wouldn't feel lonely.
Like her skin must have felt,
like bare legs in shorts
after dusk in early summer,
turning to leave the porch
when there is no more
alivelight, or during sleep
when uncovered shoulders and
smalls of backs are cold until
a sheet is pulled up. The night
my mother died I was drunk off one
glass of wine and two bourbons, a jack

and ginger, a sip
of someone's beer, and lips, and the cold
air on the terrace where I wore just a sweater
the day before winter
and warmed my hands and face with a lighter
going in for a three way kiss.
Me in one room, her in another. My mother
and I both drugged and working on leaving
our bodies. Mine
joined some cowboys, galloping
westward toward a gold rush while she
was becoming a space explorer. She was
strapped into a suit of sheets and
catheters taking charge of fluids
and functions so she could gaze
on celestial bodies through clouding
eyesight and float in the stillness
of anti-gravity.

Son Worrying About Down South

TRAVIS STEPHENS

I hope that the Texas doctors
have been trained in how to handle calves,
handle them firmly but slow,
steady as a post,
not to spook yet not to yield.
I hope they've been
trained to handle full buckets of milk,
steady walk, not to slosh,
each one a white dollar bill.
How to treat old sick men like the men
treated their dairy herds—
calm voiced and glad to see them.
Open the door and then get out of the way.
Warm hands
or you'll get kicked for sure.

I try to imagine such a doctor and worry. None I've met.
Nurses, that's another story.
Some steady on her feet,
sassy woman with the hips of fuller living.
She would joke with the old farmer to put him at ease.
A nurse like a vet he knows,
best at giving shots, giving advice.
Big animal vets don't need x-rays to know
it is time to call the mink farm.
I imagine my father talked into sitting on
the exam table, milker's hands clutch at the paper gown.
He came to Texas to get out of the cold,
not to move into a living hell.
You'd better be good, doc. Good enough for
the milk money, my blood money.
Money earned by the day, not by the "visit".
Be good or I'll come down like a
winter storm all over you.

Unrooted

HANNA SALTZMAN

"Whad'ya think? I'm the Grim Reaper," our hired driver said when I asked if he liked his job. Every few hours, we—the transplant surgeon, the surgery resident, the "Grim Reaper," and I—arrived at another small community hospital flanked by icy farmland. We changed into scrubs, power-walked to the operating room, and waited. As the only medical student, I tried to play it cool, like this was just another Saturday. I could barely breathe.

Learning clinical medicine has brought me to witness vulnerable and severe corners of humanity that I had not previously imagined. But I could not have even begun to imagine *this* experience: impatiently and fervently wanting a human being to die.

We could not hear the gasp of each dying human or see color drain from skin, but on a computer screen down the hall, we watched vital signs descend: heart rate 60, 50, 40. Like monitoring patients in the intensive care unit, except now, we pleaded for zero. My body pulsed with adrenaline, my mind with images of the hopeful recipient whom I had admitted to our main hospital early that morning: an elderly man with grandchildren and a love of swimming, now yellowed and weak, the life force of his liver robbed by a rare and aggressive disease. He might live, if only someone else would die fast enough.

Our task that day was organ "donations after cardiac death," in which death occurs after withdrawal of ventilator support. Without the ventilator, organs rapidly lose oxygen. Strict rules dictate how much time can pass between extubating and removing organs. If death and dissection happen fast, another person might live. If they take too long, the transplant team packs up, hoping to harvest an organ elsewhere.

No, not harvest, *procure*: that's the word we are instructed to use. *Procure, extubate, dissect.* Words build boundaries, neutrality, space. Words turn the profane into the sacred—or at least, the acceptable. Words insulate us from our own experience.

Fixated on vital signs from behind a computer screen, our transplant team intentionally did not think about the dying person's experience. We intentionally did not even refer to the person as a person. "A dead body," the surgeons had instructed me when we were preparing for the day. "Remember: it's a dead body."

Our first body did not die fast enough because his wife waffled about whether to extubate. A nurse came to apologize. Against the surgeons' wishes, he told us why: The husband had gone for a drive after getting in an argument with her. He was the father of three young children. On his way home, he was hit by a teenage drunk driver. Now, his wife stood (sat, collapsed) next to his intubated body, in a room mere steps from me but hidden from my sight. I imagined her sorrow and guilt as she replayed their last angry words over and over. I imagined my own fiancé, the petty annoyances that sometimes started our day. I cried under my mask.

Now I understood why transplant surgeons shun stories of organ donors. Story is what turns procurement into person.

Throughout my life, words and stories have nourished me. In medical school, my patients' words and stories have nourished me. Learning about their lives has proven just as important to my ability to find meaning in medicine as learning about their medical concerns. I believe that listening to patients' stories is crucial to helping them heal. But might stories also be my downfall in medicine? Many medical situations requirethat we buffer ourselves from the full emotional impact of our patients' stories. We need distance in order to make difficult decisions or perform difficult actions. In some situations, like organ procurement for transplant surgery, we must shut down stories entirely.

Medical school does not teach us how to switch modes; how to sometimes be open fully to a story, other times hear a story from a safe distance, and other times shut it out completely. Instead, medical school teaches us words and phrases; medical jargon and symptom checklists. We learn new words to describe things we've experienced all our lives: emesis instead of vomit, fracture instead of break, auscultate instead of listen, palpate instead of touch. Learning this language of medicine carries many purposes; one effect is unconsciously learning to inhabit more distance between self and patient.

It's just a dead body. Body, not person. Say it. Try to believe it.

Our second body did not die fast enough because his vital signs refused to budge: heart rate 80, respiratory rate 15, oxygen saturation 96 percent. Several minutes passed without change. *Vitality*: the capacity for survival; the power to endure. Quarantined from his family's grief in the room next door, our transplant team listened to '90s pop music and shared our favorite recipes—steak in a red-wine reduction for one of the surgeons, a middle-eastern tomato stew for me—while glancing every so often at the unchanging screen. *We tell ourselves stories in order to live*, Joan Didion wrote. Now, the story we told ourselves was its absence. A not-quite-dead body. Nothing more. Thirty minutes passed; too late for a liver. Ninety minutes passed; too late for a kidney. We packed up our unused freezer and left.

Our third body did die, and fast. A young woman with an opioid overdose. We could hear her family wailing through the closed operating room door as our computer finally showed those zeros that we had been waiting for. Moments later, the body was rushed into our room on a gurney with a flock of people in scrubs. Caught up in the chaos, I briefly forgot that it was not her life we were trying to save.

Her face slid to one side of her neck, her mouth half-open, starting to foam. The skin around her eyes was a disturbing green-gray, a color unrecognizable to me as human. As a child, I used to collect sea-glass, gathering bouquets of shards polished by the violence of waves. When I held the glass up to light, gray became silver, gold became sunflower. I remember standing on the beach and wondering: How come we can name colors, if they change with sun and shadow? If a piece of glass is gray one moment and silver the next, then the words we use to label colors are inadequate for depicting lived experience. I wondered: Why is there no word for gray-becoming-silver? Who gets to decide words and their meanings?

My role as the medical student on the transplant team was to create a clear visual field for the surgeons. I shoved suction hoses between scalpels, sucking up streams of blood and fluid. Overflow gushed onto our scrubs and shoes. How does this much liquid hide inside a body? I wrenched loops of bowel away from surgical instruments. More colors, this time shockingly vivid: red, yellow, green, nearly fluorescent, like watching them through an Instagram filter. All vision is filtered, my photographer brother once informed me, and thus all experience. Instagram filters just bring awareness to what our brains already do. Words and narratives, too, filter our experience. Blood and bile blurred like a sunset.

We removed her liver—a gorgeous, gleaming oyster compared to the shriveled livers of our cirrhotic patients—and put it on ice. We dissected her kidneys and searched for stenosis in the renal arteries. Pristine physiology; not a single plaque. *Cirrhosis, stenosis, hepatology, physiology*. This language I have worked so hard to learn in medical school. This language of *-osis* and *-ology*: of distance and boundary.

When we finished with her organs, we sewed up her abdomen with thick, rough stitches and pulled off the bloody sheets. Without the race against time, I saw her differently. She was wearing makeup. She had freckles on her breasts. She had a light-purple pedicure, still unchipped. Written on her body, clues to the story of the life she had lived. Where was she planning to go when she got that pedicure? Who was she hoping to see?

Freezer now full, our transplant team crammed back into the van. We ate granola bars and chatted about our weekend plans. The "Grim Reaper" played Aerosmith. The surgery resident helped me study for an upcoming exam. My elderly patient who loved swimming FaceTimed with his grandchildren and prepared for surgery. We met him in the operating room, now with the profound ambition of turning death back into life. Not just any life, *his* life; not just a body, a person. Open the gates to stories again. If he survives the surgery.

Later, I squatted in the garden, fistfuls of soil running through my hands. I held up a plant from the garden store and wriggled it free from its plastic pot. Its roots clung ferociously to each other and to the soil as I tried to shake the tangle loose. I lowered the displaced plant into the earth, covered it with soil, watched tiny life-giving earthworms wriggle toward its transplanted tendrils.

Stories root us in time and place, embed us in culture and community, help our feet feel firmly planted on rocky ground. Root, embed, plant: this language of vegetation, growth, stability. How, as a doctor, to stay rooted and stable without stories—and with them? How to turn stories on and off on command; how to transplant ourselves into our patients' lives without letting ourselves become embedded?

A Living Wall

JAN C. GROSSMAN

It takes care to make a living wall –
gauging the light, the water flow,
choosing the right plants;
judging how the umbrella tree or ficus will fare
growing from the pockets of man-made terrain,
purple-brown and damp.
It will be verdant, always Spring on this wall –
vertical stalks pushing through,
and the veins of the leaves and the filigree of the ferns,
quenching their constant thirst, and breathing.
It takes time and skill to place the source of the water,
then follow it as it filters and flows,
pumps through the wall.

In his hospital bed, the young man turns his face to the wall.
They are coming for his veins again.
The oxygen tube in his nostrils is as narrow and slippery as a stalk.
He lets it slip away, takes his own moist breath, presses the pump himself,
tries to heal.

The varieties of the plants matter.
Some are tropical, some are not.
The begonias' paper-white bells have flowered.
Tending to the seeds and sprouts,
it is important to see how the plants are responding to the sun,
or to the heat of the lights,
to watch how they soak and sip the constant stream.
Spreading the stems and leaves apart,
looking for signs of early decay,
it is crucial to prune and clip and cut,
protecting the vines.
Even at night it helps to observe in the near darkness
while listening to the soft breaths among the leaves.

In his hospital bed, he looks for a long time at his hands,
jaundiced fingers and paper-thin wrists.
His life is a desert.
The water drips and he counts each drop for a while,
but it is hard to put number after number.
They wilt as soon as he mouths them.

Finally, the wall is what it should be.
It is lit now from above and from all sides,
but also from within.
The air is always moist.
It is easy to breathe.
It takes hours to plan and build a wall.
Weeks using your hands to heal and grow the plants.
Months to keep it moving, fertile, alive.

In the silence of the morning, the living wall is audible and warm.
Its breaths could almost be those of the boy who shared the back bedroom,
a little brother, asleep,
but under his heavy green quilt,
still hungry and stretching in the early light.

My Mother and The Kamikaze

ROSANNA STAFFA

My mother had a list of husbands for me when I'd be all grown up, like a soccer coach makes up a dream team. A doctor came first, replaced by a Kamikaze when she was mad as hell at me. I was in love with Gregor Samsa, having chanced upon *Metamorphosis* like a junkie on a lucky break, and was very much enamored with Kafka himself, but that was aiming too high. I thought of marriage with scientific curiosity, as it seemed to occur in the life of adults like a kind of chemical phenomenon, both utterly surprising and inevitable.

The year I turned eight it was a scorching, humid summer in the Venetian region. During the day the heat was so fierce we had to close the shutters by 11 a.m. to get some respite, and we spent the afternoons in and out of darkened rooms like fish underwater.

That was the summer I was given a big secret to keep. I had always fantasized to be entrusted with special information by an adult. I could imagine how exciting it would feel. But it was different.

No kid ventured outside to play after lunch except Ciccino, my neighbor, his hands in his pockets, his mind absent, squinting up as if he could glimpse playmates in the sun. Ciccino had a round face with glasses and an expression of adult resignation. He had a TV set and no siblings, luxuries unheard of. Everybody avoided him but me. My family had come up North from Naples, and nobody wanted to hang out with me either. My classmates gathered in a herd-like manner at recess, observing me from afar. I pretended to be immersed in deep thoughts that required solitude.

One afternoon my doorbell rang. Ciccino stood outside, with a bloody nose and dust clinging to his T-shirt and shorts.

"I was jumped," he announced. His hands shook holding his broken glasses. Pointy shards glittered in one frame; the other was empty. He had strolled all the way to the boarded up Cinema Cristallo, curious about the sighting of cats with five legs I had made up on a whim. He had unwittingly strayed into the territory of the kids from the projects of Meggiaro Alto. "They were four. The tall one with blond hair was really mean."

I knew it had to be Sandro, who smoked cigarettes and threw live kittens in the Bisatto canal. I thought about him at night when I was alone in my room; he whispered sweet nothings to me like a threat. I knew I would succumb, to what I wouldn't know, but it would be total surrender.

Ciccino now was tearing up. I took him to the bathroom, where he washed his face and wet his hair. He sat on the edge of the bathtub and looked at me with moist desolate eyes.

"You'll be okay," I said.

He nodded. There was a silence. He burst out in sobs.

"My mother is having another baby."

"That's nothing." I said. "I promise." My tone was cold, almost formal. I knew there was no choice but watch your mother change into someone impossible to recognize. After my brother's birth, all my witty remarks found her distracted. It was four years after his birth, and we still did not dance silly around the table. I loved her to death. It was dangerous love like in the movies, it hurt.

I sat on the edge of the tub with Ciccino. We gently hammered the bathtub with our heels. I had occasionally imagined my brother walking far in the rain, get pneumonia and die. After a respectable period of mourning, things with my mother would go back to the way they used to be.

"Everything will stay the same? Promise?" said Ciccino.

I heard fast steps, and my mother peeked in. She looked alarmed.

"What is going on?" Her beautiful eyes wandered to the towel stained with blood. She covered the mouth with her hands, "*Gesu'Cristo.*"

Ciccino teared up again.

My mother hurried off. She was talking so fast her words were a blur of consonants. She was back in no time, and had Ciccino hold ice cubes to his nose.

She motioned fast for me to come closer.

"Doctor Sartori-Borotto is coming for a house visit in half an hour," she whispered, her eyes fixed on the towel soiled by Ciccino. A doctor's house visit was common in Italy back then, while hardly anybody ever came to our house. "I must go and change clothes, put lipstick on. Immediately." My mother scrubbed and cleaned every room; always wore slippers and a house dress. On special occasions, like the church service at Easter, she indulged in a dab of red lipstick and a drop of Chanel #5 behind each ear. Marilyn Monroe did precisely the same, she told me.

While my mother hurried to dress properly, I was instructed to run and bring to the bathroom the embroidered hand towels from Burano. My mother had taken them out of their box with a coquettish smile only once before, in preparation for my First Communion.

Doctor Sartori-Borotto was a tall man of few words. There was something unsettling about his long manicured fingers, immaculate. He drove a white Fiat 500 while we all whirred around on bikes like a flock of sparrows, even the old priest, Don Antonio, who hiked up his robe and pinned it with a clothespin.

Doctor Sartori-Borotto spoke exclusively in Italian like a TV announcer and never used the affable local dialect like everybody else. According to his maid he did so even in private with his two boys, who played the violin and the tuba in the prestigious Orchestra Di Padova e Del Veneto. Their early success deflated all of us in the eyes of our parents. Doctor Sartori-Borotto didn't smoke, didn't drink. His patients would rather get better on their own than suffer the discomfort of his visit.

I hurried to look for the hand towels from Burano, but just then the doorbell rang. Ciccino shuffled to open the door, and there stood Doctor Sartori-Borotto, intent on looking at his shoes, a hand to his chin. It puzzled me that he seemed to be quite early. He looked oddly troubled.

Doctor Sartori-Borotto asked me to show him where he could wash his hands. When I did, he preceded me down the hall in fast strides, with total disrespect for normal courtesy. I had to run to catch up.

In the bathroom, Doctor Sartori-Borotto closed the door behind me with a gentle click. He didn't wash his hands. Planted firmly in the middle of the room, he fixed his eyes on me. He asked me if my father was still away on a business trip. I said that he was. He asked me to tell him if I would be able to call my father on the phone with nobody hearing me and tell him to contact his office immediately. He needed to talk privately to him. It was urgent. The test results of my mother were not good. I moved back a little, saying nothing. I heard the steps of Ciccino come up to the bathroom door. The doctor heard them too, and in an instant he crouched to speak to me. Even more terrifying, Doctor Sartori-Borotto addressed me with the endearing Venetian term for a child.

"*Cea*, can you? Can you call your dad in secret?" I looked at him a bit confused and nodded. This seemed to encourage him as he blurted in perfect Venetian dialect, "Can you call him without your mom hearing? I have test results I do not like."

I promised. I was determined not to let down Doctor Sartori-Borotto. I had never been entrusted with an important job.

Doctor Sartori-Borotto stood up and walked out of the bathroom to greet my mother, who had put on her pale yellow seer sucker dress and gray sandals, her favorites.

"You two go out and play," my mother suggested, breezily, shooting me a sharp look when I hesitated. "Go, go."

Ciccino and I went outside.

"My mom is sick," I told Ciccino. "It's a secret."

We walked on to the dry canal, where the smell of dust, dead cats and excrement distracted us a bit. Ciccino clasped his hands in his lap.

"I heard that babies keep you up crying at night. The moms are tired during the day and don't want to play anymore. Is it true ?" he asked.

"Of course not," I said, looking away. Confession was coming up in two days and this lie to Ciccino would cost me two extra Hail Marys.

When I returned home, my mother was now alone, back in her house dress and slippers.

"I wonder if you'll marry a doctor," she said. This meant that she was pleased with me. She didn't know that I had not gotten the towels from Burano for Doctor Sartori-Borotto on time.

I snuck into my brother's room. He had just woken up from his nap. I told him I had thrown out his favorite toy truck and I ran off. He howled, and my mother went to attend to him, just as I hoped. I hurried to make the secret call to my father, long distance. My father and Doctor Sartori-Borotto would take charge of the problem and solve it.

I was for once relieved to see my brother on my mother's lap as usual, coloring a bunny she had drawn on a piece of paper for him. This cast a kind of spell on me, I could not move.

*

One evening after dinner, Ciccino and I took a long walk, hunting for frogs. We had no idea how to or why but the other kids did this all the time and bragged about it at school.

Ciccino and I got disoriented in the dark. We sat in the grass and fell silent. We saw in the distance the lights from bicycles cut through the night, scissoring back and forth like searchlights. Ciccino had heard that old Signor Zenere roamed at night looking for kids. Some he ate. Some he tortured.

We remained for a long time in silence, breathing hard. I confessed to Ciccino that new babies didn't sleep much but cried all day and all night, and when there is a new baby, moms don't fix you bread with Nutella anymore. I told him everything.

I stood up and started home. Ciccino followed me at a little distance.

"We should run away," Ciccino said. "You should marry me."

"That's silly," I said, "I'm going to marry a Kamikaze."

"What kind of a husband is that?"

I told him he would be strict and loyal. A bit scary too.

"A Kamikaze," I concluded my little speech with the pride of future ownership "is trained to face anything without batting an eyelash, even his own death."

"Let's train just like a Kamikaze," he blurted out.

I thought it was a good idea. It seemed to me I had somewhat suggested it.

The next morning after breakfast Ciccino stood waiting outside. The sight of his plump hands and scratched knees took me by surprise, as if I had expected him to have grown into a mature age in the course of the night.

We walked side by side with purpose, figuring out a plan. That summer the Kamikaze training took us for punishing walks all over town and in the outskirts. As we silently pushed ahead, the paths would change from the dirt roads of our neighborhood, bare of trees and shade, to the tidy gravel and landscaped villas of the doctors I would not marry one day. We scraped our hands and knees crawling over the walls of the Convento Riposo of the Cappuccini friars, leaving streaks of fresh blood on the whitewashed walls. We snuck into the friars' orchard and ate a fistful of their salad, mixed with tiny pebbles. In a week, we were crawling on our bellies under the chicken wire protecting the property of Signora Zuccotto who was reputed to own a gun and use it on anybody trespassing. We stole two fresh eggs, one each. As a final challenge, we stuck our heads in the water of the fountain at the Giardini Pubblici until we felt our lungs would burst.

We ended our days squirming with cramps. We rarely spoke. I could detect in our smell the bittersweet odor I associated with the Kamikaze. But I wasn't sure any of the training was making me stronger. I was just dirtier. I woke up at night afraid that, as my mother appeared a bit different every day, I would become different too, and one day maybe not recognize myself. I slept badly, listening for the steps of my mother who had started to get up at night and stumble, pushing herself off the walls with determination, as if the wandering had a purpose. She had become forgetful and I noticed a dark hue around her lips.

"*Gesu Christo, Gesu Christo.*" She scrubbed my back in the bathtub every evening, attacking dirt with her bare hands. "This summer is a torment, you kids are going nuts. Look at your knees." Her voice was tremulous when she added, "Thank God you'll be back in school soon."

"I can't wait," I hissed back. I was determined to spend with her as little time as possible from now on, glad that I was capable of staying away a bit longer every day. But there was such coziness to her fussing that made me look forward to it every evening. Perhaps summer would last very long.

But the heat slowly let up, and fall was in the air. Notebooks and backpacks appeared in the window of the venerable Sorelle Apostoli bookstore with cheerful notices of 'Back to school!'.

On waking up, I found my mother complaining of headaches, jabs in her ribs, *qui e qui, here and here, qui e qui e qui.*

"It's nothing. I have them too," I'd lie.

"What's new this morning?" I chided, and we giggled. Her skin was shedding under the touch, dead flakes that I hoped would leave a harder layer uncovered, tough like a shell.

One time my mother took me to the window in our tiny kitchen, opened her shirt and showed me waxy bubbles surfacing on her clavicle. She looked at me, timid.

"What do you think it is?" she said.

"Too much salt," I improvised. Maybe it was the dust in the air or the debris from all the falling stars.

Ciccino told me that his mother's belly was getting bigger and bigger. She was napping all the time. When he called for her, she would look up as if responding to a door-to-door salesman.

Ciccino and I had to go back to school. We walked there together but spent no time talking, just worried about what was to come. I strained to imagine it, but it defied my understanding. There was no mystery, no disorder but only facts to what I learned at school hour after hour; it taught me nothing. All the knowledge on the blackboard just made me clench my teeth. I walked back home on wobbly legs like a convalescent.

"I'm not sure they teach you anything interesting," My mother would greet me, "you look very upset." She worked on my coat, her increasingly trembling hands unable to help me take it off, and still trying every day.

At home I kept my brother busy, reading to him so she could nap. She slept almost nothing at night. She complained about the pillow, the mattress. Her skull hurt. It floated and wandered in the sky bumping into stray meteors. She needed water. She could not drink a thing. She heard pigeons fussing out her window. Time after time she was alarmed by someone at the door. There was a burglar who pretended to be Doctor Sartori-Borotto and strived to find her home alone. She failed to finish anything she started, from a phone call to preparing a meal. If I helped her, it made her mad.

By Christmas the pain from cancer would wake her up in the middle of the night and I'd find her wandering with a pillow under her arm. I tried to take her back to bed, as if that could be of any help. She'd fight me, hitting with baby hands, escaping to the couch. I sat by her, waiting till the night faded. With the light, the visions that made her cry disappeared: Professor Manin, the math teacher who had humiliated her at the blackboard as a child, and the German soldiers who had kicked her away from the truck where they had loaded her brother Armando.

Ciccino had a baby sister, Luisa. By the time she was able to follow him everywhere on her fours, bawling, my mother was gone.

For a while my days seemed like a landscape glimpsed from a speeding car, and my life rearranged in haste, crudely, by a stranger.

One summer day the bittersweet smell of the Kamikaze filled my room. I imagined the Kamikaze taken out of his group, singled out for a terrifying mission. I saw him fall from the sky, and the air for a moment seemed liquid, holding him, rocking him before letting go. We both opened our arms and moved them like swimming gently. We kept going together. We slowly merged with the air, fading into it.

What Becomes of a Broken Heart

GWEN E. ERKONEN

The unit clerk calls out to me, "Doctor Gwen, the heart's coming back to room 18." That's PICU (pediatric intensive care unit) speak for a patient being admitted from the operating room after an all-night open-heart operation.

"Thanks, Miss Debbie, I'm on my way."

I shuffle around the front desk of the dated pediatric intensive care unit towards the back pod that houses the cardiac patients. I stuff my hands into the pockets of my dirty white coat and let my sneakers scuff across the floor. My oversized scrubs, weighed down by a pager, drag along the faded tiles. I'm too tired to hike them back up.

I'm finishing a 24-hour call. My face is greasy, and my messy hair is pulled back into a hasty bun with a plastic hair clip that's seen better days. It's been a long night. The usual load of trauma, shock and respiratory failure seemed to have come at a heavier pace than usual. My fellow and I had been bouncing from the PICU to the ER to the general floor putting out fires all night. I didn't realize how tired I was until I sat down just moments ago. This last admission will be an emotional gut punch.

It's my husband's case. He had texted me around midnight that he was coming in for a sick newborn. He doesn't usually text me about his cases, so I called him back and asked, "What's wrong?"

"She has TAPVR (total anomalous pulmonary venous return) and she's obstructed. I don't want her to wait."

I was hit with the revelation that I will never hear those words without feeling sick to my stomach, without remembering my own baby who had that exact disease. Time stops, my body tingles with a surge of adrenaline, and I experience her devastating death all over again.

My husband said she was obstructed, meaning no oxygenated blood was returning to her heart. Other surgeons might have put the case off until the early morning, but he wouldn't let her wait. TAPVR is an emergency. Prompt diagnosis and treatment is crucial. But as he and I know, it's not always a straightforward diagnosis and it can easily be missed, confused with pneumonia.

My husband, Bob, and I work together in the shared vocation of pediatric heart surgery. He operates on babies with congenital heart defects, redirects the blood flow and makes their untenable anatomy compatible with life, then he hands them off to me so that I might usher them through the instability of the post-operative period.

An intensivist and a surgeon have a special relationship that only flourishes when there's trust on both sides. The intensivist must believe the surgeon did a good repair, and the surgeon must believe the intensivist will do everything in her power to protect the fragile reconstructed heart. As a married couple, that relationship thrives. We know each other's strengths and weaknesses, and because we love and trust each other, we are completely honest about the concerns we have in each shared case. If something goes wrong, I know he will be honest about the limitations of the surgical repair, and he knows that I will provide meticulous care to our patient during the perilous post-operative period. We've worked together this way for nearly a year. But to us TAPVR is special. I never look at a baby with that diagnosis without thinking of our own infant daughter who lived a brief nine days.

I steel myself before I walk into this new baby's room.

"Hey Gwen," David, the anesthesiologist, calls out casually. "Are you ready for handoff?"

He relays the operating room course and the baby's current doses of epinephrine, milrinone, and calcium, all crucial medicines to support an infant heart during the tenuous post-operative period. As I listen, I watch Bob from the corner of my eye. He's sitting in the alcove of the patient room, looking out the window towards the urban sprawl that is downtown Houston. The rising sun and the city pollution combine to create light in every shade of pink, purple, orange and red. He hangs back from the scrum of white-coated medical professionals buzzing around our newest patient; a sign that he isn't worried, but I know he's distracted. Our baby, Eve, went to the operating room back when we were in residency, but when she came back to the PICU, there was no ventilator or chest tubes or medicines or anesthesiologist. I remember the words of the surgeon when he told us she had died.

"I'm really sorry, we just couldn't get her heart going again. The ventricle didn't recover after that second bypass run," he said.

I recall his bony, soft hand was dangling near mine and I briefly grabbed it as I nodded my head to the cadence of his words. I'm not even sure if he actually said the word "dead." I mumbled a thank you or something close to it while I did my best impression of an understanding mother and sympathetic physician. But I couldn't look him squarely in the face. Instead, I looked down at his bloodless white sneakers and fought back the urge to puke.

Eve's lifeless body was delivered to us by a silent, reverent, assistant surgeon. His confident posture replaced with slumped shoulders as he bore the burden of this thankless task. She was wrapped in a pink blanket that was not hers, and her skin was a pale blue. The only indication that she had undergone surgery was the perfectly dressed sternotomy on her small chest. Closing the wound would have been this assistant's sad job.

That night we held her, bathed her, took pictures with her, sang her lullabies, and did our best to be brave for our other small children. In that time before smart phones, we had only two pictures of the three of us together. One, when she was first born, before we knew anything was wrong, and the other, after she had died. We left the hospital that cold, Iowa night in a fog of sorrow; at a loss as to how we would wake up the next day without our daughter.

The patient before me is good sized with pink, perfect skin, lovely petite features, and wisps of strawberry blonde hair. A white surgical bandage covers the incision on her chest that Bob had closed. Two tubes protrude from her lower chest to drain the excess fluid and blood that accumulates with major surgery. A small breathing tube, emanating from rose bud lips, is attached to a ventilator. IVs protrude from her perfect hands and a large central line extends from her short neck. Everything is held in place with strips of pristine, white tape. She is absolutely still. The vital signs on the monitor indicate temporary stability. I put my hands on her tiny pink feet and feel her strong pulses. I know that before she went to the OR, she was blue and unstable, hanging on until surgery.

The nurse hands me an initial set of labs, which confirm her reassuring vitals. I marvel at this baby, a product of my husband's cool and singular focus. He succeeded in redirecting the errant pulmonary veins allowing oxygenated blood to return to the left side of her tiny heart. He saved her.

I envy the relief her family must feel, and I can't help but wonder how different things might have been had our little girl survived. I want to scream to everyone in the room, "Why didn't my baby live? She had the same disease, why couldn't she be saved?" But that's the wrong question.

I'm not sure why we've chosen to work in a field that provides a constant reminder of the worst day of our lives. Like a self-cutter, I get relief through the pain of remembering Eve's short life and death whenever I care for a cardiac baby. Each patient is a blade cutting across my skin, providing me a brief respite from the daily pain I work so hard to control. For a moment my breath comes easy and I'm free from pain. And like a cutter, I feel shame. I am ashamed of my pain. I'm ashamed that I can't quit.

After Eve died, the pediatric intensive care unit became the only place where I felt I belonged. For those families who face the death of their baby, I have learned to quietly bear witness to their devastation, and to be present with them as they negotiate the unimaginable. I still feel my own denial, immense loss, and the inability to breathe. I recognize the same pain in their eyes that I see it in mine every morning. There are old wives' tales that say a baby girl steals her mother's beauty. But what does a baby who dies take from her mother? The answer is too frightening to contemplate; too awful to say out loud.

When this baby's tearful and exhausted mother enters the room, I lead her towards her little daughter. I place her tremulous hand on her baby's head and tell her she'll be ok. I realize my voice is shaking, and I try to swallow away the emotion. I'm both crushed by the memory of losing Eve and ecstatic for this mother.

"Really?' she asks.

"Everything looks great," I reassure her. "She's doing really well." I blink back my tears and look away. They are interminable.

Bitterness tempts me at that moment, but I push it away. I'm learning to ignore the unanswerable questions. If I indulge that inner dialogue, I would dishonor my Eve and devolve into a raving madwoman. The memory of Eve's death threatens to weigh me down, pulling me into the depths of a depression where I would easily stay were it not for my children and husband.

To keep from crying, I pick up the chest tube and strip the blood from it with swift, methodical strokes. I grab my stethoscope and listen to her heart and lungs. The muscle memory of the physical exam relieves the burning in my eyes and eases the tightness in my throat. For the moment, I am able to assume the role of competent physician and push away my broken mother self.

The grief books have it all wrong. There are no stages, and there is no beginning or end to grief. It comes at you with a steady rhythm like waves hitting the shore. You accept that you won't be spared. So, you stand paralyzed as you take the unrelenting buffeting of the icy waves. Grief has its own intrinsic rhythm that's rarely intuitive. Sometimes, the waves come at a steady, even pace with an anticipated force. Other times, their pace accelerates or slows hitting you with a surprising strength or an unexpected gentleness. Their sounds can be pleasantly soft, muted, almost bearable. While some days they roil into a crescendo until your ears ring, making you deaf to logic and coherence. Just when you learn the pattern, it shifts, and like the Greek myth of Sisyphus, you roll your rock of grief up the hill each day only to start over again the next. Progress is elusive, and the work of recovery becomes your destiny.

Yet, I understand we are lucky. We survived a loss so painful, there's no word in the English language to describe it. There are widows, widowers, and orphans but what are we? Grieving parents? War buddies? Damaged? Yes, we are all those things at the same time. Grieving differently, grieving together.

I rarely look at a family photo without mentally airbrushing Eve's silhouette into the image. I imagine her grown up features and the beauty she's become. I picture her by the Christmas tree, laughing at the beach, and lazing on the couch. When I drop my youngest daughters off at school, I indulge a reverie in which I see her walking between them. I envision her hair in a ponytail, and I think she's a brunette. This year she would be starting seventh grade. I want so badly to stay in my imaginary world where I can hold her hand, tell her I'm here, tell her I love her.

Eve is always with us. We celebrate her birthday each December with roses and balloons. As January first, the anniversary of her death, approaches, I find it more and more difficult to focus, to breathe, to function. I used to insulate myself from the outside world until the day passed. I now try to work on New Year's Day. I'd rather be in the hospital treating patients and helping families. Working gives me a second breath, a chance at humanity. Prayer-like, I try to honor her rather than shoulder the pain of her loss at home. The PICU has become my home, my place of comfort.

A beeping alarm from the monitor pulls me back to the present and the pressing needs of the baby before me. I ask the nurse to increase the dose of epinephrine and tell her to draw up a fluid bolus. I feel Bob's gaze on me. His green eyes hold me, and a peaceful half smile spreads across his handsome face. I tilt my head and return his smile. Our shared secret pulsates between us with an almost crippling pathos. I hold his gaze for one more beat, then let it go, and return my attention to the miraculous baby in front of me.

Maybe, broken hearts can heal.

What the Mostly Blind Eye Sees

CARYN MIRRIAM-GOLDBERG

Yes, it can see its way out of a paper bag
but not more than a wavering center line
on the highway the good eye has to drive solo.
It sees fast torches where once there were trees
and later, raining streaks of yellow
from the tract lighting in the restaurant.

The mostly blind eye isn't bothered by the lack
of definition between sofa and turquoise wall,
the rectangle of green punctuated by branches
filling the frame of the window,
or the absence of a word on the exit sign.
Instead, it sees trembling amoebas
that it swears it saw as a child eye
falling in love with eddies of dust
singing the sunlight. It sees right through
forced forgiveness or hyacinth exploded
into fragrance and pink too early.

It sees nothing of the future but is smart enough
not to be perturbed by this, or by the presence
of floaters that turn into faces full of better eyes
but not necessarily better views, like now
when it sees the dark green panorama of cricket song
turning into lightning bugs, the smell of cedar
between thumb and forefinger, the heavy drape
of humidity that doesn't lead to rain,
and the tumbling blue birdsong roosting
in the tree tops, begging the sky for long life.

Anamnesis

ALLISON BAXTER

Sandra stood in the shadows of a lone brick building with quaint oversized gables. She studied the perfection of the Memory Care Unit building as she tried to soothe her nausea with lukewarm water from her beat up bottle. In front, gardeners manicured boxwood bushes that rested in perfect piles of wood mulch. Behind, a copper sun set, scattering pastel colors in a blue sky. Her mother's current and future home—for whatever future she had left.

It was "nice," her mother had said when they first visited in May, back when she knew Sandra's name and her own. She'd squeezed her mother's hand and smiled, acting the part of the responsible daughter. Wasn't that who she was? Even if she hadn't visited in three weeks.

"Three weeks," Sandra whispered to herself, disgust twisting her stomach. She took another sip. Three weeks ago she'd been married to Evan, a trader gainfully employed at the Chicago Mercantile Exchange. Then, late night phone calls to his fellow traders, a suddenly empty bank account and Evan's confession. Sandra had curled into a ball and neglected everything that mattered. Even her mother. Her mother who had neither time on earth nor the permanence of memory. Sandra needed to catch—no, she needed to clutch—her fading mother and hold on tight.

The glass door slid open with a near-silent whoosh, and she was transported to hospital hominess. She walked toward the reception desk and returned a hand to her upset stomach—an assault of emotions mixed with smells of industrial-strength pine cleaner and fried food.

In front of Sandra loomed the leather-bound guest book. She signed in. A young woman in blue scrubs looked at the book and back at Sandra. Sandra placed her driver's license on the counter.

"I'm here to see my mother, Patricia Sage," Sandra choked out, pushing the bitter down.

The nurse typed something into the computer. Did she notice that Sandra hadn't visited in awhile? She was probably thinking about how she would never neglect her own mother like that.

"I'll buzz you back." Sandra heard the soft drone and walked toward the door.

She turned to thank the nurse, but the nurse's eyes were trained on a spot beyond the door where a woman wandered down the hall in a short, thin gown.

The nurse picked up her radio, "Mrs. Davis is wandering again. And she's not dressed. Who can help?"

Within seconds, an orderly was purring soft words and rerouting Mrs. Davis to her room for clothes.

The door slammed behind Sandra, the lock clicking as it engaged. Locked in, locked out. Moaning, laughing and shouting floated from rooms and tangled together in the hallway. With her mother's move to memory care came overpowering sounds, smells and loss. Loss in degrees.

Her mother's door had been left ajar. The bellow of a romantic comedy on television and floral soap greeted Sandra.

The last time she stood at the threshold, Evan rubbed her back and supported her sagging body as they walked through the door together. He was thoughtful like that. Perceptive. Would her mother notice she was alone, that her ring finger had only a white mark where her band had been? Maybe her failing memory was the one gift of her mother's illness to Sandra. Sandra could reinvent her life and, for a few hours, be a different daughter.

Sandra tapped lightly and pushed the door open. Her mother lay in the bed on top of the blankets, staring at the screen, her thin frame swimming in Sandra's father's old flannel pajamas.

"Mom. It's me, Sandra. Your daughter," she announced, closing the door.

Her mother turned to her, eyes vacant. She slid her eyes back to the TV, then closed them.

Sandra leaned over in an attempt to hug her. "Do you want to walk to the cafeteria?" Yes or no questions, just like the staff social worker had said.

Her mother sat up, pushed her feet into slippers, and stood. She stared at Sandra, her eyes empty.

The pajamas were tatters now. Sandra tensed remembering how her father, in those red and green pajamas, reclined in his brown leather armchair with his *Chicago Tribune* obscuring his face. Her mother, usually serious bordering on grim, would ask her father when he was to play bagpipe, and Sandra and her brother, Tim, joined in with surprise and delight. He'd lower the paper, squint in pretend irritation, then raise it over his face again. But they could hear his soft, airy chuckle.

Now, Tim and her father were gone, taken out violently. Sandra's mind and heart held them and her mother for safe-keeping .

She needed to get her mother some pajamas that fit. Something that didn't make Sandra want to cry.

"Do you want to get dressed? You don't want to wear pajamas." That was too much information. "Do you want to put on some clothes?" she corrected herself.

Sandra opened the small closet and grabbed some elasticized black pants and a knit shirt. She handed them to her mother who obediently slipped them on. At least she remembered how to dress—for now

"Let's go," Sandra said, reaching for her mother's cold, wrinkled hand.

Her mother looked down at their clasped hands and up into Sandra's eyes. "You're Sandra. I remember you. I used to live with you."

Sandra's heart filled with bitter and sweet. She wiped the mist from her eyes with her free hand.

They strolled down the hall in the direction of clatter and conversation. Her mother stumbled, so Sandra linked arms with her for more support, a tree supporting a vine.

In the cafeteria, orderlies fed patients, encouraging them to eat and talk. Adult children forced smiles as they spoke to parents who may or may not have known them.

A waitress greeted them. "Good evening. I'm Ellie." She stooped over and spoke softly to Sandra's mother. "Hi there, Patricia. You want the chicken-fried steak, right? And a little cherry Jell-O? And some apple juice to drink?"

"Oh, yes. I love chicken-fried steak," her mother said with a single head bob.

Her mother liked chicken-fried steak? Jello? Apple juice? Since when? Now, this stranger knew more than she did about her own mother.

Sandra looked up and smiled at Ellie. "You know my mother was quite a cook when I was growing up. She hated red meat and fried food. I'm surprised she'll eat it here." Ellie didn't really know her mother.

"Oh, she eats French fries, fried fish on Friday during Lent, of course. She loves it. She asks for seconds on the French fries. Then we play bingo, and she's into the potato chip bowl. Right, Patricia?"

Her mother bobbed her head in agreement.

Sandra bit her bottom lip. She wanted to shout, *Who are you?* Who did she want to shout at? Ellie or her mother? Why was she so angry at this poor woman who cared for her mother? This woman made her elderly, sick mother comfortable. Sandra's face warmed. Ellie's care was more than Sandra could do—had done recently.

Sandra sipped her iced tea, cleared her head, and smiled at Ellie, a middle-aged woman standing over their table, helping both of them. "Thanks so much for spending time with my mother. I have to work full-time, so I can't always get here for a visit."

Ellie smiled, but her face was strained. "It's my pleasure. My calling. My own mother had dementia, you know. It was hard keeping her at home, but I did. I enjoyed those last months. Just like she was the kid and I was the adult. I'm just helping where I can. Now, what can I get you to eat, young lady?"

Keep her mother home. Guilt cascaded over Sandra's head as she avoided Ellie's gaze and bowed to look at the menu. It would be harder to get her professional care at home. Sandra would be there for her but she didn't have that luxury. Sentiment wouldn't pay the bills.

Not many choices on the menu. Meatloaf or chicken-fried steak. She glanced up at Ellie and winked. "I'll have what she's having."

Ellie left and Sandra smiled at her mother. She wanted to cry, to heave in the arms of this half stranger sitting across from her. She wanted to talk about the pain of putting her mother in a home, of Sandra's contentious divorce, of being the last in their family to remember their family. She wanted to cry on her mother's shoulder to tell her how much she missed Evan and hated being alone. Would her mother have approved of her decision?

Instead, Sandra asked, "Do you like Oak Park?"

Her mother shrugged as if she didn't understand the question.

"Mom, you always wanted to live in the suburbs."

Her mother had no idea that she'd finally made it out of the city to her dream village. Patricia blinked a few times and focused on Sandra as if she'd noticed her daughter for the first time. She moved her mouth, a mime, but nothing came out.

Keep the conversation moving, draw her mother in. At least she seemed to be half-lucid. "Maybe I'll come to movie night next time. Would you like that?" She'd come to see *On Golden Pond*, the last movie she saw with her ex-husband. The three of them sat nestled in the rec room, her mother in the middle, hugging her skeletal arms around a tub of buttered popcorn. A movie with the two people she loved the most. Now, Sandra was single, nearly orphaned.

"I miss Tim," her mom said, voice trembling. The social worker told her to play along, especially if the truth might upset her, but thinking of Tim alive folded her stomach in two. He would be doing art, would be an artist. Such talent, dedication to his acrylic paints that he lay in thick impasto lines on huge canvases. In a flash of an officer's gun, gone forever. Death by mental illness. And Sandra and her mom, the last alive.

Please don't remember he's dead, Sandra prayed silently. Her mother cleared her throat "Is he still painting?"

Sandra sighed softly into a heavy grief but also a contentment that he lived in his mother's mind. "You know Tim. Painting is his life." Her mother was remembering things.

Ellie delivered their piping-hot fried steaks, smothered in gravy, with small mounds of overcooked green beans. And two bowls of red Jell-O.

They ate in silence. Sandra saved the Jell-O for last, repulsed by the unnatural red. Finally, she balanced a little cube on her spoon and dropped it on her tongue. She chuckled quietly. Sugar and fictional strawberry flavor were childhood parties and kids' menus in restaurants. Long summers and knock-knock jokes. Before violence ripped them apart.

Sandra studied the other families. Married couples with kids, adult siblings. All the things that she was no longer a part of. She reached across the table to touch her mother's hand. Her mother was laughing as she tried to balance her own jiggly cubes in the tiny spoon and failed. The smile, it was her mother. At least she had her mother today.

Finally, her mother ate the last cube and exhaled with satisfaction.

"All done?" Sandra asked.

Her mother's face clouded suddenly. She leaned in. "I miss the one before Tim. My other son."

Sandra leaned back in her chair. How could she be surprised by this? Maybe she'd seen something on TV. The social worker told her that could happen. Her mother was confused.

Sandra nodded. She should change the subject.

"Mom, do you remember that time Tim and I decorated the house for Christmas while you guys were asleep?"

Her mother swallowed with effort, then continued. Her face was drawn. She put a shriveled hand to her throat, the way she'd always done when she was upset. "You never knew the one before. I never told you about him."

"We set my little watch alarm to go off at midnight, but you guys were still awake," Sandra said more loudly than she intended.

The rims of her mother's eyes filled with tears. Sandra picked up a clean napkin and leaned over the table to dry them. "Sandra, I want to tell you right now, while I remember it."

"Mom, I don't want you to get upset."

"I named him. Before."

Had her mother miscarried?

Tears streamed down her mother's face and fell onto her plate. Sandra dabbed. She might suffocate in sadness if her mother continued whether this was true or not.

"Sandra. Listen to me. I want to tell you about your brother." Her mother spoke with such force and conviction. She studied Sandra's face. "I want to tell you. I need to tell you."

Sandra stiffened, trying not to cry herself. She could only honor her mother's wish. Her mother had lived through so much pain, losing her son and husband and then fighting Alzheimer's. It was unbearable to see her suffer with some memory, especially since it was probably not real. Sandra moved to sit next to her mother and put an arm around her shoulders.

Her mother cleared her throat. "My parents, they were so ashamed. They sent me away."

"Sent you away?"

"I left Chicago. Had the baby in Nebraska. Aunt Freida. It was a secret."

Aunt Freida died before Sandra was born, so she'd only heard the name.

Her mother continued, speaking in a near whisper now. "At the hospital in Nebraska, these people from California came. They took the baby. I was only seventeen. My aunt. She made me sign the papers. I named him Charles. They said they'd keep the name. Charles."

Sandra closed her eyes, then opened them to see her mother, face drawn, eyes wet and pained. What if…? Sandra felt as if she'd fallen from a height and had the wind knocked out of her.

"But Mom, where's the baby?" Sandra asked, regretting that she was encouraging her mother but being pulled into this possibility.

"Adoptions were closed. I didn't even have a picture."

Sandra waited, in her mind urging her mother to continue.

"I never told. Not even your father."

Her mother looked crumpled, destroyed. If it was true, the monster of Alzheimer's left her the most painful memory. The cruelty was complete.

"But there must be something else. A last name?"

"Only a letter they sent Aunt Freida. She wouldn't give it to me. Aunt Freida was not a nice woman."

Was this the glimmer of anguish Sandra noticed on her mother's face when they talked about Aunt Freida? Her puffy, red eyes on mornings when

Sandra woke early and her father was at work? Now, her own tears flowed with her mother's agony. All these years she'd wondered. Worried.

Sandra needed to know the truth, but she didn't have time to process. Her mother needed her. She rubbed her mother's back. "It's OK, Mom. It's OK."

Her mother took another bite then pushed the plate away.

"Done?" Sandra asked, taking her mother's face with soft hands and turning it towards her own. "Mom, who would know something?"

Her mother shrugged, closed her eyes, and swayed back and forth. After a minute, she opened them and pushed herself up from the chair, nearly falling over.

"Wait. I'll help you." Sandra jumped up and steadied her mother, linking arms with her for the walk back.

In the room, they sat side-by-side on the bed. "Mom, tell me everything you remember."

She looked at Sandra blankly, her face pale. She lay down and her lids slowly closed. It was over. The neurotransmitters used up. Self-preservation.

"Mom," Sandra said, pleading as she stood up.

Her mother lay still, her chest rising and falling.

"Mom, please." Please don't leave again. I need to know. Sandra waited, rubbing her eyes, wiping away the emotion she'd spent. "Let's get you into your pajamas."

Sandra got a nightgown out of the drawer. She put an arm under her mother's body and helped her sit up and get undressed.

"Sandra, are you married?"

Maybe Sandra was still reeling from the revelation of the baby, but the question had a knife tip. She recovered herself. Her mother had been through enough. Sandra herself had been through enough. "No, Mom. I'm not." And with that, her ten-year marriage and its cruel ending disappeared.

"You should get married. My parents were so happy."

It was true. Like her parents, her grandparents doted on each other. But had her grandparents argued about the baby? Had they agreed to send their daughter away and give the baby to strangers because it was the sixties?

Then her mother was silent again, as if she'd left her body.

She tucked her mother in and said goodnight.

On the drive home she didn't notice the potholes or the ample late-summer trees. She played the evening's conversation and saw her mother's tears over and over in her mind. The details of the adoption seemed solid. Sandra's intuition was ripe. Or was it wishful thinking? Distraction? It felt true. How could she track him down? If...

She entered her house with only a forlorn echo as greeting and the thud of her shoes across the wood floor as welcome. In her bedroom, above her half-unmade bed with one pillow, hung a huge expressionistic painting, Tim's last and best. What if she wasn't alone in the world? What if Charles had been desperately searching for her the way she would search for him? She had contacts, tools. She had cousins who lived in Aunt Freida's house where there must be documents, notes, answers. Maybe she had a brother with no memory of her or her mother, but what an exquisite idea. To be connected.

On the Fence

SHERI REDA

I was sick of sitting alone at a desk. I was working at a seminary library—and slowly losing my mind to the solitude and dysfunctional bitterness there. I also had a successful freelance writing business, but that operated largely online. Most mornings, I worked alone at a desk in the library until it was time to pick up my son. I'd drive him home and then write at my other desk. I took a break to cook for my family, had dinner, then worked alone at night.

Something had to change. So I called my dad at his restaurant and offered to work there part-time. He said no.

To be fair, my two sisters and I had just encouraged my dad to hire our two younger brothers. One feared a layoff. The other had lost a series of jobs and was deeply unhappy. We didn't want our little brothers on the streets. And that was all the "help" my dad said he could afford. Anyway, he observed, astutely, I was a mother. He added, in a "case closed" kind of way, "You can't be gone at night."

After a few moments of chewing and chatting, my dad looked at me thoughtfully. If you think you can handle it, you could hostess on the weekends," he said. He seemed to be missing that fact that weekends are the latest nights of all.

"Friday, Sunday . . . Saturday, Sunday . . ." Tom could go to chef school. I want him to go to chef school," he said.

He peered at me. "Think you can handle it?" he demanded.

I said I thought three master's degrees, two kids, and a thriving free-lance business had probably prepared me OK to lead people to tables.

"Yeah, you're smart, he said, almost accusingly. But this isn't book-learnin'." He said this in the same tone he used when he used to proclaim, "It's not what you know, it's who you know." It still drives me crazy that he was partly right.

Then he sighed. "Ehhh, OK," he said. "Give it a try." He assigned eighteen-year-old Leslie, the pretty little Roma girl, to show me the ropes, since she'd been hanging out at the restaurant since she was thirteen. I knew there was humiliation in all of this. But it also seemed like a fairly fun way to hang out with people and make a few bucks at the same time. So I shrugged, "OK."

And it was . . . OK. Except for the indignity of my baby brothers lording it over me, it was a good way to visit with my dad, who was always there. It was a hilarious window into the antics of the Old Town regulars, the Viagra Triangulators, the tourists who dropped in on their way to Second City.

I did discover fairly quickly that no one had really known I existed. They thought my dad only had two sons. Never heard of his three daughters. That was kind of uncomfortable. But now that I was there, he would walk me around the place, introduce me with pride to his friends: "Here's my daughter, the writer. She has three master's degrees."

Still, it was annoying to witness the changing narrative in my dad's conversation about the place. Over the months that I worked there, he stopped talking about how he'd given "the boys" a chance to escape their bad situations—and he started bragging that his sons had stepped into help him out.

About two years in, my dad had a stroke, from which he mostly recovered. He needed a walker after that, but he continued to hold court in the dining room, at Table One, or on the outside patio, at Table Ninety. Regulars still vied to sit with him while he curmudgeoned.

Then, a year and a half later, came stroke number two. My dad's best waiter and loyal friend, Miguel, saw it coming and called an ambulance, so my dad got treatment right away. First, the staff at Northwestern pumped so much saline into his system that it seeped into his lungs. He developed pneumonia and nearly died of it. Then they dried him out so thoroughly that he became—I think the medical term would be *unhinged*. He had panic attacks and hallucinations and was generally out of his mind.

One morning in the middle of the pneumonia fiasco, I got a phone call from my sister, Linda. "Dad's mad at you," she said, laughing.

"What did *I* do?" I practically squealed it. I'd been coming by almost every day, despite my dad's efforts to make me and other visitors feel unwelcome. I darted uncomfortably in and out, just long enough to make sure my dad was OK.

My sisters came a little less often, but for nice, long visits, though they had unforgiving jobs, and they live out in the suburbs. My youngest brother—the one who was supposed to become a chef—brought food or sent food made by other people on the days he worked at the restaurant. My other brother came once. Maybe twice. "I can't handle it," he said.

Still, Linda said I was the one charged with neglect.

"What did I *do*—or not do?"

"You've been bad," Linda teased. "Apparently, Dad had a dream last night, and he thinks it was real. He thinks you left him at Holy Ghost Church in Wood Dale. You abandoned him there or something. He's *really* mad."

He really was. That afternoon, I made my way to the ICU to find my dad unconscious, or anyway laboring so hard to breath that he paid no attention to events in the room. I gazed at him a moment, then brought a chair to his bedside, took his hand, and just hung out. It was a little easier, actually, when he was asleep.

But he looked pretty scary. My brother, Tom, showed up and said he looked way better than he had the night before. And the nurse agreed. She was brisk and cheery, checking lines and attending to data, and she just started talking to my unconscious dad.

"Frank—how are you doing, Frank? Are you breathing OK?"

My dad opened his eyes, looked at her, and muttered that he was OK. Then he turned his head and saw *me*, and his brow darkened. With tremendous effort, he raised his right arm, pointed a finger at me and, beaming a laser of rage, he whisper-yelled, "You!"

I thought maybe he was joking. "I smiled and rubbed his hand. "Hi, Dad," I said.

"You." He repeated. "Left me hangin'.

"Dad," I said, "I've been here almost every day."

"In Wood Dale," he insisted. "Yesterday. Got stuck on that fence and you wouldn't get me down."

I didn't know what to say.

"On the fence by Holy Ghost. You left me there."

"Dad!" I protested. "I didn't!"

He glared at me.

"Dad, I'm sorry you dreamed I did that. But I would never."

Silence.

"Dad!" I exclaimed. "It was a dream!"

"Dream?"

"Yeah, Dad. A dream. You didn't leave the hospital. You've been in the hospital since Friday."

"Dream."

"Yeah. A dream. And anyway," I added for good measure, "I would never leave you."

"You left me hangin'..."

"Yeah." I was a little exasperated now. "Dad, I promise: If you were ever on a chain link fence—if you were trapped on a fence, I would get you off it. Somehow."

"But you didn't!" My dad was nearly sitting up for emphasis. Maybe this rage was good for him? But I had to defend myself.

"Dad!" I said. "It was a dream."

My conversations with my dad went on this way for the next four or five days. So did everyone's. My dad complained to everyone that I had betrayed him. Nurses told him it was a dream. My brother, Tom, and my sisters told him it was a dream. But the reality was almost impossible for him to shake. It made my husband laugh, because I've blamed *him* for his behavior in *my* dreams....

But I was worried—about my dad's lucidity, on the one hand, and the dream, on the other. Even as time passed, the dream didn't fade much. After those first four or five days, my dad wasn't mad at me anymore. But then he wanted to sue the hospital for causing that dream. He was still focused on it the next week, when his doctor moved him into the Rehab Institute, where he was scheduled now for several therapies a day, though he insisted he wasn't well enough yet.

The move to rehab seemed like a turning point. My dad was getting more visitors. His best friend smuggled him a bottle of whiskey. Other friends and fans stopped by to hang. And then on August 14, at 3:30 in the afternoon, someone called the restaurant to say my dad had had a heart attack during rehab. From a medical point of view, he'd died. His heart had stopped for a significant amount of time and not started up again on its own. An emergency team revived him and hooked him up to an epinephrine drip, but they said it didn't look good.

My brother, Frank, was working that day, so he got the call and then called me. He got to the ER in fifteen minutes, just time to witness a second heart attack. Again, my dad died. For a second time, the staff brought him back.

I got there in twenty-three minutes, in time to witness the third death and resurrection. My dad on the gurney, in deep repose. Five people surrounding him. Two of them—big men—pounding on him, smashing against his chest until his whole body bounced up and down in reply. It looked like a scene from *Goodfellas*.

My dad's heart started up again, but no one cheered. Instead, the lead doctor turned to me. He was breathing heavily, like an athlete, mid-run. My brother was pacing, so the doctor held my gaze. "We have to know what to do if he has another one," he said.

I stood there, trying to understand.

"He *is* going to have another one," he said. "He's only alive because of the epinephrine drip.

I was silent.

"And he's still having heart attacks, even with the drip." He leaned in, in a fairly unfriendly way, and repeated—slowly, "You have to tell us whether to revive him or not."

I was trying to conjure clarity, but I'd just watched some people beat the shit out of my dad. To save him. He had refused all offers of a DNR, but he had already died three times. Did Dad mean this? Even this?

"What about his brain?" I asked the doctor.

Since I had summoned science, he looked at me with a little more respect. "We don't know . . ." he trailed off. "But he's been without oxygen three times already. And we know *this* will happened again." He looked at me with impatience—or was it just urgency?—and I glanced at my brother, Frank, who threw up his hands, like this: V

. . . and said, "I can't." And scrambled away.

Christi, Linda, and Tom were yet to arrive. It was all on me. *Are you sure you can handle it?* my dad had asked me.

Then he died again. Fourth time. I remember thinking, *the fourth time is not funny*.

The ER doctor looked at me in a television-drama kind of way, but I couldn't speak. So he turned to my dad and started beating on him again. And then I remembered the dream and the chain link fence between Holy Ghost and the world, and—here we were. On the fence.

I'd promised I wouldn't leave him there, so I shouted, "Stop!"

The lead ER doc twisted around to make eye contact, while the staff kept beating my dad. Kept dragging him back.

"Stop!" I said it like I was saying *Uncle*. "Just—Just don't," I said. "Just let him be."

The men and women around him straightened up. They unhooked the connection points between my dad and the defibrillator. Then they removed the drip, snapped off their gloves, and left.

I stood there, alone, my hands resting on my dad's naked body. My other siblings came, and went. They were on their way to take care of all the details that pop up when somebody dies.

Alone with him after everyone else had gone, I felt impelled to murmur, I'm sorry, Daddy." And I was sorry. About so many things.

But not about letting him go.

Stroke

JO ANN BENDA

You fell into your bowl of soup
You rode unaware to the hospital
You mumbled—home?

We kept you comfortable
We sang you hymns of your childhood
We washed your hair

You drifted and came back
You waited and prayed
You breathed until you stopped

We watched your body shrink
We watched your spirit leave

Your ghost lingered awhile

Then you were gone

Family Education at Ground Zero

KATHRYN TRUEBLOOD

Ask any parent in this room if they'd rather their kid had cancer, and they'd probably tell you yes. Because there's so much support, and money, and sympathy if you say your kid has cancer. Not so, if you say they're sick in the head. You want to know why you can't find a support group for teens with OCD or bipolar or depression? Because the therapist is liable for anything that happens. That's why your kid has got to be on lockdown to find a support group. And I count us lucky. If my kid hadn't tried to off himself before he turned eighteen, he'd be in a state hospital. Or jail. Or on the streets. The hospital psych nurse said to me, "State hospitals are often more traumatizing than the original incident." She was visibly pregnant and her hands were loosely clasped beneath her belly. She sounded like she was reporting on a toxic spill across state lines.

So now we're in this Family Education Room at Ground Zero. You can picture it easily enough. Once you pass through the waiting room of bright foam furniture, there's a conference table, a screen, a white board—plenty of blank waiting to be filled. Everyone in here looks some version of beat, except for the Education Consultant leading our Safety and Crisis Prevention Planning Meeting aka *What to Do When We Get Home*. She looks like she should be leading us in a volleyball clinic—a strapping tall gal, swinging pony tail, bronzed arms— the same age as the brothers and sisters who have come here with their parents. Our goal in this class is "to replace negative coping skills with positive coping skills."

First thing when you get home, say goodbye to belts, scarves, sheets, cords, ropes, knives, bleach, ammonia, weed killer, knives, razors, X-Acto knives, craft supplies, tools. Firearms? None. Pills? On lockdown already, in a black plastic safe guaranteed to float in a river.

My sixteen-year-old son, Sid, took an entire bottle of Lexapro and half a bottle of Wellbutrin. Fortunately, he threw up three times before he told me. Even though I was half-asleep, I knew something was going on because he woke me up for work that morning. *That* never happens. Then, immediately after telling me, he began seizing. A swift wind seemed to lift his arms, hands, and fingers, then he buckled as though a tree limb had hit him square in the rib cage. He was lying on his side on the bed. His eyes were flashing back towards me like a spooked horse's. I had my hands on his hip and shoulder, then he began to jerk as though a negatively charged wire inside him were being touched to a positively charged one. It flipped my switch; I called 911.

"Get rid of gallon size baggies, extension cords, paper clips and pencil sharpeners." Molly, our leader, is ticking off a bulleted list. I remember now that Sid had melted the pencil sharpener I put in his Christmas stocking in order to get the razor out.

"How will my kid read if she doesn't have a lamp by her bedside cause I took away the extension cord," one parent says. She is plain-faced, stripped of adornment, her hair a blunt cut grey, and she sits beside her substantial husband who occasionally rolls his neck. He has a Polynesian tattoo banding one cheek in an interlocking pattern of shark's teeth or spearheads.

"Well, maybe for awhile that's okay," says Molly, our leader. "Give her a flashlight. The goal is to buy time. Less access, more time. You want to give the teenager time to cool off."

Who is going to argue with that? No one. We are left to our dread remembrances. The thermostat ticks. The power point letters hum: "Remove sharps and tools, including items that can be broken or used as a weapon."

Sid once carved tic-tac-toe into his arm. Another morning he came home with a dollar sign shaved onto his scalp. Sometimes he came in with a bruised face. He laughed it off. He and his buds liked to scrabble when drunk. I counted myself lucky that on the nights he went out to party, he came home in the mornings; that it was a point of discipline with him to crash on the floor or sleep in the car and not endanger himself or worry me by driving under the influence.

"The three leading methods of suicides in children and adolescents are..."

The seventeen-page handout accords with every page of the power point projected. Our dog was staked to the front lawn when the paramedics took Sid—the dog was the family witness and the reason Sid felt sad for trying. "*Firearms account for 45% of suicides in the U.S. Suffocation (Strangulation) accounts for 40%. Poisoning (Overdose/Ingestion) accounts for 8%.*"

You admire the parentheses. You imagine trying them out on someone who might not realize the nuances —*oh, by the way, did you know that suffocation includes strangulation? Or that overdose is technically poisoning*? At parent night or book club or around the Xerox machine. What a way to throw a pity party. You want pity. You want it like caramel sauce on vanilla ice cream, big gooey sweet globs of it. Afterwards, you don't care about the ice cream; it's just the gluey bottom of the jar you're going after with a spoon.

The night you came home from the hospital to gather some things, you found the jar of Wellbutrin. There were only a few pills left in the bottle; they appeared larger now that the others were gone. You poked a finger inside. The pills were damp. Sid had poured water directly into the vial. Chug-a-lug.

The shark-tooth-tatted father shakes his head. "She sure tried to die."

A woman in the opposite corner puts down her needlepoint and looks up. "When I cry or seem scared she says 'please don't make this about you.'"

You smile at them both. You take notes in fits and starts, like a dog that doesn't know if it's the flea that bit him or the thought of the flea. The lady to my left keeps a cheery face on. She has rouged it onto her cheeks. There are tiny cherries embroidered on her button-down shirt. She is a version of perky past its prime. She is alert like a star pupil, a fifty-year-old one whose bra long ago lost its elastic. I will come to appreciate her.

"You'll want to set up a schedule for meds," the education consultant says.

No dur, you hear your inner self say, Sid's words, teenaged words. *No duh* became *No dur*. But Sid is on five meds, and you are on four, and keeping schedules never was your strong suit. You wonder if keeping to a schedule now will be like breast feeding, if you will receive an inner signal that will cause a life-preserving rush of hormone, of cortisol. Sid thinks the lithium is working. The other meds weren't working—for months and months and months. Fortunately, the meds for your MS are working. You called the psychiatrist's office—for months and months and months. Sid wouldn't get out of bed and go to school. He claimed migraines, clamored for the dark. They tested him for mononucleosis. You hoped he had it. You couldn't stand to call the Attendance Office at school anymore. You finally told them, "School depresses him."

"Is there something in particular about it that depresses him?"

"No," you said, "just everything." When the robo-calls came in at dinnertime about attendance—"your student missed 1st, 2nd and 3rd period today"— you yelled things like, "Tell me something else I don't know."

"Who was that?" Sid asked.

"Have you tried not excusing his absences?" the doctor said. Sid complained of nausea, stomachache, migraine. One day he said he had a fever. "Take him to the doctor every time," the psychiatrist's nurse advised. A pretty expensive consequence to provide, but you were out of ideas. You took Sid to your family doc. "You're taking a lot of medicines," he told him. "I don't want you to rattle like a pill bottle if I shake you." You agreed with him. Who ever heard of a child taking this many medications?

You want to shake yourself for this comment now. First your son averaged three days a week of school, then two, then one, then none. You had no idea it could be so exhausting to watch another human lie down and refuse to get up. You comforted, cajoled, catered, bribed, cheered, threatened, consoled, intimidated, raged, and regretted.

Molly, the Education Consultant is talking. "Put your kid on a check-in, check-out system with razors."

"Or buy a cheap electric razor," the woman with vaccination scars on her arm says. She's a hefty weight woman with plenty of bosom to show. She wears the wife-beater in the household. Her voice is smoke and syrup. Pour Southern Comfort over coke. I will come to appreciate her.

"Assume your child knows where the guns, sharps, and meds are hidden. Valuable or sentimental items may be targets for youth who engage in property destruction."

You allow yourself to sigh here. Your child does not tear up the house, knife the couch, or smash the tchotchkes. He did try to jump off the balcony at his father's when he was grounded because he wanted to see a girl. His father relented, still panting after pulling Sid off the ledge. I see Sid now striding in the tall gold grass, antelope interlocutor, legs swinging over a crescent moon on the rise.

"Our kids are non-verbal autistic," the woman across the table says. Above her brow is a mark like a crosshatch, a pound sign, or as Sid would see it, a hashtag. "There's nothing left to break." She shrugs.

"We need to move along," says Molly. This is her go-to line. We are being herded to the end. You know she is being paid to get to the end. You are not unsympathetic. She is not unsympathetic.

At his bedside, you watched Sid sleep, alert to the eye movement behind his lids that seemed to signal whole schools of fish swimming. What did you know of him, this man-child, dark in the way of the Southern French or Italian, but with cobalt eyes limned by a thin vein of crystal around the iris. You remembered that tall gal in a print shift who strode toward him in the school parking lot. You watched them embrace. She must have dived deep inside him to mine that mineral. Even heartbreak, you welcomed, so long as it wasn't now, today, final.

"Runaway behavior is hard to manage," our leader says. If Molly even has a child, it can't be more than two years old, easy enough to sweep off its feet and carry back to its room.

"Preventative strategies include purchasing alarms or chimes for doors and windows."

Southern Comfort crosses her arms and lets out an audible snort.

"What good will that do if he's six foot two and weighs 250 pounds? Like I'm going to catch him." She looks around at us as if we're a bunch of liars and betrayers. No one moves a pen.

"My six-year-old just crawled out the dog door," says a bouffant blonde with a boob job and a submissive lilt to her voice. You can feel everyone in the room register a sudden Ah-ha. This is the parent of the youngest child on the ward, the six-year-old slamming himself into walls so hard he wears a helmet. She radiates a tormented loveliness.

"We also recommend calling 911 and filing an At-Risk-Youth Petition," says Molly, who is by now reading directly from the notebook that repeats verbatim the power point.

"What?" Southern Comfort says flatly, "the two burly guys in the white van who manhandle your kid into the back?"

The woman with cherries on her shirt puts down her needlepoint. "My daughter ended up in juvy for nine months at a center 200 miles from home. How's that supposed to help?"

Molly looks stunned, like someone hit the mute button on her mouth.

The professorial Asian dude, who is actually wearing a tweed marl cap, clears his throat. "What helps," he says in a surprisingly resonant tenor, "is that you're her mother, and your child knows you will see her through anything."

Southern Comfort nods briefly at him as she wipes under her eyes. "They didn't treat him like they do here," she said. "That's for sure."

"My son has seen the abuse," the bouffant blonde says, apropos of nothing. "I always let his father come back."

Tweed Cap leans back, choosing his words. "Whoo boy, I'm going to have a double bourbon tonight."

"It's like bleach on your hands." The blonde stares down at her blue gel nails. "You can smell it for hours no matter how many times you wash."

Molly is looking around the room for someone to take this up, but no one says anything. Her mouth is holding back all the additional risk factors in this room.

I reach over and pat the woman's hand. "Someday this will all seem like a bad dream." It's something my mother used to say to me. The woman turns her huge baby blues on me, and I have the sensation of tripping into a kiddie pool.

"We need to talk about social media," Molly asserts. "You need to obtain all your children's passwords, codes, and accounts and do random checks."

A striking black woman wearing Egyptian eye makeup—heavy lines of kohl that flick out and upwards—wrestles in her seat as though she were itching to get out of her magenta power blazer. She jumps in while Molly's eyes sweep the room.

"Don't think your kids aren't into it. Cutting clubs and fake suicides on the Internet. Girls all crying over someone who isn't real. They help each other out. This way," the woman draws her pointer finger across her wrist, "to the hospital. This way," she draws her pointer down the vein, "to the morgue."

The woman knitting is suddenly riled up. "I tell my kids their phones are on lease. I paid for them; they're mine. I take 'em when I want."

Tough, smart lady, I think. I'm betting on her horse for now.

Then Bouffant Blonde speaks up: "What if your ex gave the kids their cell phones and says you can't have the codes. You can't take the phones away then."

"There may be parts of this that just aren't possible," Molly says, finally abandoning the power point to sit in a chair at the table. "We're not really saying you can do all this."

Southern Comfort shifts on her haunches and pivots her knees towards the Education Consultant.

"This whole deal you have here is a set-up, unless it comes with a in-home nurse and a prison guard, and I suspicion it don't."

"It don't," the beauty in the magenta blazer says. "So just remember, whatever happens, it's gonna be your fault."

I look around the table. Against the white of the walls, the fluorescents, and the blank board, we are visibly fading. Somewhere Sid is sitting in a circle with kids who have bruises on their foreheads, hair in their eyes, feeding tubes in their nostrils.

"I'm calling this bullshit meeting over with," says Southern Comfort, and she rises to her full stature.

We stumble to our feet and rise with her.

Extractions

KAIN KIM

> "The inferno of the living is not something that will be; if there is one, it is what is already here, the inferno where we live every day, that we form by being together. There are two ways to escape suffering it. The first is easy for many: accept the inferno and become such a part of it that you can no longer see it. The second is risky and demands constant vigilance and apprehension: seek and learn to recognize who and what, in the midst of the inferno, are not inferno, then make them endure, give them space."
> Italo Calvino, *Invisible Cities*

I am told to arrive at the sleep lab exhausted. The room they do the study in is obscured behind two large steel-grey doors, the kind you see on television when they wheel the invalid in on a stretcher without stopping, the doors flapping about on either side like monolithic wings. But I am not maimed or mutilated. I walk in just fine on my own two legs, and when the nurse sits me down in the neatly made twin bed not too unlike my own and begins taping wires to my face, I keep still, a docile lab rat. The nurse wears long, red fake fingernails to match her red hair and keeps raking my cheeks with them as she fidgets with the tape. She leaves. The lights go down. Behind my eyelids I follow the needle tracings on graph paper of my respiration, heart rate, brain activity. The capillaries of another me unspooling, thread to thread, spider-webbing in long streams down the page.

That night, for the first night in months, I dream. I dream that dark matter coagulated into a dense mass and reshaped itself, like clods of oil shifting on a black pan, strewing the planets and the asteroids and the stars in a hotchpotch about the universe. Pluto appears like a smudge of blue ink at the corner of my window. Mars quavers, huge and monstrous, on the horizon, blotting out the moon and flooding our planet with war vibes. You can see everything on its mottled, bruised surface, right down to every speck of red cindery dust. Its gravitational pull draws ocean tides to tsunami proportions, and the great black, briny tongue of reeling water swallows up our cities and towns and homes in one gulp, the sound and static of the world muted in an instant.

When I finally wake, my face is bloated with tears. I follow the luminous course of the second hand on the clock through its rotations without missing a single second until daybreak blues the room into view.

After the nurse again goes through the arduous process of unrigging me from the machine, the doctor comes to see about me.

"Did you get it?" I ask.

"It was perfect."

Great, I say, and I walk out past those grey double doors, down the back stairwell onto the colonnade into the bright December morning and into my waiting cab, into plush grey seats and the smell of cigarette smoke. The tinted windows of the cab cast the serpentine wriggle of the Hudson under a grayed, gaseous light. Behind me to my left is the vast asthmatic rattle of a diesel truck grinding by. The roar of its engine pitches higher, then lower, as it sidles up alongside us and passes by. This is called the Doppler effect, the shift in frequency as viewed by an observer moving relative to the wave source. It applies to space too, used to measure the velocity at which entire galaxies approach or recede from us. Right now, in this giant ashtray of a cab, I am moving sixty miles an hour but relative to my universe I don't budge an inch. Negligible difference.

On this day I am sixteen. I don't know much, but today I know this: Not all those free-fall doors on the television immure the frenzied rattle of snapping vials, the low keens of dipping blood pressure monitors. A few will house just maybe a few beds, beds made and empty, the lights turned off.

The sleep test was Doctor X's idea, Doctor X being the unforeseen consequence of my mother's self-steered course on How to Deal with an Incompetent Child: make it someone else's problem.

Something throws me about Doctor X from the very beginning. Maybe it's the casual name-dropping of famous depressives in literature after I told him my intended major.

Today, X says, "But is that really you talking, or is it your illness?"

I look at him blankly. "Is there a difference?"

X stares down his long walnut desk at me, rheumy eyes shelled in coke-bottle lenses. Cradled in his cavernous hands is a pen like a silver needle, like a chrome bullet. His office smells like turpentine.

If I could, I'd peel this feeling off like a cheap swimsuit to play in the sea alone and feel the sharp slice of water on legs. I'd unsheathe myself like a knife. I'd hinge off this topmost version of me like stapled paper and read the underside inscription. Maybe that girl would have something useful to say. A book with a spine you can crack, instead of a shivering thing bound in one uninterrupted skin.

From behind the desk I hear my voice respond, "I guess it's the illness."

What I hear at the end of six two-hour sessions: textbook depression. Pistons clink into place and engine the plot onward: ce-lex-a-pro-zac-zol-oft. The diagnosis feels redundant, a restatement of the obvious. I see my graduation portrait shrunk down and formatted into the margins of one of my psychology textbooks. It would be outfitted with its own cramped, scorpion-lettered caption. *Fig. 2, Case Study #21. Subject presents typical symptoms of adolescent depression, including apathy, inappropriate guilt, withdrawal, and extreme fatigue.* My illness is sourced material. What can I possibly say about it that hasn't been said before?

When I actively boycott my own therapy, my mother's last offer of advice is to tell me the best cure for thinking too much about yourself is to help somebody worse off than you. Most parents jump at the opportunity to tell their child they are special, irreplaceable. One of a kind. My mother loves to remind me that I am a Small Pinprick on the space-time fabric of all existence. Think of the *size*, she says. If the universe is infinite, then the difference between you and the next person, some malnourished kid in a third-world country, is basically negligible. This should be encouraging! Mom is always sliding off into the distress of the infinite: the contingencies of life pared to absolutes, the I and the not-I. To clothe oneself in the not-I is to know the bigness of the universe in all its entirety, its radically accidental nature. A life lived through all eyes – all 'I's – at once is a heroism to strive for.

Icky thought: If getting better means shoving further and further away from the self, how many degrees of not-I will I have to scale until I am finally *me*, again?

In the end, I take my mom's advice and apply to volunteer with a program that offers pro-bono medical services to rural communities in Honduras. She thinks it's smart of me to distract myself with clinical service. Like knocking down two birds with one stone, she says. Even when it comes to my illness, productivity is paramount. Maybe even especially so in the case of my illness.

Selfish thought, here for only a moment: Isn't it asking too much that I toggle between all human dangers and pains? Isn't one enough to inconvenience a person a lifetime?

While writing the mandatory entrance essays, I feel involuntarily sick. I Google pictures of derelict shanties and water browned with grime, trying to scrounge up an ounce of magnanimity from the bottomless well of myself. Children with the weathered and world-weary faces of old men stare out at me from behind the computer screen, eyes blown wide with accusation.

The program site's page for volunteers is worse. They have an index of volunteer alum on their e-records, and they all look positively febrile. Their hair is as yellow as their eyes are blue as their lips are red as their shirts are white, collars crisp and clean, their likeliness captured and crystallized from the neck up into pristine pixelated statues. I mimic their expression. My face feels as stiff as sandpaper and my smile fissures at the corners.

I wake up at Toncontin International.

With the window sleeve edged back and squinting like a newborn baby at the unfamiliar terrain below, all I can think is that this must be the black hole event horizon of the world. This is where all manmade information comes to die.

The suction is enormous. Think red giants, burning helium and eating up the hydrogen at its core. Think Mars. Underneath runs in every-which-way stretches of burnt-umber colored ground, as flat and level as a sheen of rust. As we gradually draw closer, I see that it isn't the ground, but in fact the houses and their rooftops, crammed so closely together it coagulates into illusory hardpan. There's a sense of deadweight to it. The only sign of dimensionality is the occasional Spanish cedar tree banking the clustered houses. Their dark fronds bow as they struggle to maintain buoyancy under the unforgiving midday sun, shielded somewhat by the dishwater clouds that scud lazily across the horizon.

In astronomical terms, an obliquity is the angle of the Earth's axis of rotation. Obliquity here is zero. If you were to walk to the end of that plain, just beyond that bend of mountain, you'd drop off the surface of the earth. The land is a hot press, a screen.

Starting day two, our mobile brigade will set up shop in a children's schoolhouse. Our destination is Chirina, a rural community distanced a few hours from the center of Danli, its municipality. Population: 1,500. The community houses a single health center, staffed with one doctor and several nurses.

Relative to the resources of its sister villages, it is considered well off.

The other volunteers, all thirty-something of us, remain within the confines of the compound for the first day, nibbling on fried plantains. The dorms are low-slung shanties roofed with corrugated iron the shade of old blood. I wait for a turn in the outdoor toilet, of which we have but only two. I wait, I wait. I watch dull-eyed girls with flyaway hair and airplane-seat-creased clothing disappear into the bathroom and emerge again, backed by a diaphanous cloud of muggy, sweet-smelling steam. My nails dig into the granulated sweat of my palms. I count the backs of fifteen heads. Then I realize, the same way you realize you're not wearing any pants in a dream, that I've left my toiletries behind in the dorms, and while I stand there gaping the girl behind huffs testily and pushes past me into the bathroom.

Back in the dorms, moonlight seeps through slats in the roof and checkers anonymous white beds in sulfurous yellow. The choral whine of cicadas outside surge upon my ears. I crawl in between the covers of my cot and collapse into a fitful sleep, just like that, filthy and gross from travel. The cot has sterile, white sheets fitted in perfect hospital corners.

I dream less that night, fitful because of the heat but deep despite my unease. In this one I am sitting crisscross-applesauce on my mother's oriental carpet. Another me is running circles around dream-me like a rogue planet, or some crazed rendition of Duck, Duck, Goose. I measure out the obliquities of myself against myself until I grow dizzy and slip into a heavier, duller sleep.

The heat is incendiary. On the long stretch between compound and community, we traverse on foot over rolling, dusty hills, taking swigs from insulating thermoses and lining up at the coolers during water breaks with the glaze-eyed complacency of cattle. Molten asphalt sucks at our soles. Untethered goats shoulder through the high-growing brown grass and pass us without interest, fine rings of tea-colored dust rising in their wake. We wait for our bus, squatting in the meager shade. When it arrives, it brings no solace. The little ventilation there is seems to be sucking the air back into its ducts for all the good it does, and when we bother to speak, words refuse to carry and instead drop limply at sweat-beaded chins. Breaths come short, little whistling inhalations. The anonymous bus driver, face shrouded by a thick mesh net hanging from his visor, blasts old Spanish pop songs one after another, the cheerful litany of melodies trundling us along the unpaved road, guiding us in an unfamiliar tongue.

On the first clinic day, we arrive at the school to find a long line of people leaning against the walls of the courtyard, already waiting to be seen. Few raise their heads to acknowledge us; you would think our meeting coincidental. Nearly every face remains bowed beneath a wide-brimmed straw cap. No one wears a watch. Ambient air wavers and snaps above the blazing concrete, stewing the lot. I know that among the throng there must be wives and husbands and skinny teenage adolescents, but they look indistinguishable at first, their liveliness and sexuality snuffed out from behind the leathery creases with which each browned face is graven. The only ones I can pick out right away are the children who dangle precariously from the sagging arcs of their mothers' arms. Their expressions are shut away, bodies restless as they follow our bus with pinched glares. Spoiled bananas perfume the air.

The volunteers are split into cohorts that rotate between stations every hour, and within the first ten minutes we're put to work. I feel silly in my olive-green volunteer's uniform, a size too big because I hadn't known I needed scrubs until the night before, after the others had already gotten to the regular sizes at the compound's necessities store. I look superfluous beside the uniformed doctors and nurses, who bustle by shouting in Spanish without sparing me a single glance.

Of all the rotations, I like pharmacy best. They keep you busy there. Prescriptions are collected from patients lined up at the door and allocated accordingly to the volunteers. We then unsnarl the physician's knotted tangle of ink scribble into long, beautiful words that spill from the tongue like small pebbles plinking into water. Loratadine. Cetirizine. Medications lie packed in cardboard boxes that crowd the perimeter of the room, pills of all colors scrupulously counted and sealed off in labeled Ziploc bags. We rush pell-mell from one corner of the room to another, faces buried in pink prescription slips and juggling plastic bags of antihistamines and eye drops and Claritin. Every person gets multivitamins. To a thin, dark girl of no more than thirteen, I hand a plastic baggie of Clomiphene citrate, a fertility drug. The girl has earlobes that pucker around thin gold hoops. A shapeless dress that could have been her mother's drags from her tiny frame, at risk of slipping down her arms. Her breasts and hips scarcely make imprints on the sun-bleached cloth. She has a filthy rag pressed to her mouth as if trying to staunch some flow. Her eyes evade mine as she reaches for the bag. She chokes it in her hands, hands yellow like a skeleton dipped in wax. Nods. Leaves.

Lunchtime. We gorge on slightly mushed peanut butter and jelly sandwiches, washed down with sweaty cans of lukewarm Coke. We watch the schoolchildren play soccer in the grassy outback of the courtyard. They are surprisingly good. It is quickly becoming clear that in the pantheon of the compound, preteen boys hold a special kind of court. Adults pay them no heed but they operate like little savants of their own kind of profession, darting between legs and filching shiny things off tables. Within the first day, our team is missing two watches, one plastic folding fan, and several cans of bug spray. A sharp tug on my scrub bottoms. I look down, and a bony kid snarls up at me:

"Enséñame, Enséñame!"

"What, this? You want to see this?" I hold up my hand with the thin gold band on the middle finger. A graduation present from dad. Behind the boy, cheers erupt as a soccer ball sails through the air and lobs neatly into the net.

I meet his burning gaze and struggle to twist the ring from my finger, then hold it just out of his reach. "How do I know you won't run if I show it to you?"

The boy bares his teeth and gnashes his little pearls at me.

Working the triage table means marinating in the near-constant stream of smoke that arises in great black plumes from a massive pile of burning garbage that sits nearby.

To Jenny, this is a gross misdemeanor of the highest order. Jenny is my cohort leader and both her parents work in the United Nations Environmental Program. Last year her self-directed documentary on bee extinction was shown in six different Brooklyn arthouses. I know this because she told me at our first dinner.

"You can't do that," she says incredulously to one of the old men who stokes the fire. "That's, like, direct pollution. Global warming," she enunciates. "Have you heard of global warming?"

The man's craggy face remains averted; he breathes into a blackened bandana tied around his ears. His gaunt, sunspot-darkened arms don't buckle as he heaves a crate of aluminum cans into the mound. Jenny could have stood there and preached about carbon dioxide emissions and greenhouse gases for years, and he wouldn't blink.

At lunch, he lights a cigarette. The smoke from his breath mingles with the smoke from the bigger fire nearby. It hangs in the air, ribboning like gossamer snakeskin.

Our last day. Soggy plantains and carrot juice for breakfast. A dead dog, squirming with maggots and flies, a small grayish lump on the side of the road. Its tongue coated white in dust. A few kids venture a look and leap back, screaming. A sudden rain-darkened noon, water a thin pulse on the window, the shingles on our cabin blistering, curling, buckling, warm pneumatic wet dripping down between the light fixtures.

We close out the week with a campfire circle. Somebody is popping kettle corn in a skillet over the embers. Everyone talks at least once.

The first one that volunteers to speak is Devyn, who led my dental hygienist station Tuesday. Devyn carries the vague, indelible reassurance of someone who has given this speech before, who has been returning year after year to help, only to see the treated afflictions replicated, multiplied throughout the community in malignant autogenesis. I wonder how she does it. This girl describes her last day in the dental station. The patients in the dental station have teeth rotted to the core, cavities in their cavities, from drinking too much Coke. Devyn wants to start a nonprofit that would advocate for children's health awareness through teaching fundamental preventative measures, like drinking water and milk instead of soda. And flossing. Of course. All around the circle, bright, knowledgeable heads bob in empathy and mouths quirk up automatically.

In my mind's eye I see my last patient from that day, a five-year-old girl with rot tunneled all the way through three of her tiny moonstone teeth. It's not very hard to imagine, the yearlong harvest of bacteria climbing the hairline fissures in her mouth.

"Open wide," the dentist says.

Nothing opens—lips airtight, hermetically sealed. The dentist seizes her jaw between thumb and forefinger until bright points of white appear where dimples should be. A flinty resolve works its way over the girl's eyes and scrapes the pupils black.

"Hand me the needle," the dentist says.

Limbs thrash, galvanized to action. The hammering molars of her fists, staccato hiccups reeling high and loud. The dentist has to eventually pull out her teeth without the anesthetic because they couldn't get her still enough for the needle. When they'd done it—when his hands, shrink-wrapped in latex, had pried her maw apart and affixed the cold steel around the offending tooth—her voice had steadily risen in an agonized scream, hurting our ears. When it was done she was inconsolable.

I also remember the dull, gray solution puddled in the white porcelain sinks of the outdoor bathrooms. That unnamable something, something worse than sewage water.

I try to focus my gaze on the next person speaking but the fire belches its fumes at me and my vision swims. Around me, the dark drop into cliffside breathes the noises of a cool night beaded wet with rain, and nestled within its blue wilderness, the campfire seems an abstract ceremony.

What is fast emerging: the fetishization of story. Everyone is rippling at the seams with a need to talk, but these "personal" accounts seem so rinsed of difference that it's hard to remember who felt what. Perspectives get slippery: one can never leave the self quickly enough, never wade deeply enough through the alien waters. My own thoughts, on the other hand, are curdling around themselves. If there is a lesson to be learned, an epiphany to be had, I have but managed to access its mere shadow through my own grotesque language, a language in which everything has a meaning only in the context of my sickness.

Their watery selflessness loosens my subjectivity like a rotten tooth.

Wisps of dialogue float atop swirling, too-close images of smiling faces and crackling fire. Robert, a haggle-toothed supersenior who is on the brigade for his third time, is waxing poetic about how, during the public health brigade, a woman for whom he had been building a stove had briefly invited him in for a drink and showed him around her house. "It was awe-inspiring," Robert says, the pride he'd seen in her eyes- eyes clouded milky with glaucoma, but still.

He says, "Her vitality taught me a lot. Even with the bare minimum, it felt like a home... they're not so different from us... united in a common need... circumstance..." Robert's glaucoma-less eyes are enameled in tears. A polite smatter of applause ensues.

Out of the dark a voice says, "And what about you?" The cohort leader is looking at me. Her teeth bared in a perfect Magic Brite smile. No cavities. She says, "Have any thoughts to share?"

But I am writ small and illegible. I have no out-flung anecdotes to tell about the locals. My every encounter with them has only served in making me keenly aware of my lone reality, how everything is always lensed too tight and narrow–and this, in turn, seems only to emphasize the sheer *un*-reality of their reality. Somehow I sense this revelation would not fly with the other volunteers.

All around me, embers glow and die. Air shimmers in the space around the fire, wavy and surreal. Warped, like I'm a planet warping the space-time around me. The vague outlines of the other volunteers' bodies lean into one another, crash together, the boundaries atomized, in a big bang, and the cohort leader's words ring dully across the fire like one big, communal voice hiked up from the back of all their melded throats.

I open my mouth, and my voice is drowned in the sea of cicadas and wind and fire.

I am in the waiting room of the hospital. This morning I crossed back upwards of some two thousand miles and parked myself here, in the waiting room in front of the sleep disorders center. It's still early enough that most of the seats are vacated, the few patients in attendance chugging lazily around the wood-paneled-coffin chill like fish food about to settle.

The TSA agent had flashed me a big smile at the airport and stamped my passport like it was a report card.

"Is there a Mrs. Rodriguez here," calls out the receptionist. No one answers.

Here in the dark gut of the hospital it smells fusty and wet, congested with the sewer abscess of urban transportation people have tracked in with them on their shoes and hair. Diagonally across from me, a bilious-faced woman deposits herself in one of the disabled seats and rhythmically works her atrophied jaw away at nothing. She's thin. Not quite Honduras thin, but getting there. Early-stages-of-cancer thin, perhaps. Methadone-addict thin. Loose sheets of skin tacked tightly onto bone. I look her up and down; her coat is open, showing a strip of faded T-shirt with absolutely any logo on it, kind of blending into the inane turquoise swirl of 90s upholstery patterning on the seat behind her.

I smile at her. She averts her eyes, face like a refugee's, distressed and foreign.

"Would you like me to explain it to you?"

The internist with the ordinary face waits for my reply. She's holding out to me the results of the sleep lab, the one from right before I left for my trip. We're not alone; the lab technician stands a few feet away with his back to us, facing a machine that is quietly informing him of my diagnosis in a series of whirring clicks and beeps. Beyond his head I can make out the window, and beyond that, falling snow. The snow is fat with water; it scrolls past the frame and sticks to the glass like a bad painting.

The internist is raising her pencil-raked eyebrow at me, and I shake my head decisively. I would be more interested, but just looking at those skittering lines makes me tired. I say,

"Just tell me what I have to do."

I pick my way across the parking lot, newly sheeted in snow as if in sleep. The world sinks into a pale marbled calm, an alien planet. I wonder what kind of animals must be hibernating in this cold.

Before there was even ground or sea to fall on, there was snow. In the total darkness and silence, about 300,000 years after The Big Bang, hydrogen molecules coupled up into flakes and littered the universe with its first cosmic winter. Snow in space. Half a billion years before the invention of light, so you couldn't have seen them, but they were there.

Standing in this parking lot feels not unlike the first time I stood on the airplane tarmac in Honduras, hot garbage ash snow blowing up my lungs, dark slurry on my tongue. I am no more convinced than when I left of a universal kinship, cannot enter any further into the cooperative delusion that our stories—mine, the locals, the volunteers, the doctors– might already be netted, interlinked. To invent this kind of sibling sympathy seems to presuppose a naturalness, an ease, an innateness to ties, as if they have always been there and will always remain. My body aches from constantly striving to conjure some phantom pain for a limb that never existed in the first place.

I can't touch the farthest length of the universe, and yet I do feel *larger* in myself: a compressed fullness that seems soaked up, an inner swelling that pushes to all my edges and pressurizes my eyes. I see things harder: dirt; dogs; little baggies of pills; stark, pyrrhic scream of bonfire.

The fire especially. I am thinking of that last night. After our ceremony, a gaggle of local teenage boys had swarmed upon its dregs to claim some warmth. I lingered pointlessly, wanting to say something but alone in the language. The boy closest to me made an active effort to pretend I was not there, laughing with his friends. His face was only half lit, the side turned toward me. Firelight incised his profile into the night air—beakish nose, outline hard and unusual and exact. I could see him studying me, surreptitiously, out of the corner of a slit eye. His bramble hair stuck up every which way; without thinking I smoothed mine down, as if gazing into a mirror. He did the same, and we smiled.

PQRST

JOANNE M. CLARKSON

When the body is mallet and blade,
letter from a war zone,
a burning saint,
as nurse I rely on a mnemonic
I was taught labeled *Pain Assessment.*
None of us can feel, at nerve level,
the cruelest sensations in another,
not lover or mother or healer.
I begin with

P, Precipitating/Palliating. What makes pain
worse or lessened?
Q, Quality, a descriptor like thrusting, drumming,
crushing or the breathless smother?

I take notes, typing, already deep in remedy.

R means Region and where it travels, Radiating.
S is Severity, the 1-to-10 scale
which is a joke really since all agony
is a ten in the moment.

I watch for nonverbal cues: Smile pulled
grotesque. Fists. Forehead folding tight.
Tears and sweat.

T equals Timing. When does it start? How long
does it last? How often does it menace
forever?

I present my fleshed-out alphabet
to the Hospice Team.
Construct a Treatment Plan

to still the hammer, stay the sword.
Rescue running through the liver,
across the blood-brain barrier.
Creating sensation, not exactly pleasure,
more truce. The ravaged body
making peace within itself.

A Gradual Process

REBECCA GROSSMAN-KAHN

On a hot June morning, my sandals tentatively crunched gravel beneath my feet as I walked towards the infamous gate of Auschwitz. Our tour guide launched into a history of the war, but I didn't pay attention at first, as I took in the rows of red brick buildings, the barbed wire fencing, the tourists, the birds in the trees above us, oblivious. The camp felt somehow smaller than I imagined; I could hear the traffic on a road outside the boundaries of the camp. I tried to imagine 13,000 bodies in this space at one time, this rectangle you could walk across in five minutes. The group started moving down a gravel path and I tuned back in to the tour.

We arrived at the medical experiments building late in the morning. Our guide said, "go inside and look to your left. This is where doctors injected poison into people's hearts." Inside, I saw a stainless steel table with drains, designed for dissections. There were two white coats hanging up on the wall. They were identical to the coat I would soon don as a medical resident, cloaking myself with a fresh new power. I learned about the systematic dehumanization that happened where I stood: the hair-shearing, the striped pajamas. Deliberate techniques for stripping the victims of their humanity, to make acts of atrocity somehow less impossible for the young Nazi soldiers. It was the end of medical school, and I was on an ethics fellowship with other students to visit the sites of the Holocaust. We came here to learn about Nazi physicians, to reflect on the crimes of our chosen profession.

Throughout Auschwitz, there are rows upon rows of photos. Endless faces. Beneath each: a name, a hometown, a year of birth. Or is it year of death? Who were these women? I notice a patch of wallpaper in one of the barracks: a delicate pattern of brown lines and pink shells, an unexpected detail of beauty. How many girls in these photos counted the shells of this wallpaper as they lay awake? Their identities are not the focus of the exhibition, so we must move on, into the next curated barrack. Behind glass, we see hair piled from the floor to the ceiling. Thousands of pounds of hair. We are shown disembodied hair, hundreds of eyeglasses without faces, a room full of shoes, and mounds of kitchenware. It is designed to compound the nauseating emotional impact of the daily items from the lives of the dead, left behind.

What strikes me is how quickly we adapt, how quickly our shock subsides. On day one, we are hesitant to sit down on a bench as our guide lectures. How could we relieve our aching feet in the face of what happened here? We produce impenetrable silence on the bus ride to the hotel; there are no words to express the horror. On our second day, we act more like tourists in a museum and feel less of the dreadful weight of the experience. We sit down in the dry grass near the train tracks at Birkenau and soak in the warmth of the sun. Silence is replaced with mundane chatter on the bus. We have our delicious freedom to feel the cool breeze from an open window and ask a friend a meaningless question.

The night after I visited Auschwitz, after seeing all those photos of the bodies, I found my mind drifting to my anatomy donor from the first year of medical school. The information I knew about my donor was limited to her age and cause of death. Nothing else. It is enough. At that point in training, the sight of fuchsia nail polish on a donor's fingers pushes us over the edge, tears blurring our ability to finish the lab. The body is preserved in chemicals, an unhumanly grayish yellow, just foreign enough to make the act of cutting bearable. But the nail polish is pink and chipped—identical to our own nail-bitten fingers. We notice the indentation on our donor's ring finger, a pale halo left from years of wearing a wedding band. Further in the semester, just as we start to gain comfort in our role of cutting flesh in order to help us heal future patients, we uncover objects that disarm us. A pacemaker, a Foley catheter. The long tentacles of an IUD still lodged in the uterus. It is an invitation to imagine a life, too full, too busy, too heartbreaking for childbearing. The medical devices lodged in our donors bodies shock us back to the reality that these bodies once pumped blood, drained urine, got married, did not desire a pregnancy. It is too much humanity to bear.

Some say Anatomy is our entrée into the violence of medicine, systematically desensitizing us to each intimate piece of the human body. Knuckle, breast, eyeball. After my first day of anatomy lab, I asked my instructor for tips to tamper my emotional response. Despite eating two lunches and drinking plenty of water, I felt lightheaded and unable to concentrate. He detailed a four step approach: *First, enter the lab when no bodies are exposed to help get used to the room, the smell, etc. Next, look at plasticized specimens. Then, expose a small part of the body for a short time. Finally, expose the whole body but don't stare—study your notes next to the body. I am almost positive this gradual approach will work!* It worked. A few months later, I eagerly signed up for optional dissections of the brain. From exposing the fat, white spinal cord, I ran straight to my kitchen to cut butternut squash for dinner. How quickly I adapted; how quickly my shock subsided.

Medical training slowly built upon this tolerance by launching me into progressively more raw encounters. I reported to the basement autopsy room on my Pathology rotation. I adapted to the hum of the air conditioner, incessantly devoted to keeping the room at 55 degrees. With gloved hands, I explored the borders of a mesothelioma that took a life. I learned to expect the buzz of fluorescent lights, the rustle of plastic gowns, the juicy swoosh the knife makes cutting each irregular slab. The slap, slap slap, of squishy, liquidy slices of organs hitting the metal table.

Yet I was still not prepared for what I saw one snowy, Sunday morning on my surgery rotation. I was at a transplant center to retrieve a set of lungs from an organ donor. In a cold operating room, the donor's body was uncovered. When I first saw the donor's body, still intact, I asked my supervising surgeon for a moment to gather myself, to process the enormity of cutting organs out of this young woman. He did not seem to understand. He quizzically scrunched his eyes at me and walked briskly into the operating room.

The organ donor coordinators didn't tell us many details about the circumstances of her death, only the direct cause of death because it might affect the organs that are retrievable. I imagine they don't want us knowing too much, about where she was driving in her Jeep, or what detritus of daily living they found in her backpack. This would make it too hard to make the incision from throat to pelvis. Too hard to drain her entire body of blood, to watch the organs turn pale, and then white. From her birth date, I calculated she was nineteen years old. I heard her body was brought down from up north. She was from the rural part of the state, an area that must be desolate this time of year, without the clatter of tourists that transforms the region in the summer. Perhaps she lived in a lakeside town, or maybe by the gas station where vans full of families stop for popsicles on their way to vacation.

Aren't these the same details I was trying to uncover in Auschwitz? A young girl, nineteen, her name is all we have. Was she shy or gregarious? Did she braid her father's *tallis tzitzit* on Yom Kippur? These details are purposefully hidden—to smooth our clinical duty at the transplant center, to facilitate the physician-assisted atrocities in the barracks. For the physicians at Auschwitz, did their medical training – this process that teaches us to temper our emotional response, to section the body into discrete labs—make it easier to carry out their crimes? Perhaps the doctor whose white coat hangs in the long wooden building secretly cried over his anatomy donor as a sensitive medical student.

In medical school, we are instructed to seek out details about each patient, to preserve humanity in the hospital, to put a temporary plug on the slow leak of our empathy. We ask about grandchildren and pets. Volunteers tell their stories in preclinical curriculum to put a face on a diagnosis. And yet, haven't we all been shocked at that moment on day of discharge when we suddenly do not recognize our patient? He is now showered, wearing a fresh shirt from home, glasses on and pacing the room. After months of seeing him in the standard hospital gown, in the same supine position we expect to find every patient in each morning. Now, the white and blue hospital gown crumpled in a corner, we are jolted to see who he is.

Medical education slowly, yet deliberately, teaches us to splice the body from the person. I've been instructed to see every patient as a whole person, and I've been taught to ignore the hints of identity, in order to dissect, to cut, to harvest. *First, learn to stomach the signs of life in lifeless body. Next, ignore what gnaws at you as you observe morning rounds. Then, suppress emotion in step with your attending. Finally, look back and see this process was so gradual you didn't notice the change.* This gradual process will almost always work. Walking through the gravel paths of Auschwitz, I saw glimpses of my own education. I learned to detach the body from a life—it is at once necessary and appalling. We visited Auschwitz to ponder: how did this happen? A clue is in my unforeseen desire to dissect a brain; a clue is the transplant surgeon losing sight of the violence in his work. A clue is in our own bodies, shocked stiff entering the infamous gate, later relaxed as we sit by the deadly tracks at Birkenau, evidence of our all too human, malleable tolerance.

Short Coat Sonnet

LIANA MEFFERT

I'm peering into your mouth by the light
of my iphone your pronged pinked muscle
slick with saliva & freshly stitched I shouldn't
but I say oh, wow, saliva flies from a fresh hole
in your trachea when you laugh & I don't mind
making you laugh I'm timid weaving my stethoscope
through the tubes making a trellis of your chest you say
 you can't hurt me anymore looking to the skin grafts taken
from one place to make another whole how many ways
can a body be a body sucking a spittle-soaked sponge
blooming on a stem of white plastic that in my
ignorance & optimism I'd mistaken for a lollipop
with a bouquet of twenty more on the table
saying, saying of all things, *what luck!*

A Single Drop of Water

ALEC FEUERBACH

What's that noise? That high-pitched beeping coming from my left. Over my shoulder. There, at the head of the bed. It wasn't there a minute ago, and I was just beginning to get some rest. After these last few days here, I've needed it. So please, could someone just turn it off?

I would do it (you see, I hate being a bother) but right now I seem to be finding myself a bit stuck. I can't even turn my head to look at it. Moving my arm to shut it off, well, that hardly computes. Odd, though I've felt something like this before. Years ago. Turns out I was only dreaming then.

Water: I needed it more than ever. In my dream, I watched my tongue dry, shrivel, and prune until it was almost a raisin. All I needed to stop it, I knew, was one drop of water from the faux-crystal glass by my bed, but I couldn't turn and get it. I knew it was there, on the table next to me, and I knew Mary was reading at my side, her light still on, like always. I waited for a cough or sneeze to wake me from the dream. When it did, I knew she'd set her book down – pages face down on her lap – bend over, and kiss my temple. She'd say goodnight and get lost again in the words of her novel. I'd grab a drink and drift back into a new dream, one colored soft and warm, kissed with the pink hue of her lips. But she never did. She read silently and I dreamed, still, of a drying, cracking throat like sand. I tried, then, to move, thinking that even a small shift in the bed might get her attention. But still nothing. I was completely stuck, paralyzed, going to die of dehydration, I knew. But then finally, and without warning, with a sudden deep breath, I woke and sat up. I realized that yes, I was thirsty but no, my tongue was hardly any more raisin-like than usual. My throat was no longer cracked sand. I grabbed a drink and told Mary. "Sleep paralysis?" she asked.

Maybe it was, but this feels different. In that dream, I knew I couldn't wake and was dying to; now, I have been awakened and would die to get some more rest if only I could turn off that incessant beeping.

At last. Though she doesn't need to run. I have a flair for the dramatic, I know, but this is not a situation of life or death. Not a sprinting-in-here-to-turn-it-off kind of situation. Yes, it is a nuisance, this chiming that woke me from the deepest, fullest, most peaceful, most needed sleep of my life (sleep like winter around a fire cracking and popping) but she did not need to bring them all with her. And the lights, they could stay off. I could tell her: the beeping is right here by my head, just press the button to shut it off, and I will go back to sleep. I would do it myself but, well, you know my problem already.

I guess the machine must be broken. Though, if they are going to wheel her out perhaps they could take me too. I'd love to go with her (a lovely lady, my roommate), and she had just the cutest little granddaughter; a literal bundle of joy and love and energy wrapped in that blanket yesterday. She told me it was her first, and I told her it is a treat and that every day with a grandkid her world would grow brighter; brighter than she could ever imagine. I told her that as far as I'm concerned, the glory days aren't your days in high school, or your single twenties, or your married-without-kids days. They aren't moving up your respective career ladder, or even watching your kid transform from a teenager to an adult exploring the world. No, rather the glory days are every second after your kid is an adult and has decided that he, too, thinks it is worth bringing one more soul here to this ball of rock. You get to spoil them, sure, that part is great. But you also see in them proof that the world you gave your kid is enough. That it's okay. That it's worth living in.

What's she doing there? I wonder. Massaging my neck, my groin? She is getting a little too close for comfort. No, I see now. She's looking for something.

Another difference between that dream years ago and this here, tonight: when I was dreaming then and trying to wake, I was trying with all my might to move my arm. Then, with all my might to move my lips, to let a soft sound come out that could maybe alert Mary to my situation. But with this, the block—if it could be called that—between my mind and the movements is much earlier. Then, it felt like my brain sent signals through its tiny connections, down my spine, out through the highways and roads and cul-de-sacs of my nerves, until there at my muscles, the signal hit a wall. Now, it's as though the signals have nowhere to go. As if this connection between my thoughts and actions isn't just blocked but has ceased to exist altogether. Mind and body, two now; no longer one. Never was, it seems. That's the type of disconnect this is. It's completeness.

But maybe that means that if I really tried, really focused (if I thought not about moving my arm or head but rather moving *me*) perhaps I could get a little distance, a little space, from these hands searching various areas of my now-naked body. A little space from the shaking heads "no."

But where to go?

The room is packed. Three in blue stand to my side in a line. A woman stands down at the foot of the bed. My nurse in his light green, and, of course, the student was the first (Sarah, she told me). She looks so young—though I suppose she is; right out of college—standing at the end of the line in the corner behind me.

Behind me? I can turn again, look: left, right, in front, behind, up, down. Down? That's new.

And look at me. (Look at me?). There, on the bed.

I stand over myself.

What was that? What is she saying?

Any pulse?

Oh.

The answer's no.

Which I suppose explains them putting needles in my arms, taping pads to my chest, ripping them off (gray hairs dangle, precariously; a few float to the bed), replacing them anew. That mask over my face with that blue bag one of the nurses in green is squeezing. And one of the young doctors in blue, fingers interlocked, hands on my chest. I step off the bed to give them space and see Sarah wince with the crack of compressions. She needn't worry, though; I don't feel any pain over here.

But still, I may not watch. It's not that I don't appreciate the effort, or that I'm disgusted by this treatment, or worried about some perceived lack of dignity. Not that I'm scared. No, not at all. A little embarrassed, sure. I wish someone would toss a towel over my penis. It'd be nice to have it covered, not flopping back and forth limply with each compression. But I get it (priorities). It's just, well, watching myself is strange. I'm not used to that.

Okay anything? Alright two more minutes.

You know what's funny? The first morning I got here Sarah and I talked for a while. Before she left, she asked me what I would want if my heart were to stop, if I were to stop breathing. I shrugged. I didn't know. I hadn't really thought about that before. She said she would come back. We talked about it three or four more times.

Sarah tried hard not to show it, but something in the way her eyes squinted, and her face flinched ever so subtly with each shrug of mine, told me she didn't understand. I'm sure she wanted to avoid this violent demonstration; she wanted me to drift peacefully; she wanted to spare me the indignity of all this; she wanted me to be at home. But I think there was a part of her (a part she would never acknowledge) that must have also thought "what's the point?" I think that because there was a part of me that thought "what's the point?" as well. What's the point of starting my heart beating again only for it to stop an hour, or a day, or a week later? (We have reached that point, now).

But you know what's funny?

Watching this now I know the answer. Yes, it's violent and degrading. But I know why I shrugged. Why something tugged at me. What's the point? Well it's exactly what the woman at the foot of the bed said: *two more minutes.*

Because think about two minutes. I mean the entire world can fit into two minutes.

Like, I remember when Robby was born. So tiny, born a little early. Collin was letting Megan rest. He was changing diapers and filling bottles and scrambling all over their little apartment; trying to bounce him and burp him and do anything to get him to stop crying. His eyes: they were bright red. That's how I remember them. Overflowing with crimson exhaustion. He was holding Robby and sitting on that dark blue couch his mom and I had bought them. Mary sat next to him on the left. I was in my chair, rocking to his right. I told him to let me have Robby. He did. We rocked, and eventually Robby fell asleep. Collin didn't notice but he started drifting, too. In doing so he started listing ever so slightly to his left. As his eyes grew heavier and eyelids drifted together he continued to fall left until at last he was sleeping. His head fell onto Mary's shoulder, who reached over and brushed the hair out of his eyes. I watched as she let his hair sift through her fingers (golden sand on the beach). With him asleep on her, Robby asleep on me, we knew that the world was good. At least this one we had created together that now slept between us.

For a little bit, everyone slept. Mary and I, we just looked at each other, my eyes shifting focus from her left eye to her right, the way they would when we lay in bed together looking for new spaces to get lost on the nights we made love. No sound back then but a soft breath from her or me. None that day either except the sound of our breath, and the soft putter of Collin's and Robby's sleep. The world was perfectly still for about two minutes. Two minutes swelled with an entire lifetime of love.

Then Robby woke up.

Anything?

No.

I am starting to drift. I am still here, fully, in this room. But this is the transition I've been through over the last hour.

First, I was me, lying on the bed, confined to that body. Unable to move. Listening to the beeping. Watching the flashing. They all ran in.

Then, I left my body, but I was still confined to its shape. Meaning my awareness of me and the space I occupied was the same it had been for many years as I walked around the room.

But now, my awareness of me spreads (or does it fade?) no longer confined by the shape of my shell. I expand to occupy the empty space in the room. The air above each of them working on that shell: it opens up, it lets me in.

Anything?

And I start to realize that this is not the transition that points towards life; not the transition that points to two more minutes.

No.

Not the transition that points to more time with Collin, more time with Robby. And suddenly I understand how desperately I want that: to hear another laugh, to break another smile, to see one of theirs. Even a hug, or a tear.

Hell, just one more good meal, even. A cup or two of black, thick coffee. The smell of red wine, a movie about to start.

Anything?

One more kiss on my temple.

No.

All of that, it seems impossible now; hardly more achievable than reaching over and shutting off that damn beeping did an hour ago. No more attainable than a single drop of water from that faux-crystal glass when I was dreaming, all those years ago.

My hope for two more minutes is fading and I don't know if I'm ready.

Anything?

Because I worry: have I just traded the peace and serenity of a death at home for this?

Why am I here and not with Mary? With Collin? With Robby? Is this what Sarah's creased face was trying to tell me?

It is, isn't it?

No.

I am just scared. It's done so why regret now? Have courage to accept the things we cannot change. Right? I am as ready as I will ever be. Which is to say, scared but not regretting.

Still nothing.

Which is to say, scared shitless and I cannot shake this.

I cannot shake the feeling that in the end, all I did was trade two very real minutes for two imagined. Two minutes by Mary's side for two minutes alone.

My death could have been colored soft as my dreams by the pink hue of her kiss but instead it will be here imprinted white by these sterile walls.

I listen for the sound of any familiar voices down the hall.

One more round and I think we have to call it.

All is quiet.

I traded two very real minutes for two wholly imagined and I realize, now, that I am going to die alone.

The student, Sarah, is the last at my body's side and I don't know, but maybe I was wrong before. Maybe what I thought I saw (her questioning "what's the point?") wasn't really there. Maybe she too, understands that two minutes is everything. Or maybe she is just scared. But when the woman at the foot of the bed says stop compressions, Sarah keeps going for five or six or seven drawn-out, long seconds. One of them behind her touches her shoulder. Sweat drips off her brow onto the bed.

They all walk out of the room, thanking each other, but Sarah stays behind, staring blankly with me at my body. I know she won't always stay. I remember the first time Collin got hurt. Back when he couldn't really walk as much as accelerate into my wife's arms. He would pivot on straight legs holding onto invisible rungs over his head, only he missed one. He fell and bumped that pristine head of light-blond fuzz on the dark wood floor. His cry stopped me cold. It sent electric shocks through every nerve in my body. I was frozen. Paralyzed. But then he grew and it became an almost weekly thing. Some little injury or other, a bruise here, a scrape there, and after a year or so the injuries barely fazed me. I got used to it. I didn't love him any less just because I wasn't frozen by his cry any more. And Sarah won't be any less human when she doesn't shed a tear every time someone dies. But I am glad she did today.

When she wasn't stopping compressions. When the man behind her rested his hand on her shoulder, a tear rolled from her dark brown eyes down the curve of her cheek and onto her tongue, stretched to her left to catch it. She quickly swallowed it, pressing down one more time with her clasped hands before turning around nervously, perhaps hoping nobody noticed. But I did. And I am forever grateful for it. Her one tear tonight: worth more than she could ever know. That single drop of water? Well, it was worth even more to me tonight than it would have been in that dream I had, so many years ago.

Because to me that one drop of water became an ocean. It became everything: a flood reminding me I was not alone. And yet, it was nothing; no more than a drop of water, quickly wiped away before anyone else could see it.

And that's just it. That single drop was never an ocean at all, no, but somehow Sarah filled it with the weight of one. So I realize now: love can fill two minutes with a lifetime, but two minutes is nothing to a lifetime of love.

I hear Sarah take a deep breath and turn around. The hall is quiet. The air around me – which is me, now – glows softly pink. I'm as ready as I'll ever be. We leave the room together.

Untangling

CHRISTINE STEWART-NUÑEZ

I cleave to what it won't become:
this body-snarl, a chromosomal tangle.
In the toilet, the product of conception—
these red, interlaced threads—sink.

This body snarls. A chromosomal tangle
flummoxes me again when my son seizes.
These red, interlaced threads sync
on the grid of his neuronal pathways.

Flummoxed me. Again, when my son seizes
his enigmatic brain moves me, too.
On the grid of his neuronal pathways
I tease truth from the tangle one strand at time.

His enigmatic brain moves me to
squint, see anew—terrible and necessary.
I tease truth from the tangle one strand at time
until the sense of loss is gone.

Squint, see anew—terrible and necessary
in the toilet, the product of conception.
Now the sense of loss is gone;
I cleave what it won't become.

A Night on Staten Island

ELLIOT WILNER

The Val Chem, a World War II-vintage oil tanker, tied up at the pier on Staten Island at one-thirty a.m. It was mid-August of 1958, and my summer job in the merchant marine was coming to an end. Within the hour I would be summoned to the bridge, where I would collect my pay, and I would be on my way to my parents' home in Washington, D.C. The night was balmy, the waterfront was shrouded in a stagnant mist, and a chance breeze barely ruffled the feathers of a pelican sitting motionless atop a piling by the pier. Yet I felt a slight queasiness when the wake from a passing tugboat caused the Val Chem to roll sluggishly in the dock. Isn't it strange, I thought, that after two months at sea, and this, my second summer aboard a merchant ship, I haven't yet managed to overcome my susceptibility to seasickness?

At least, I consoled myself, this is one problem I wouldn't have to deal with two weeks from now, when I was scheduled to begin medical school. On the other hand, might I prove to be one of those medical students who was liable to become queasy at the sight of blood? That would no doubt constitute a bigger career problem for me than queasiness at sea.

"Yo, doc, we gonna miss y'all roun' this place. But good luck to y'all in medical school. Y'all think you might come back some day as the doc on a ship?"

That was Cookie's voice. I was crouched on the floor, occupied with stuffing all my clothing and books into a brown duffle bag, when Cookie approached from behind me. I was surprised that he had wakened, since I had been moving about very cautiously, and I had always known him to be a sound sleeper. Cookie bent down to squeeze my neck with his thick fingers, and when I stood up, he drew me into a big bear hug and then handed me a scrap of paper on which he had scrawled his home address and his name, Thomas Henderson. Funny, I had never known his real name, only "Cookie." He was the cook in the crew's mess, a heavy-set black man, from Houston, with whom I had worked and shared sleeping quarters on the Val Chem for these past two months. I hadn't expected him to show me that much affection, even though we had had a cordial relationship from the beginning. Soon we would be parting company, probably forever, and I was touched that he had roused himself from his bunk in order to say goodbye.

"I don't know, Cookie, a ship's doctor sounds like a great idea, but I don't know. It'll be a long time before I finish medical school. Maybe I'll meet up with you next summer on some rustbucket tanker like the Val Chem. And I'll remember to bring a lot more books."

Cookie was an avid reader, who had long ago finished reading everything on the shelves of the ship's modest library, as well as the books that he had brought with him for this voyage. He had eagerly accepted my suggestion that he help himself to the books I had carried onboard. He loved Jack London's *Call of the Wild*, and he was even more impressed with Hemingway's *Old Man and the Sea*. He and I spent a lot of hours discussing those books and the books' authors. I had participated in discussions in my English 101 class that were much less enlightening.

"Yeah, and when y'all do come back, y'all be sure and bring that big book you got with all them pictures of bones, muscles, nerves and stuff. I ain't finished reading it yet."

After Cookie had read every book that was available on the ship, he had even begun browsing through my copy of *Gray's Anatomy*, probably absorbing more of it than I did that summer.

"Sure, I'll remember the anatomy book. And, you know, Cookie, I'm really going to miss our conversations. I'll miss you a lot. So, in case we don't meet up on the Val Chem next summer, here's my phone number, it's in Washington. That's where I'll be living for the next few years. Call me if you ever come that way."

It was obvious Cookie was a man with an intellectual bent, even though he had quit school to join the U.S. Navy midway through the eleventh grade, after he turned seventeen. He said he had never liked school. It wasn't so much that he was eager to go to war as he was eager to get away from school. In the Navy, he was a steward's mate aboard the USS Boston, a cruiser in the Pacific fleet, where he served for a year and a half. Realizing that, as a black sailor, there was no prospect for his advancement in the U.S. Navy, Cookie took an honorable discharge soon after the war ended and transitioned to the merchant marine.

This seemed to be a common story amongst the crew of the Val Chem. Nearly everyone I talked to had run away from something, from school, or a woman, or a debt collector, or a dead-end job. Many had, like Cookie, previously served in the Navy, but a career in the merchant marine appealed more because it didn't require any long-term commitment, the work wasn't especially demanding, and the pay was good. Even so, I got the impression that Cookie was tiring of the seafaring life, because from time to time he would mention that his dream was to open a restaurant in Houston and settle down. He was married to a woman in Houston, and he would usually stay with her for a couple of months between voyages.

I was going to miss Cookie, and a lot of the other crew members, too -- the deck hands, the oilers and all the rest. But I wasn't going to miss another ocean voyage, because I was frustrated by my propensity to become queasy almost every day at sea, including some days when I was actually sick with *mal de mer.* These guys were mariners, I was not. True, I was a card-carrying member of the Seafarers International Union, and on my union card, next to my photograph and date of birth, I could read my rating, "Apprentice Seaman." That's what the card said, but I knew it wasn't true. I was a fraud; real mariners didn't become seasick. During my two summers at sea, sailing the Atlantic or Mediterranean, the surface of the sea was sometimes as smooth and flat as a glass tabletop, and then I could spend hours happily standing in the bow of the ship, watching a pod of dolphins cavorting just ahead of the prow. But whenever the wind picked up and there were swells of three feet or more, I would be revisited by that familiar queasy sensation.

At first the crew had treated me suspiciously – how had I managed to land this union job, just a week after graduating college? – but they soon accepted my presence and contributed generously to my post-graduate education. Not only did I learn to tie a bowline knot and a clove hitch, but one of the deckhands even taught me to play chess, so he could have someone to play with, and beat, every day of the voyage. (This same seaman also read from *The Life of Reason*, by George Santayana, on a daily basis.). I enjoyed especially the occasions when we would reach a port and "take on stores," which meant loading galley supplies and other goods aboard the ship from a re-supply tender. Only then, when I worked alongside the rest of the crew, could I indulge in the fantasy that I, too, was a real merchant mariner; moreover, I earned overtime pay in the process.

My glimpses of working-class life in the Texas and Louisiana refinery towns, to which I was escorted by various crew members during our off-duty hours, were also educational. Those dusty, sweaty, bawdy towns appeared to me—raised in Washington, D.C. and educated at a college in New York City—every bit as exotic as Port Said, Egypt, or Ceuta, Spanish Morocco, had appeared to me the previous summer when I sailed to the Mediterranean aboard an old Liberty Ship and visited those ports. My tour on the Val Chem contributed to my education in another way, too, since the pay was substantial—averaging, with overtime, about $100 per week, far exceeding the pay that I had received for any previous summertime job—and my total earnings would nearly cover the tuition for my first year of medical school, where I would be beginning classes less than two weeks after disembarking from the ship.

Within an hour after the ship had docked in Staten Island, bringing my career as a messman to an end, I was paid off by the ship's captain and discharged. I recall walking up the ladder to the captain's office on the bridge—only the second occasion during my entire time aboard the ship that I had been permitted on the bridge—and being handed a white envelope that contained one $500 bill and three $100 bills, in addition to a few $5s and $1s, and was promptly directed to collect my belongings and disembark. It was only some while later that I figured out the meaning of "paid off": you received your *pay* and you had to get *off* the ship. Four or five other crew members were paid off and discharged at the same time, and I observed them gathered together on the wharf where, after a few minutes, a car arrived to pick them up. Somehow they all managed to stuff themselves and their luggage into the car, which chugged off and disappeared behind the warehouses on the wharf, leaving me alone on a dimly lit dock at 2:30 a.m. So I was not sure of how I ought to proceed. It would have made sense to remain aboard the ship a few more hours, until daybreak, but that was not an option: once you were paid off, you had to get off.

My destination was my parents' home in Washington, D.C., and to get there I would have to find my way to the Staten Island ferry, and upon reaching lower Manhattan I would ride the subway to the Port Authority terminal in midtown, where I would board a Greyhound bus bound for Washington. The immediate challenge was finding a way to the ferry terminal, which was approximately three miles from the dock. There was no bus service anywhere in the vicinity—at least not in the early hours of the morning—nor was there a taxi in sight. There was a public telephone on the wharf, so I might have called a taxi, but I was reluctant to pay the taxi fare since I had only a few small bills with which to buy the Greyhound bus ticket and food on the way home. I had no intention of breaking one of the $100 bills, so I decided to walk the three miles to the ferry terminal, traversing a waterfront that was now totally deserted and illuminated eerily by the light of a half moon. (The light was enough, however, for me to discern a couple of rats scurrying up the pilings of the pier to which the Val Chem was moored.)

There was a good chance, I reckoned, that I would be mugged on the wharves before I could reach the ferry terminal, so I devised a plan to save the $800 that was in the white envelope, wrapped the $500 bill around the three $100 bills, fashioning a wad that I placed in my right shoe wedged between my heel and the insole of the shoe. If I were to be mugged, I assured myself, the assailant would find only the small bills that I had placed in my wallet; he would never think to look inside my shoe, right? This was probably a tactic that I had gleaned from some crime novel or action movie, although I realized it wasn't a tactic that would have occurred to a tough guy like Robert Mitchum (nor would Robert Mitchum have been walking three miles to the ferry; a blonde driving a Corvette would have been waiting for him as he walked down the ship's gangway.)

I started my trek to the ferry terminal, lugging my duffle bag which no doubt weighed at least fifty pounds since it was loaded with several books, including my hardcover edition of *Gray's Anatomy*, in addition to my clothing and toiletries. I was apprehensive all the while, and my eyes constantly scanned the dark hulks of the warehouses on the wharves, searching for any sign of a human figure that might be moving in my direction. Yet, I was also sensible of the dramatic—even romantic—quality of the waterfront about me, as I walked past the docked ships and the Narrows on my left and the wharves on my right. The early morning air was warm and damp, the moonlit water in the empty slips rippled gently, and across the Narrows the lights of Brooklyn glittered. Once or twice I saw a dog skulking about, not paying me any mind, and there was the occasional rat scampering up or down the pilings, but only once did I encounter another human being—and that was a night watchman who emerged from the shadows of a warehouse and asked where I was going. I told him of my destination, and he advised me that the first ferry of the day from Staten Island to Manhattan did not depart until six a.m.

By the time I met up with the night watchman, I had been walking for an hour, had covered a little more than half the distance to the ferry terminal, and my duffle bag had become a progressively heavier burden. Although I was switching the bag from one shoulder to the other at increasingly frequent intervals, I had to stop every five minutes in order to put down the bag and stretch my aching shoulders and arms. I was also becoming more and more aware of a tenderness in my right heel, which, I would later discover, was due to a blister that had developed from the repetitive friction of my heel against the wad of bills in my shoe. I was tempted to remove my shoe and transfer the wad to my wallet or to a pocket, but, ever mindful of the perils that still lay ahead of me, I resisted the temptation. My mouth and throat were parched, so I was grateful to the night watchman when he directed me to a water tap nearby. After another hour's walk I did, to my surprise, reach the ferry terminal altogether unharmed.

There was already a ferryboat moored in the slip at the front of the terminal, but it would not be departing for another hour and a half. Exhausted and hungry, I entered the terminal and collapsed onto a bench in the waiting room, too weary even to bend down and unlace my shoe so that I might retrieve the wad of bills inside. I nodded off to sleep almost immediately. All too soon I was awakened by the commotion of passengers entering the waiting room and by announcements that crackled over the public address system. Yanking my duffle bag over my shoulder once again, I shuffled over to the ticket window, paid the five-cent fare and boarded the ferry. Entering the passenger lounge, I located the concession stand where I splurged on a cup of coffee and a couple of donuts, and then wearily dropped onto one of the wooden benches nearby.

Soon the ferry eased away from the slip and, turning about, began motoring toward lower Manhattan. Then, and only then, did I unlace my right shoe and reach for the wad of bills inside. Taking the wad in my left hand, I began to unfold the individual bills and – in disbelief – I identified only half of the $500 bill! Where was the other half of the bill? The three $100 bills were whole, but half of the $500 bill was missing! Panicked, I picked up the shoe and slid my fingers along the insole, up to the toe – but there was not another half of a bill! Where, dammit, where was it? Holding the shoe in front of my face, as the morning light streamed through the window behind me, I looked closely inside and observed…a small grayish-green pile of… what? dust? powder? Could that be…?

Yes, that's exactly what it could be, no doubt. The little pile of dust represented the missing half of the $500 bill, which had been pulverized, micronized, ground to powder by the relentless action of my heel crushing the wad of bills against the insole of my shoe, like a pestle crushing coca leaves in a mortar. I calculated that, over the distance of three miles, I had come down on my right heel close to three thousand times, producing enough friction that my heel blistered and the uppermost bill in the wad simply disintegrated. Not knowing precisely what purpose I had in mind, I poured the pathetic little pile of dust from my shoe into the empty envelope that I was carrying in my shirt pocket, while my body sagged against the bench and I sank into a slough of despondency—totally fatigued and totally dejected. Had I just managed to turn $500 into dust, $500 which represented more than half of my wages for the summer and which also would have constituted half of my tuition payment for the coming year? What could I do with $500 worth of dust? Ruefully, I imagined that after my return home I might find a decorative, solemn-looking urn into which I would place the dust, and it would remain on my desk forever as a *memento mori*. But my reverie was soon interrupted by several loud blasts of the ferryboat's horn, signaling our approach to the terminal in Manhattan.

A few minutes later, after the ferry had docked, I trudged ashore, lugging my ponderous duffle bag, yearning for my parents' house where a bed with clean sheets and a soft pillow awaited, yet knowing that several hours of bus travel lay ahead before I would reach my destination. The subway fare from the Battery to the Port Authority terminal in mid-Manhattan was fifteen cents, and I had still a couple of five-dollar bills and enough one-dollar bills with which to pay the bus fare to Washington. The bus route included many stops along the way, not only in the major cities between New York and Washington but in a number of small towns and a few obscure crossroads along the way, so it was early evening before we reached the Greyhound depot in downtown Washington.

I boarded a D.C. Transit bus near the depot, and when we reached Connecticut Avenue, I transferred to a second bus that eventually, close to sunset, brought me to the bus stop near my parents' house. I could barely lug my duffle bag the last five hundred feet to the house, where my parents were awaiting my arrival. As my mother was preparing a hot meal for me, I spilled my tale of woe quietly and confidentially to my father, for I was sure that if my mother were to learn of my situation, all my relatives and the whole town would soon know, and during the rest of my life I would hear, over and over, "I can't believe you actually put the money in your shoe..."

My father listened thoughtfully and empathetically, as I told him about the damaged $500 bill, and when I had finished he said, "There is a place where you can exchange paper currency that has been damaged."

"What place is that?" I replied.

"The Bureau of Engraving and Printing. It's on Fourteenth Street, a couple of blocks south of Independence Avenue."

"Do you really think they'll give me a new $500 bill?"

"I can't say for sure, since I'm not familiar with their rules. But it's your best hope...probably your only hope."

After eating dinner, I showered and flopped onto the bed with fresh linens that I had been craving for the previous twenty-one hours, ever since I disembarked from the Val Chem, and I slept until ten o'clock the next morning. Soon after breakfast, I was again on a D.C. Transit bus, on my way downtown to the Bureau of Engraving and Printing. The whole while I was on the bus I held the intact portion of the $500 bill in my hands and scrutinized it intently. The torn margin wasn't sharply edged or straight, it was sort of frayed, and what remained of the bill wasn't, in truth, exactly half. It was more like 49%, maybe 47%, of the bill. But President McKinley's engraved portrait was placed a little off-center on the bill, mostly on the intact portion, so most of his facial features were preserved. His face had a somber expression. Didn't that count for something, that the president's portrait was largely intact? And even if the government people were to suspect that I had deliberately torn the bill in half, with the intention of cheating the government by bringing in the other half at a later date, wouldn't I at least deserve $250 for the half of the bill that I presented? I alighted from the bus at Pennsylvania Avenue and Fourteenth Street and walked the final nine or ten blocks, across the Mall and across Independence Avenue, to the building that housed the Bureau of Engraving and Printing.

There were a lot of security guards posted at the entrance and inside the building. They seemed to be more concerned with checking people who were leaving the building than with people who were entering. I recalled having read stories about employees who had contrived to smuggle out freshly printed paper currency. At the information desk I asked where I should go to inquire about an exchange of paper currency, and I was instructed to take an elevator to the second floor, to the Office of Mutilated Money. Did I hear right, was it really named the Office of Mutilated Money? How absolutely right that name was, I thought, and how compassionate is the government of the United States of America! Only in this country could there be found a government that cared -- compassionately cared! -- about paper currency that, through no fault of its own, had been crushed, pulverized, wounded, yea mutilated. The United States government would provide it a refuge -- and wouldn't the government also extend its compassion to the person who had been the devoted caretaker of that mutilated paper currency? My spirits were raised, for no rational reason, as I headed in the direction of the Office of Mutilated Money.

Riding up the elevator to the second floor, and walking down a long corridor to the designated office, I realized that I was glancing frequently downward, on the chance that some one, perhaps an employee who had purloined some freshly printed currency, had carelessly dropped a $500 bill on the floor. Nothing caught my eye, and I made a note to myself that I should start thinking more rationally. When I entered the Office of

Mutilated Money I was greeted by a secretary, who told me that a currency examiner would meet with me shortly. The office was decorated with enlarged photographs of various treasury notes and federal reserve notes, and I quickly spotted the by-now familiar portrait of President McKinley, still looking somber, on a facsimile (non-mutilated) of the bill that I had brought with me. A door toward the rear of the office soon opened and a stout, smiling man approached, informing me that he was the currency examiner and inviting me to accompany him into his office.

"Well, what sort of problem do we have here?" inquired the currency examiner, who appeared to have a friendly, unpretentious manner.

I told him the whole story, in my most plaintive voice, not sparing any details about my ordeal on Staten Island and my subsequent pathos. Then I produced the intact portion of the $500 bill and showed it to the examiner: The damage was obvious; in fact there was mutilation of the bill, wasn't there?

The examiner took the mutilated bill in his hand, placed it on his desk, and, producing a ruler, took a couple of measurements. "Well," he said, "you have maybe one half of the bill remaining, probably a little bit less than that." He paused and looked directly at me. "You know, our rule is that we will replace a bill if three fifths of the bill remains intact. I'm sure you understand why that is."

"No, I'm not sure I do," I responded forlornly. My response was also somewhat disingenuous, since the reason for the rule was obvious.

"So, I'm not sure that we will be able to help you," said the examiner. There was a long pause, while he looked at me with what seemed to be genuine pity. "Don't you have any idea what became of the other part of the bill?" he asked, almost as an afterthought.

"Yes sir, I do."

"You do have an idea?"

"Yes, I have an idea, in fact I have the rest of the bill." I then pulled the white envelope from my pocket and cautiously poured out the greenish-gray dust that was inside onto the table.

The examiner stared at the little pile of dust for a full half-minute, and then he looked intently at me. "Did you say that you will be entering medical school next month?" he asked.

"Yes, sir. And next week my tuition payment is due."

Again, the examiner looked at me intently, for what seemed to be an eternity but was probably only a few seconds. It occurred to me that he was spending more time examining me than examining the mutilated bill. He then arose from his chair and, without saying anything more than "wait here," opened the door to his office and disappeared from my view. I sat by myself in the office for perhaps a couple of minutes, my body almost motionless while all sorts of ideas raced through my mind. Did he believe my story, or did he think it was bogus and I was a liar and a crook? Could he have me arrested for trying to defraud the government?

When the examiner returned to the office, he sat down and said, simply, "Give me your bill." I handed him the mutilated bill, and he then produced a fresh, crisp, immaculate, whole $500 bill that he handed to me. "It's yours. Let me wish you good luck in medical school." He smiled warmly. "And you can keep the dust, too." I quickly swept the little pile of dust on his desk back into the white envelope, and, too stunned to articulate my feeling of elation in any meaningful way, I just clasped the examiners hand with both my hands and muttered, "Thank you, thank you so much," before floating out of his office.

Once I had exited the building of the Bureau of Engraving and Printing, I removed the fresh $500 bill from my wallet and took a long, admiring look at the portrait of President McKinley: He didn't appear so somber, after all. He was actually a good-looking man, and I felt sad that he had been assassinated.

A Long-term Patient Leaves a Veterans Hospital

RICHARD KRAVITZ

I've been here too long, and it's time for me to go.
Summer's ended, leaves have begun to fall.
It's almost cold enough to snow.

So thank you for the homemade throw
I'll use on whatever bed I'll sprawl.
It's been too long, I know, and time for me to go.

I'm sorry that my mood has been low,
my face a mask, my voice a growl,
and my heart puckered like graveled snow.

But I've loved the chocolate and espresso,
I've mumbled, rather than howl,
and yes, I've stayed too long, so it's time for me to go,

which is fine. What's left to grow
but the ache inside, my rumbling bowel,
and my knuckles whiter than snow?

So forgive me if my bitter tears show,
or if you think my behavior a stall.
This has been my home, and time to go
I know, but it's so cold, almost cold enough to snow.

The Emu Wars

KEVIN MCKIM

Following the Great War, and in the earliest days of what would become the Great Depression, but may have only been the Bad October at that point, Australia had a series of problems. The government based in Canberra was faced with an overabundance of men who knew how to use rifles and fight, as despite the Kaiser's best efforts, some of the Boys from Oz had gone home. Canberra had struck a deal with the veterans to give them huge parcels of land to farm on the far western coast of the Lost Continent. The soldiers established farmsteads across the fertile West, and spread into the desert West, and just as in another young continent, Manifest Destiny was met with resistance by hostile natives. The soldier farmers took up rifles they had learned to use on the killing fields of Europe, or to lasting fame at Gallipoli, and felled thousands of the natives without ever seeming to stem their reconquista. The farmers, overwhelmed by enemy numbers, and unable to supply themselves with enough ammunition to continue the fight, appealed to the capitol which had given them the mission of settling the unforgiving West. Canberra responded to this existential threat by deploying an army, really just a battalion, equipped with the most cutting edge technology of armored cars, biplanes, and machine guns. The best that the world had to offer at the time. The natives were primitive at best, unable to respond to the killing power of the machine gun, but they had their own cunning and guile. They were able to harness the chaos of the battlefield, by scrambling out of trouble, using the very same thick stalks of grain they were raiding like a smoke screen to cover their retreats. In the first engagement with the Australian army, only 10 or 12 were killed, and only a few hundred were slain after the army had expended nearly a quarter of its supplies. Reports of the conflict even included frustrated musings that the natives were as bulletproof as Zulu warriors, that an army of the natives could conquer the world. Confusion abounds in sources as to why they didn't charge machine gun nests like the men fighting in Ypres, Nantes and all across Europe. A journal entry even includes a report of a successful ambush by guerrillas against an overnight camp that resulted in several injuries so grievous the men needed to be sent back East. In the end, Canberra recalled the army, gave the soldier farmers more ammunition, and wished them luck. Despite the best efforts of everyone involved, despite the best equipment, the best soldiers, the best intentions, thus concluded the Great Emu War.

And the emus won.

*

She sat in the car, listening to the faint breathing of the sleeping infant in the car seat they had needed to borrow from someone else for the ride. Worried, and tired, and troubled about her baby, her husband had given her the money for the first two trips by cab to the doctor's office, but this time, she had worried him enough through her persistence that he came along too before his double shift at the restaurant where he worked to cover their room in the larger apartment his cousins rented them. The child just didn't seem right. She fed him several times a day at her breast, and felt the milk let down, saw him shift the fussy, mewling cries of hunger to the sleepy, mumbling noises he made as she set him into his second hand bassinet. He would make such a mess after each feed though, spitting up and stooling out, worrying her that he wasn't getting enough, that something was wrong in him. The worry ate at her, but her husband was certain things were going to be okay. His son was so strong, he would remark, he would grow tall, he would enjoy the life in America they would build for him. She leaned into that strength, found comfort in the sense that her husband would provide for them all. He was a good man, her mother had promised her before their engagement was arranged. Now, as they drove to the hospital, she hoped the worry that filled her head was wrong, and that memories of her mother, and her aunts and cousins telling her things would be okay could soothe her fears. All their voices joined the cacophony in her head, with the shouting, nagging thoughts. She looked at the infant, worried, and rocked his car seat gently as they sat at a red light, and he roused slightly with the change in engine tenor.

*

Damien and I sat on the desk outside the room. The attending and fellow had put on gown, mask, gloves, and entered into the isolation room to meet the patient. To limit the amount of horrible pests dragged along, the medical student and I had remained outside the pressurized room. She was undergoing chemotherapy and was suspected to have acquired some fungal infection, so Damien and I were helping by keeping our germs to ourselves. And the most helpful spot for us in that moment was on the desk. Perching out of the way of nurses busying back and forth between more open rooms and discussions. I turned to Damien, our medical student, ready to ask questions I could remember from the pediatrics clerkship exams, enthusiastic about teaching as only someone who just changed trainee levels can be. He struck me as halfway engaged and at best pretending to listen to us versus the ticking off the time that had to pass before he could ask to leave the hospital. In an effort to connect, I ventured," I guess I should give you some reading to do at home, right?"

Damien startled to the sound of my voice, annoyed he had lost count of the passing seconds, and turned to me,"Do you?" He didn't seem to think it was on the syllabus.

"Yeah, that's my job as the resident, to teach you stuff."

"Is it?" He knew it wasn't on the syllabus.

I ignored him and persisted. "We'll be done soon, go home tonight and read about the Emu War."

"Really, though, you don't have to do anything."

I pushed on, "No, really, go home and look it up. We can talk about it later."

The infectious disease attending stepped out of the room, and the conversation turned to the overly-wide differential of things that eat someone without an immune system.

*

The big, happy, Caucasian doctor from the first two times saw them right away this time. The two times she had brought the boy in, she had had to talk to the phone on the wall to have any conversations with the younger doctors, someone different both times. No one in the office spoke Bengali, and the translator spoke with a funny accent, but was passable. None of the voices of her memories sounded like him, except maybe her aunties from far off who had married into the family. This time, the big happy Caucasian doctor came in first, and was very serious, his broad smile gone, his manner more serious from the start. Her husband and the big doctor spoke back and forth in English and she vaguely followed. She would answer questions directed to her, but otherwise, she held their son, asleep, and so small, and her worries sang out, he was so, so worrying. Something was wrong. She interrupted her husband and made sure he said that to the doctor, but he soothed her, motioned with his hands that all was well, and smiled his toothsome grin, with the one gold capped tooth in the front glinting in the summer sunshine pouring through the windows of the appointment room. The big doctor's smile came back, starting with the well-worn creases in his cheeks, then mostly spreading up to his eyes. She quieted down, taking a deep breath, and focused on settling the worried voices and their screeching. The big doctor took the sleeping baby from her gently, placed him on a scale as he woke, examined him as he screamed and cried at the intrusions. She held herself still, wondering when the noise should worry her, and why his screaming didn't. Her husband and the big doctor had a rushed conversation, a flurry of English, with the same sounds, and she caught on enough. The child was going to be admitted to the hospital. She felt relief. Something was wrong. They heard it too.

*

The next morning, Damien met up with the infectious disease team, saw me, and made a face. His usual face was that of contentedly deaf isolation. He didn't hear and didn't care, and didn't care to hear things happening around him other than, "Well, why don't you get out of here early, Damien? Here's five dollars."

Today, he looked like perhaps he felt another emotion, but as it turned out, it was the same. More annoyance.

I opened with, "Did you read about the Emu Wars?"

"Yes," end of sentence, and no further conversation needed was suggested.

"And? What'd you find?"

"Emus are surprisingly bullet absorbent."

"So you did read about it!" I was thrilled, he had passed the first test. I hadn't thought the surly young man I had met on the rotation would do anything of the sort, but he had gone off and done what I had asked.

"Wait," he paused, and turned to actually make eye contact for the first time," was that a test?" He had a good glare.

"Kind of," I admitted, more proud than sheepish, quite against protocol," I didn't want to try and teach you if you wouldn't engage. So, I gave you something," I paused, "*different*, to read about."

"And what lessons did you think were there?" Damien was more genuinely curious than miffed, another first. We talked from there about antibiotic resistances, about choosing the right weapon for the job, and about how important knowing your enemy was before trying to fight them. That sometimes, even the best ideas and the most comprehensive plans wouldn't work. He nodded, content enough with the lesson, and we went off to see another patient without him realizing I had panicked and ad-libbed the whole thing.

*

So many voices, so much was being said. She knew some English; everyone did, living in America now, coming from a legacy of British rule. But the people here had such funny accents, were all so different, and then so many of the words they used that were medical. She presumed they were; she couldn't tell what language they were. Her husband had been here most of the time, though, and had thankfully done all the talking, so she didn't need to shout into the phone and talk to some strange, tinny Bengali voice who sounded like an auntie from far away. Nurses took care of the baby, and so did he, and sometimes, even the doctors. They would parade in, touch, remark, discuss, then march out. And she would worry, worry, worry, and the sounds of that anxiety would just get louder, louder, louder. Her husband reassured her that things were getting better, but the baby still seemed *wrong*. Something wasn't right. Yes, yes, yes, he had gained weight, he was eating, but they didn't hear her worries. People came in, not doctors, not nurses, friendly people who asked her and her husband through the tinny voice or bad American accented Bengali, if they needed help with housing, food, bills. People came in and watched her feed her son, weighed him, looked at his diapers. Even the day they were sent home, the doctors and nurses, some of them vaguely familiar looking, others Caucasian, like the big doctor from the clinic, all seemed so happy. Her husband was happy with them too. No one was able to hear her aunties, her mother, her cousins, all the worries that her son wasn't right. He was broken, broken, broken. But they went home, with her son and her worries, worries, worries.

*

Friday, Damien and I met up for our usual morning, forced conversation. We discussed the cases from the day before, some of the reading I had set before him Thursday afternoon, and then lapsed into the silence Damien preferred to better hear the passage of time. We sat in the bigger resident work room, taking up space, and idly wasting the batteries on our phones, when the Chief Resident walked in. In pediatrics, true to most matrilineal societies, the head chief was the most matronly woman, wise and possessed of great wisdoms and magics, and she was brightly clothed in feathers, stunning colors and ornate sartorial choices. This Chief whirled in, skirt edges dancing and flashing, her large personality, in a large frame, in a dress with colors that demanded a larger rainbow," Voluntary code lavender for noon conference, attendance is mandatory," then whirled out and slammed the door before the fear of her sudden appearance had dissipated. I looked at Damien, hoping he knew what that meant. He looked at his phone and sighed heavily, knowing it would only lengthen his day here.

*

Sarah and I met in the hallway, heading to the noon conference. Damien, somewhere behind in tow, like a puppy sulking at the indignity of being on a leash for the first time. Sarah looked at him, then at me, raising an eyebrow. I shrugged. She knew about how I sent him home to read about nonsense, about how I was trying to teach, and I think she was more sympathetic to him than to me, but she had held her tongue. Neither of us knew what it meant to have a code lavender, but the room was packed, and we got seats along the back wall, grabbing two and saving one for Damien, who at this point had looked up long enough to realize something was different. A general pediatrics attending was at the front of room. His face normally wore a wide smile, but today was gaunt and hanging; creases normally flexed in a grin, eyes normally full of mirth, drained. Several social workers and a pastor started to unwind a story before us all, detailing that code lavenders are to discuss a loss, a painful death, or just an outcome that wasn't what we all wanted. That it wasn't to blame anyone, but rather, to help us all process a loss, a defeat, that we couldn't otherwise have stopped. Deaths in pediatrics are hard for people not in medicine to understand, and even those within medicine may not fully grasp the impact of a child's death, of that thick, syrupy silence that fills the halls and heads of those who came into that child's care and didn't get to send them home.

*

A patient, after presenting to the clinic three times, with maternal complaints of something not right, but with his mother unable to explain further through rough English and translators, had been admitted. The attending had trusted the mother's instincts, and not seeing something wrong beyond slower than normal growth, admitted the child to the inpatient unit to figure out her concerns. His feeding was optimized, breast feedings observed, stools counted, weights measured before and after, and gains recorded. Social work had been in and out of the room to talk with the father, a gregarious local cook with a shining golden tooth where a cricket ball had knocked out his original. They lived with fellow immigrants, but had their own room for their small family, and the mother, quiet and reserved, had left most of the talking to the glinting, gilded smile of her husband. The infant boy was quiet, fed well, and gained weight promisingly, much to his father's exclamatory pride. They were discharged home with little concern, and told to follow up at the clinic. But the mother had been so worried, worried, worried. The voices of her anxieties, of her aunts, mother, grandparents, family she had never met, of the crowds in her head were still so loud, and the cacophony of the crowd finally quieted to a clear drumbeat. A command. She tried to feed the boy, to care for him as best she could, but the worries, the worries, the worries. The worries warned her. Something was coming for him, for the small boy against her breast. They would fill the small room she and the man with the golden tooth who was her husband shared and they warned of harm to the small boy child. Her worry, worry, worry was misplaced, no wonder the doctors, nurses, tinny voices on the phone that sounded like her aunt, had all failed to help. It was here, now, in the room with them, with her and the boy. He was perfect, but he would befall such great injury if she let the worries get to him. She had to help him, had to get out. She clutched the boy against her. He squirmed in discomfort at her tight grasp, as she squeezed him tighter and tighter to her heart, to keep him from the worry, the worry, the worrying of the voices, now shrieking and shrill and screaming at her and him and them. Closer, closer, closer still. She fled in the small space as the voices rose further. She couldn't so much hear them as individual sounds anymore, or hear his fearful cries, or hear the blood rushing in her ears and behind her eyes, or the sounds of her own pulse blended with the voices of her family back home, and everywhere else the sound crept in. The roar ablated all things but one. And so she set him free, cast him out and saved him from the shrieking, the crying horrible noises and after a moment, felt the noises slowly drain away. Hot, thick air of the deep summer crept in the open window. A single scream continued as all the others drained away, as she closed her eyes to sleep without the worry, worry, worry. Finally, silence.

*

Despite everything everyone had done, from doctors checking in on the family frequently, to nurses working with the mother through pantomime and proper translators; despite social work and case managers assessing the family for needs and trying to see any concerns in their home life, everyone had missed what in hindsight was a clear case of postpartum depression. The husband was charming, gregarious, and the wife, reserved. He was as open to the world as any new convert to our American dreams, and she was quiet, because of traditional values, or as it would turn out, because of a deep depression that filled her head with voices, conversations and finally with the deadly impulse to hurl her boy to safety from the demons and darkness that stalked him out a 9th story window into the humid August night sky. They talked to us about how hard it is to lose a patient in pediatrics, how people don't hear you when you try to talk to them about your pain, and how you end up consoling someone you made cry with a sad story about a sick kid. Seniors discussed losses, people cried. Sarah and I looked at each other, both quiet with shock. As the room began to clear out, I turned to check on Damien, who I thought might be even less equipped to deal with such a heavy moment. He sat in the chair, not stirring for a moment, even as Sarah and I stood, as chairs squeaked against the floor and people rustled out of the room.

He looked up at me, blinked, and slowly said, "Sometimes, the emus win," the shine in his eyes showing he had finally solved some larger riddle.

It was my turn to stand silent, feeling Sarah looking between me and Damien.

I answered," Yeah, sometimes. Despite doing everything you can, despite having everything, sometimes, the emus win."

Damien nodded, made sincere eye contact for the first time all month, and we walked out, to join the thrum of residents and students headed back to the in patient wings.

The Knockers

JAMES W. GIRARDY

The ancient green landscape now rightfully reclaims the entries to the
Cornwall mines.
There are still some who remember the days when peals from clanking
machinery
echoed from the belfries that crowned the gouges in the hillsides
where the tin was torn from the earth's veins in exchange for the bodies of
the Cornishmen.
It is still told, that deep in the now abandoned shafts reside those in limbo
not good enough for heaven nor bad enough for hell,
they dwelt next to the toiling souls in their former realm.
Their rapping led miners from the cave-in's crush
and toward the richest lodes.
The knockers presence marked by pasty crusts
left by blackened hands in thanks, tribute and solidarity.
With what souls are we now in communion,
as we toil in digital shafts capped by a new machinery dinning across our
landscapes
and with what acknowledgments,
exchanged for what protections
are spirits in abeyance recognized?
Surely there are knockers lingering in our data mines
whose presence might lead us from the false passages of misconception
their message a warning
to ascend from the constricting shafts and avoid the cave-in's crush.

Davy lamps now replaced by monitor's glow
still insufficient to illuminate the pitch black of spiritual depletion where
moral residue clings.
Do we not hear echoes of old souls
who inhabit the stories encrypted by the electron glimmers
digital crumbs of sustenance
left in the shafts where we spend our working hours searching for veins of
meaning?

Would we not be wise to look and listen ?

I try, surreptitiously, to leave keyed in signs
to mark the crystalline details
of my patient's lives,
hoping these coalesce, forming flows of meaning meandering through the
backlit monitor walls.
We crave these stories no less than our sooted predecessors.
We are just as compelled to leave fragments behind
so those who follow will recognize our presence
crumbs still necessary for sustenance
of their souls and ours.

Plague of Pain

AMY ZIMMERMAN

I got off a plane and heard that Zac Efron had been rushed to the hospital with a deadly infection while filming his new reality TV show, *Killing Zac Efron*. The end of the world is routinely absurd. Y2K was the widespread belief that computers would not be able to comprehend the year 2000, that 1999 would culminate in the world's last and loudest fireworks. The typical grab-bag of post-apocalyptic imagery: violence, chaos, death and desperation, nuclear war triggered on a technicality, big scary arrows plunging through the bottom of their stock market charts.

In 1780, a morning that should have been like any other morning, New England went dark. The air went strange and heavy, the sun never rose, and the likeliest conclusion was that Judgement Day had come in the night. Eventually the world came back—it was all just forest fire smoke, or so they say—but those who lived until and through the end of days never quite forgot it. Strange religions sprung up from the ash, enough morbid minerals to sustain a hundred doomsday cults, prophetic preachers, separatist sects.

Every apocalypse reminds me of my own, and I can't distinguish between flashback and present, memory and premonition. My ex and I dated for three years, maybe four—the timeline is hazy, bombed out, and memories surrounding that time in my life don't work right. I lost my appetite for a few months, and he told me that he would stop seeing me if I didn't start eating. We went for bagels and argued about who was killing who.

I knew I wasn't living, wasn't quite sure if I was haunting my own life or haunting his, if we were haunting each other.

We waited outside of my house and his, broke up on park benches and in garages, on buses and in his grandparent's basement after a rainstorm (I was wearing his Bubbe's sweatpants, he was wearing his Zayde's). The morning after, everything would look softer, blush-pink light and sleeping bodies, and it was not so hard to convince myself to stay. What no one tells you about the end is that it never really is.

I read books about what happens when apocalyptic prophecies fail; study the psychological state of doomsday believers when the world doesn't end. Usually, they just push back the date of the apocalypse. You get so fixated on the end that you can't admit it's over.

The earliest apocalyptic warning is said to have come from an Assyrian tablet. In 2800 B.C., they allegedly took stylus to clay, carving, "Our earth is degenerate in these late days; there are signs that the world is speedily coming to an end; bribery and corruption are common; children no longer obey their parents; every man wants to write a book, and the end of the world is evidently approaching."

Now it's 2020 and the sky is often the wrong color, grey like dirty paint water or orange/red and fluorescent. Instagram influencers are selling nudes for 700k to fight the advancing fires. Flames swallow entire species whole and GoFundMe's flood the timeline. A man self-immolated in Prospect Park as a protest against the use of fossil fuels. I read the other day that the ocean was boiling; and here we are, somehow, all cooking together like Martha Stewart's famous one-pot pasta.

A girl I follow tweeted that she had almost killed herself the night before, but then she thought about all the content she could make tomorrow. Two years after the Parkland massacre, the father of a high schooler who was shot down was removed, screaming, from the State of the Union. Teenagers in homeroom never think that they might die today, and kids hiding from an active shooter under their desks are probably certain that they won't make it. The thing about the end is that some people have to keep living.

During a rare slow Saturday at the bookstore, Ellie and I sit behind the counter angling our bodies away from customers. Ellie, who has many interests, tells me about a gnarly plague that I had never heard of. Amputation was overwhelmingly the treatment of choice for Civil War battlefield medics. Between 1861 and 1865, surgeons attempted amputation on roughly 60,000 soldiers, and about 35,000 survived it. This limb-lessness was so widespread that eventually it was legislated, with a Congressional act in 1862 granting one artificial limb to each sailor or soldier. A new "arms race" quickly followed, businessmen chomping at the prosthetics market like hungry hungry hippos. This burgeoning industry struggled to deliver on advertising claims; prosthetics just weren't very advanced, were irritating and clumsy, often caused more trouble.

With so many amputees coming in to claim free treatment, there was an increased interest in and access to this category of patient. A Civil War surgeon studied soldiers at the stump hospital—exactly what it sounds like—studies that legitimized the concept of "phantom limb pain" within the medical community. The existence of phantom sensation—feelings in a lost limb—had previously been unexplained, but more or less accepted.

Ellie says that before the standardization of amputee care, before large-scale studies and leading surveys that signaled to patients what they should be feeling, people often experienced their severed limbs in strange and magical ways. They swore that they could feel their lost fingers wiggling in the Promised Land, their amputated feet pressing down on the velvet white of the Celestial City.

I reach for a piece of scrap paper under the register and jot down—love lost/lost limb? I feel ridiculous comparing my pain to a Civil War era amputee's, even though all pain is incomparable, incalculable.

There's this clusterfuck that Ellie is trying to untangle, something having to do with these government contracts, these thousands of men trying to cash in on Congress's impulsive gesture. Doctors and entrepreneurs offering solutions for that which previously may not have been seen as a problem—clumsy prosthetics, morphine for "pain" that used to be a miracle. An explosion of medical publications on phantom limb pain led to a public panic; this massive population of amputees, amputees seeking pledged prosthetics, were met with frightening new language. Asked to describe their phantom limb sensations using the language of pain, Ellie reports, the amputees were diagnosed in droves. It is difficult to separate the growing awareness of suffering from the affliction itself. They called it "The plague of pain," Ellie tells me. When I Google this later, nothing comes up.

This takes us into about five separate conversation threads, one of which is the relationship between industrialization and the rise in endemic and epidemic disease. Ellie says that anti-civs are sometimes labeled ableist, but that's not how they see it. They grant that they need medicine to live, but think that society is simultaneously making us sick and selling cures back to us. It's like, you don't thank your jailer for letting you use the yard, they say. You have to remember that you're in fucking prison.

The first time I realized I was in an abusive relationship was when my best friend told me so. "You keep getting sucked back into this, like, abusive thing," she said. That was about two years in. I could tell you that there were good days, that that was why I did it, but that wouldn't really be true. It's more that there were days when I wasn't dead yet, the last polar ice cap floating in a warming ocean. I walked to therapy every week to hear my therapist say I shouldn't sleep with him, or even talk to him anymore. "She says we shouldn't have sex," I texted him while I was leaving her office. "She says I shouldn't talk to you anymore." He would come over and fuck me and leave, and I would think about all the things about myself that I hated: I loved people who I despised, and I knew that meant it wasn't them I wanted, but this kind of love: The kind where you get to hurt yourself and pretend it serves a higher purpose.

For a long time, I was so much more afraid of losing him than I was of dying. Or maybe I was just convinced that they were the same. When we were together there was pain, but also momentary relief from the nothingness I felt when we were apart, when I would sleep all day or forget to take a shower, or forget to take myself out of the shower once I finally got in it. From these pains and depressions I could extrapolate the end of everything. But no matter how post-apocalyptic my visions, I could not imagine a world without the sensation of him. Past the upper limits of pain, past the pass-out point, there would still be love, which defies cure and articulation.

Think of pain as the tip of sensation—the feeling that announces itself first, that we verbalize fastest. Pain—unlike a strange, individualized phantom sensation, a lost limb off holding hands with a cherub, can be classified, logged, systemized. Suddenly, you have a medical diagnosis, resources, a community—peers in pain. Most importantly, pain demands a cure. Optimistically, we tell ourselves, this pain must end, or at the very least lessen.

"Every step you take I feel it in my side," I wrote, two years ago. "I will give up any limb, any organ, to avoid the severance of whatever sentiment is still between us."

"Many amputees welcome a phantom limb," I read. There's a fine line, medically and metaphorically speaking, between phantom limb sensation and phantom limb pain. Even if it hurts, a memory can be its own kind of comfort. The International Association for the Study of Pain: "Experiences which resemble pain but are not unpleasant should not be called pain."

One recent study shows that half of a sample of new amputees report pain in the residual limb in the immediate aftermath of amputation. However, 13 months later, the percentage drops to just 13. I remember a pain that was so everyday it didn't feel like pain; a time afterwards, armed with therapy and language, in which the pain was triaged and diagnosed, and the years that followed, when I found so much pleasure in writing about the pain, holding fast to the chalk outlines I traced around its absence.

Ellie and I trade doomsday cults and end of days imaginings. I say that shit is already so strange—flat earthers and anti-vaxxers, guys who don't have sex because they want it too badly, infected cruise ships floating indefinitely in oceanic limbo...Ellie says that things are just going to keep getting worse, and we'll live through it. Think about the Black Death, they say, the

Holocaust, the mass-murder of Native Americans. The apocalypse happens in segments, in silos. Everyone around you is dying or they aren't; you do or you don't. Everything will get worse, Ellie says, and weirder, and you'll keep coming to work.

I don't fantasize about stopping the apocalypse, real or imaginary; instead, I think about tiny, tender moments that scuttle in the shadows of all of this suffering. Small salves, homemade balms. These used to be those mornings after with my ex, the little stale-mates that gave me the strength to face the next great shit storm—but you don't thank your jailer for letting you use the yard, right? I'm learning this new language. I'm trying to differentiate between a banishment and a summoning, a zombie and a body of work. I rewrite my relationship over and over again, endlessly repeating the coda; with every right word I wonder if I am saving my own life or just building myself a crutch, something new to hold on to. I picture the amputees rushing the hospital to ask for new treatment, for morphine, for fresh shiny limbs that might not remember. What might we do to momentarily lessen suffering, our own and each other's?

For centuries, it seems, we've banked on the apocalypse taking us out of our collective misery. And, if not the end of days, then some miraculous cure. But maybe what we really want is the calm that comes right after, or even during, calamity; pain-tinged memories reminding us that we are, at least for now, on the better side of suffering. In the case of Civil War-era amputees, drugs were used to momentarily dull the pain, but only time, really, "treats" sensation. Before there was phantom limb pain, a standardized medical diagnosis, there was phantom limb sensation—excruciating, revelatory, divine, degrading. Before the plague of pain, as much grace as you can handle.

Trapped Bird, Locked Door

SHERI REDA

Iowa City, 2018

Starlings commonly bang into windows,
fall senseless, and die.
This one dives and rises.
Uses beak and wing in the glassy well
of the outdoor parking garage
to feel its way to the edge
of North, guardian of safety;
South, gatekeeper of opportunity;
East and West, the bounds of play.
Upward to the limits of soul,
downward to the cement wall of desire—

It must have got carried away
by a vicissitude,
a stream of air
slipped through an opening
or closing door
held back or propped in place
by one of those wingless, who thump along
stair steps to go up and down,
who walk from prison to prison,
whose flight, even, is enclosed.
Who walk away.

Tired now, it undertakes a rescue
by rows like a farmer
planting an escape from hunger:
spirals in ascending squares,
takes an intentional dive,
begins again. It doesn't defy.
Doesn't bash against glass and die.
It flutters a wing against hard nothing,

taps its beak into warm ice, continues
flying, oxygen-starved,
in case a door opens in time.

Quality Control

MIKE OPPENHEIM

"Do you have a moment, Doctor? I'd like to discuss a patient."

Martin's heart sank. The speaker was the quality control nurse. When she asked for a moment, you gave.

"You were treating this young man for acne," she continued.

Martin's heart rose again. What sort of catastrophe could pimples lead to?

"According to the chart, he complained that the cream burned. You changed to another."

"So?"

"As you know from the last meeting, we're concerned about documenting allergies.

We noticed you didn't enter the medication on his allergy sheet or mark it in red on the cover of the chart."

"Because that reaction isn't an allergy. The cream is irritating; it bothers lots of patients."

"I just thought I'd bring it to your attention," she replied on her way out.

Martin gnashed his teeth. He'd broken his vow never to contradict the quality control nurse. She never argued back. She merely reported any uncooperative attitude to the medical director. Minor infractions like this weren't worthy of his attention. Martin would probably not receive a phone call, memo, or tactful follow-up visit from the nurse herself. But the director might remember during the yearly salary review. He had remembered in the past.

As soon as she left, a genuine quality control problem turned up: a student with a cold.

"It's not a cold. It's bronchitis," said the student.

Martin's heart sank again. Bronchitis was a diagnosis doctors used to justify giving antibiotics. Since patients preferred antibiotics to no drugs, they eagerly repeated it on future colds. This promised to be a no-gratitude visit. Martin explained that a cold with a cough was bronchitis. Treatment was the same.

"I didn't come here to get cough medicine. Doctor Brown gives me Cipro. That knocks it out." A glance at the chart confirmed this. Like most doctors, Brown prescribed antibiotics generously. Martin stuck to his guns; the student's jaw tightened. "I have a paper due in three days, and I can't afford to be sick. Since you won't give me anything, do you mind if I wait for Doctor Brown?"

The student sat in the hall for the next hour, glaring at him whenever he left the office.

The clinic's quality control campaign was in full swing, filling doctors' mailboxes with memos, protocols, and surveys, packing charts with extra forms and colorful stickers, occupying much of the weekly educational meeting. At first Martin approved. Doctors grew sloppy dealing with patients unlikely to have serious illness which was the case in a student health clinic.

"Do you have a minute? I'd like to discuss a patient." Gloomily, Martin gestured at a seat.

When the medical director appeared at the door carrying a chart, the news was never good. "You saw this young man for a foot injury last week. According to the chart you didn't order an X-ray."

"It wasn't an impressive injury. I told him to come back if it wasn't better in a few days."

"And you documented it. Good. Unfortunately, he didn't come back. He went to an emergency room last night, and they found a fractured metatarsal."

"Unless I X-ray everyone, I'll miss one now and then. A metatarsal fracture isn't serious."

"You're right. They didn't even cast it. But laymen think fractures are a big deal. I just spent half an hour with his father, explaining that you didn't do anything wrong. I'm sure he understood."

This did not make Martin feel better.

The director continued: "There's no question of a settlement here. It's not like Jack Whitney." Jack had jammed a finger. Another doctor took an X-ray and found nothing wrong but didn't read the radiologist's report that arrived the next week. Three months later, Jack returned to ask why he still couldn't bend the finger. Naturally, the corrective surgery was gratis, and his parents bought a vacation home with the settlement.

"Mostly it's a headache dealing with angry patients. Remember, X-rays are cheap." Giving Martin a friendly slap on the shoulder, the director left.

`X-rays are cheap!' Was that a command to X-ray all injuries, Martin wondered. Should he ask? Of course not; that wasn't the important question. Which was: did he want to risk another patient giving his boss a hard time over a missed fracture, however trivial?

Quality control was especially important because student health clinics do not attract outstanding doctors. They appeal to those fresh out of training, happy to take an easy job while planning their next move. They appeal to old doctors, tired of running a practice but unwilling to retire.

When Martin arrived twenty years earlier, the position offered regular hours, a below average salary, four weeks vacation, and a week's educational leave. Since then, universities had tightened their belts, eliminating frills such as cultural activities, minor sports, profitless fields of study, as well as services such as counseling and student health clinics. Martin's clinic survived, but salaries stagnated, vacations dropped to two weeks, education to zero. Turnover increased.

The last hired before the cutbacks, Martin enjoyed six weeks of vacation (a benefit after ten years service under the old system) and a salary larger than anyone's including the director. Lacking ambition, he saw no reason to leave. During his long tenure, he observed a number of doctors hired, then fired: young doctors with a drug problem or obnoxious personality, old doctors who had worked solo so long they practiced a strange, outmoded style of medicine, foreign to everyone except their patients who had grown old with them.

Martin blamed the unreasonable features of the current quality control campaign on Gerald Mays, the last unsatisfactory doctor. Although no less unqualified than previous fired doctors, Doctor Mays had left under spectacular circumstances a month earlier. The fallout had not settled, but Martin suspected the university was exploiting the situation in an effort to eliminate health services and convert the clinic building to profitable use. Student government (which exerted considerable influence) opposed closure, but an HMO two miles away was tempting it by offering a forty percent reduction in the student health fee.

Martin took the summer off, so he didn't meet newcomers until orientation week in September. Doctor Mays was Martin's age but taller and fatter, with a full head of pure white hair, surprisingly smooth skin for a middle-aged man, and rosy cheeks. He looked Irish and spoke with a lilt redolent of New England.

The week before classes was slow. Doctor Mays kept to his office, usually reading a magazine. He listened quietly during staff meetings and responded politely when addressed. His last job had been at a Veteran's Administration clinic, easy work that attracted the same sort of doctor as a student health clinic. No one asked why he left.

On Friday of the first week, students signed up for classes, so almost no one came to the clinic. In late afternoon, a dozen bored doctors and nurses sat on benches in the corridor normally occupied by students. A game of Trivial Pursuit had run its course. One doctor told a joke. Someone told another. Attracted by the sound of laughter, Doctor Mays appeared in his doorway.

"Could I contribute?" he asked and then launched into a long, offensive story featuring sex and the clergy. He recited energetically, his face animated, waving his arms, impersonating male and female voices. When, with great gusto, he delivered the punch line, the roar of laughter emptied all the offices on the first floor. He told a second joke, no less amusing. With perfect timing, he bowed, thanked his audience, and disappeared into his office. It was five, time to leave, and the crowd broke up, buzzing at this delightful side of Doctor Mays. Martin noticed another feature of Doctor Mays that remained after his departure: the smell of alcohol.

Staff consulted each other and chatted about medicine, giving Martin an idea of how much they knew. Mays rarely socialized. Martin learned about other doctors by reading older chart entries when seeing a patient. Mays' notes were almost nonexistent and always illegible.

In the end, one judged a doctor by what happened to patients. This was a terrible way because outpatient medicine was so easy. Ninety-five percent of students arrived with minor illnesses. Almost all the remaining five percent were genuinely sick, but they looked sick. Even a fool would pay attention. Only rarely did a student arrive with a serious illness that wasn't obvious, and not all of these came to grief. Imposters with fake credentials and a professional manner often practice years before getting into trouble; an unfit doctor can do the same.

Mostly, Mays stayed in his office. Now and then he became sociable, but it was the sociability of the barroom. He stood too close, talked too loudly, and tried to be amusing. In the latter he was successful, so the staff enjoyed his company. Since everyone smelled the alcohol on his breath, they assumed his days were numbered.

Two months into the year, the medical director appeared during one of Mays' performances and asked him to step into the office. It was three o'clock, and Mays did not reappear by closing time. Fired doctors simply vanished, so no one considered this unusual. To everyone's surprise, he was in his office the next morning. But the performances stopped.

Martin learned through the grapevine what had happened. According to the Americans with Disability Act, an employer cannot discriminate against a disabled employee as long as the employee can do his job. Alcoholism qualifies as a disability, so firing Doctor Mays for a single transgression was grounds for legal action. Knowing this, the director warned him never to drink on the job again. Mays promised.

Martin had a veteran physician's knowledge of alcoholism. He assumed Mays had been obsessed with drinking all his life. When he wasn't drinking, life was tedious. When he drank, he felt good, but drinking got him into trouble: lost jobs, accidents, medical problems as he reached middle age. Unlike a skid row alcoholic, Mays lived comfortably and wanted this to continue. That required an income, which meant practicing medicine, an activity which gave him far less pleasure than drinking, probably none at all.

An impaired physician undergoes a steady career decline. Jobs caring for hospitalized patients disappear first, but that leaves plenty of nine-to-five positions. Large organizations check out doctors, so these soon become unavailable. Smaller but legitimate clinics can be surprisingly casual, offering shelter for decades. Finally he reaches the end of the line: diet clinics, Medicaid mills in the ghetto, shady clinics that dispense drugs and require only a body with an MD to sign prescriptions.

Medicine bored Mays, but a lifetime of practice gave him the correct moves. Knowing the current patient would be replaced by the next, he felt no urge to keep things moving, so he sat quietly as the patient talked. Patients liked that. On a good day he might never leave his chair, so his door was often open and Martin could see him, leaning back, hands clasped over his generous abdomen, nodding genially at the student. During slow periods, he closed his door, and no one doubted he was drinking again.

Doctors heard from the director if a student complained. No student complained about Doctor Mays, because he never hurried, never contradicted their opinions, never refused a test or medication a student wanted. Students with a cough or sore throat wanted an antibiotic, so they got one. Upset stomachs received stomach medicines. Painful body parts were X-rayed and given pain medication. Insomnia received sleeping pills, anxiety tranquilizers. Students who wanted a note to drop a class, retake a final, or exchange an airline ticket without penalty knew they could depend on Doctor Mays.

He was generous with referrals. The clinic's specialists came in one or two afternoons a week. Highly paid and scarce, they were not supposed to see simple problems, but no student considered his or her pimples, backache, or hay fever simple. All believed specialists possess healing powers unknown to a G.P., so there was persistent pressure for referrals. Most staff resisted when it wasn't appropriate, but Mays didn't. Students liked that.

One day our dermatologist, elderly and not even-tempered, marched into Mays' office. "You seem to have difficulty treating dandruff," he snapped. "I'll teach you. It will take one minute." The door slammed. A minute later it flew open, and the dermatologist marched off. The medical director summoned Mays to his office, but this didn't help. Unlike drinking on the job, inappropriate referring wasn't an offense that got a doctor fired.

By the end of the semester, the director concluded that Doctor Mays did not measure up. Unfortunately, three months had passed, the probationary period for university employees. Firing after probation was a complex procedure requiring documented evidence, written warnings, counseling. The director often persuaded substandard doctors to resign, but Doctor Mays declined.

Student health doctors joke that college students suffer eight medical problems; a doctor who knows only these will do fine. While astute, this is not a rule, so a good doctor stays alert. Doctor Mays made diagnoses quickly then went on automatic pilot, so he occasionally missed something. A student with a backache turned out to have a kidney stone. One who suggested she had bleeding hemorrhoids and left with a hemorrhoid remedy returned with hemorrhagic colitis. A student announced he had gone blind in one eye. Doctor Mays sent him to an ophthalmologist. The clinic didn't employ one, so this required an outside visit, paid for by the clinic from its meager budget. A simple exam revealed normal vision, and the ophthalmologist advised a psychiatric referral. None of these students made a fuss, so the director could only document each incident in Doctor Mays' file for use in his eventual dismissal. They were never needed.

The clinic buzzed one February morning over a headline in the student newspaper: three students had died the previous night. All had seen Doctor Mays the day before.

One was doing poorly in class and felt generally unhappy. He left with a prescription for a tranquilizer and hanged himself that evening. A woman with abdominal pain suggested she had eaten something bad.

Obligingly, Mays prescribed a digestive remedy. A stoic, the woman tolerated the pain of her ectopic pregnancy until it ruptured that night, and she died of internal bleeding before reaching the hospital. The third had AIDS, one of a dozen at the university. Maintained on medication, such cases were usually followed by our internist but saw the regular staff for minor problems. This student had a headache. An aide took every student's temperature before delivering him to the doctor, and his showed a fever. Fever in an AIDS patient is a red flag, but Mays paid little attention to charts, so the patient left with headache pills. That night he had a seizure and died of an overwhelming brain infection by one of the odd organisms that thrive in AIDS. He would have died if Mays had taken proper action, but combined with the other deaths it made a bad impression.

Doctor Mays was fired. The staff worried about their jobs as the university extolled the virtues of privatization. No less worried, the medical director ratcheted up the quality control program. Experts delivered lectures on topics Martin already knew. Depressed patients commit suicide, and a doctor must pay attention. A young woman with low abdominal pain has an ectopic pregnancy until proven otherwise. AIDS patients can go downhill quickly.

The lawsuits were settled without trial, but the university made no secret of the expense which would, ultimately, be reflected in increased student fees. Another proposal by the HMO to take over for half the current health fee split opposition among student leaders and allowed the university to close the clinic.

The HMO offered to hire the doctors. Martin accepted despite a cut in salary and vacation time. Soon he discovered that twenty years caring for college students had atrophied his skill with patients of other ages. Brushing up would not be difficult, but he decided he preferred students. Jobs at other student health clinics were scarce and paid even less than the HMO, and few wanted a fifty-five year old doctor. After debating whether to accept a position in Tempe, Arizona, Martin decided to retire.

Students complained about the distance to the new clinic, and they hated the waiting room, full of noisy children and the depressing elderly. Requests for a specialist or a note to avoid a test were evaluated on their merits and usually denied. Students remembered the campus clinic fondly, but they were not competent to judge the quality of their care.

Prop

GABRIELLE MONTESANTI

Dad and I are driving through a coal town in West Virginia when he asks me what's so special about Tom Hanks. It's spring break, and in a few weeks, I'll be the first in my family to graduate from college. This road trip was Dad's idea. He says he wants to spend time with me before I find some fancy job and move to God-knows-where, but I suspect he's just trying to shield me from my mother. Six months from now, he'll apologize for never protecting me. Whisking me away like this is the closest he'll ever get.

I'm grateful for something to talk about, but I don't know why Tom Hanks is on Dad's mind. It's impossible to track the way his thoughts meander; we've been virtually silent since we set off from Michigan two days ago. He asked about the last math class I need to complete my major, but I can't say much about Real Analysis that Dad will understand.

Without much thought, I say, "I'd really like to sit on the bench from *Forrest Gump*."

Dad knows the bench I'm talking about. It's the place Forrest lingers while he waits for the bus that will take him to his love. Strangers come and go as Forrest describes every moment that has led to his arrival there. In his memories, cruel people call Forrest names, all of which Mom has called me. I'm stupid. I'm selfish. I'm slow. Now, I'm quiet. The most I offer strangers is a strained smile. I rarely look anyone in the eye.

So Dad and I decide to go to Savannah to sit on the Forrest Gump bench. I can tell he's relieved that we're done driving aimlessly. In a McDonald's parking lot, Dad scrutinizes the map, traces his bony finger down the roads that will take us to the Peach State. Neither of us has been there before. Mom doesn't travel and doesn't like us to leave her. I don't know what Dad had to say to untangle himself. I worry what will happen after he drops me back at college. I imagine him driving down Academy Street and through the rough neighborhoods of Kalamazoo. If he sees someone begging for change at a stop light, he'll pull out a bill he can't afford to give away and say, "God Bless." He'll retreat somewhere deep in himself, or maybe outside himself, as he crosses the palm of Michigan at exactly sixty-one miles per hour. He'll pass thirteen confederate flags and the dealership where he works. He'll drive right past St. Agnes Catholic Church and the Pepsi plant where we let our dog run free in the parking lot. He'll pull open the back door and enter the house where I grew up and from which I escaped. Here is where I stop imagining. Here is where my body goes cold.

Still at the wheel, Dad whistles as he examines the map. I offer to take a turn driving, but my words hang between us like the long, wooden cross dangling from the rearview. I wait a few seconds and then ask Dad if he wants a Dr. Pepper before we set off again, but he shakes his head. High fructose corn syrup is on the list of things Mom won't let him eat, along with bread and croutons.

We stop somewhere in North Carolina for the night. The inn is almost full, and the only room left with two beds is in the smoking section. I extract fifty dollars cash from my Goodwill wallet and Dad mutters that he'll pay tomorrow. Up in our room, we crawl under blankets that Dad says feel like forty-grit sandpaper. I'm not bothered by the staleness or the scratchiness. I wish I had a cigarette.

Even though it's late and we're exhausted, neither of us can sleep. I try to slow my breathing and imagine my girlfriend's body pressing into my back. Her hot breath on my neck. Her arm wrapped around me, her fingers dancing under my shirt and then under the waistband of my shorts. I imagine the way she grips me as my muscles tighten and relax, tighten and relax—but the squeeze I feel in this moment is not love or lust, it's suffocation. I'm too aware of my dad's body in the neighboring bed, too tense to let myself imagine my girlfriend or her embrace. "Meeting her would kill your mother," Dad once told me.

I snap the silence by asking Dad if he wants to watch a movie. We find a bootleg copy of *Forrest Gump* in some dark corner of the internet and watch from our separate beds. A white feather. A wooden bench. Two strangers. I say to Dad, "We'll be there tomorrow." We both fall asleep before Forrest learns he can run.

When Dad and I arrive in Savannah, it's raining, but we pretend it's not. Water collects in the crevices of brick roads and pools underneath black fences. The streets are canopied by Southern Live Oaks. A fountain of cherubs blow horns that spray water. We think we should say something, so we say, "This is beautiful."

The bench is supposed to be on the north edge of Chippewa square. I expect it to be marked, memorialized maybe, but when we approach, there is nothing. All that is left is a One-Way sign. A woman passing by looks at us with pity. We're not the first who have stood here, searching for something that doesn't exist. In a deep drawl, the stranger tells us the bench was just a movie prop. "Wound up in some museum," she says.

Dad wanders off without speaking. I know not to follow. He does this at home—goes to find a quiet space to pray. Unlike Forrest's girlfriend, Dad doesn't have a cornfield to hide in when things get too bad. Instead, he sits in the mouth of the garage in an old lawn chair, head down, hands together.

Right here, in the rain, I imagine living in a place she can't find us. We wouldn't have to be brave. Like Forrest tells Ginny, we could sleep when we got tired. Eat when we were hungry. Go when we needed to go.

There are six other benches lining Chippewa Square and Dad sits on all of them. I lower myself onto the wet ground by the One-Way sign to watch. I expect his head to bow, his hands to find each other in his lap. But this time, he doesn't pray. At each bench, he sits for only a few seconds, looking around as though expecting things to be different. He ends up right back where he started.

Sonnet for the Pandemic

JAKE TAXIS

And just like that, this loud world tripped and fell.
Lives on pause—but not still—saw cities shut.
The fine threads of faces, with hopeful spell,
smiled through screens for weeks with their lifelines cut.
This quiet kill with creeping, rhythmed step
marched into bodies wise, and loved, and known.
With covered mouths and guarded eyes they wept—
website eulogies for brown and black bone.
We, the quarantined souls, stumbled on facts,
with vast illusions fractured, severed, torn.
Our strength is not in lonely, callused acts,
but in strange allied breath with bright lungs born.
What will be said of what this place became?
They surfaced new, or sank again, the same?

After Video Touring the Brooklyn Japanese Garden During the Time of the Virus

GAIL GOEPFERT

—Cinematographer Nic Petry of Dancing Camera

I swoop and swoon with the camera
through the hill-and-pond garden—
a slow reveal of lift and slide.

Blue sky, and hanging above the blushing
cherry trees—cotton-candy blossoms. *Sakura.*
Only one god's-eye milky cloud.

No one walks here.

Cherry blossoms—symbols of birth
and death—sway in clusters on dark limbs.
The trunks have learned to dip and rise.

Birdspeak, lilting calls and strings
of notes without urgency. Lullabies.
Finch and chickadee and catbird.

All the people told to stay home.

Only the insistent Canadian geese
parade themselves, their honks lukewarm
as they toddle unchased.

Media voices toll the deaths.

Edging the pond, fiddlehead ferns,
camellias in pink, and a vermilion-red
wooden *tori*, gateway to a Shinto shrine.

The sun glimmers through the arms of trees.
Komorebi. I revel in this deluge of beauty
offered up by the camera's lens.

A swell of sound intrudes.
From somewhere beyond, a siren keens—

the world outside still sorrows.

Forever and Ever, Kaboom

DAVID HC CORRELL

When I was a little boy, my family and I celebrated the Fourth of July with the same reverence that other families celebrate Christmas. The three of us, Dad, Mom, and I, would gather every year at a little lake in Iowa to watch the fireworks light up the night, and the water. Since my Cancer — and then his — I look back at those moments, his big hand on my little shoulders, pointing my gaze upward from the airy black toward the color, and the bursting light, as my father's first lessons in how a man handles his own sickness. And since Cancer took him, that's how I'm going to remember my Father: training my gaze upward. Dad was mostly a quiet man. But sometimes, on those Summer nights when an especially big firework would explode against the night sky, he would smile and give my shoulders a genuinely excited shake, and mimic the explosion, "*kaboooom!*". The Fourth of July was when he started training me to look ever upward, beyond the airy night, toward the color and the light, in sickness and in health, forever and ever, kaboom.

*

Tonight, I'm sitting at dinner. Across this Mexican-themed hole-in-the-wall's glossy two-top from me is a beautiful blonde woman, perched expectantly over the steaming plate of tortillas and cheese that she's just been served. She and I love places like this, with their unlimited salty chips and so-cold-they're-sweating imported beers. She is my best friend, and my fiancée, and we're planning for our wedding, and pipe-dreaming about all the couples *entertaining* that we'll do in the home that we plan to make together. But, when conversation turns to crockery, to which serving trays and sauce boats we would need for *entertaining* which imagined holiday's configuration of supposed dinner guests, I have to pause myself: *Entertaining? Sauce Boats?*

Contrary to what one might expect, my change was not some sort of gradual maturing and settling down with time; or even some gendered acquiescence to my partner's wishes. Rather, it was an abrupt change of heart over a painful, year-long re-birthing that transformed my feelings about family and death — and even serving pitchers.

My lesson started early one early September morning, before I had even left my apartment for my new job at a University in the Boston area. At my first appointment with my new General Practitioner, the physician noticed subtle irregularities in the shape of my neck and calmly referred me to a specialist. It could be nothing, he said, but we should probably check. That morning, the specialist had just rung my cell phone, as he promised me he would.

"It is certainly Cancer," he said.

"*It is certainly Cancer.*" I remember that sentence vividly. I wondered then if he had rehearsed it. Or, if there is a handbook for physicians somewhere that suggests using the word, 'certainly' when conveying a Cancer diagnosis. It was certainly right to say it in the way that he did. I needed to know, definitively — to begin to steel myself and my family for the gauntlet now before us.

In my experience that morning, the immediate aftermath of a Cancer diagnosis leads a man to more questions than it does answers. For me, some of these questions were quite banal. For example: *that's how you find out you have Cancer, some guy just calls you?* Other questions, though, were less silly, like: *how am I going to tell my Mother?*

I've always had trouble saying emotionally charged things straight to the faces of the people I love. A lump grows in my throat when I have something personal to convey, and I get choked up in all the cliché ways. So, in those moments, I sit quiet and distant, plotting the most effective and personally achievable way of speaking from the heart. At times, the lump in my throat has made "I love you" awkward for me. "I was wrong," has similarly struggled to launch from my lips. The morning of my diagnosis, before I even had time to think about how Cancer would change my own life, I remember worrying: "*...Mom, I have Cancer*" — could those words even come out?

But, later that morning, the words did come out, born breech and broken up with sniffles and pregnant pauses over long distance lines. I called my parents back home in Iowa and there was crying and there was gasping and we called each other back later the same day. Exasperated with heartache and fear, my mother said things in desperation that I had previously only ever heard her say reverently in church. My father, being my father, marshalled his and our whole family's strength and proposed a sensible plan of action. We would gather more information about my disease and my treatment, re-group later that afternoon, and we would stay positive — whatever Cancer may bring.

We had no idea.

*

Tonight at the Mexican restaurant, seven months after my Cancer diagnosis, I look across the table at my dining companion. She wasn't expecting my gaze, and looks back with that unintentional wink-and-a-smile that comes when one is caught angling the remains of a beer bottle down the hatch. So fresh. So cold.

Another round?

*

My beautiful best friend, then my fiancé at dinner and now my wife, was there for all of it. She was the first person I called after I heard, '*It is certainly Cancer*' and, later, she stood with my parents when they opened the curtain on my limp, life-supported body for the first time after my surgery. Survival rates for my type of Cancer are very high, but the treatment could have crippled me, both figuratively and literally. Going in, we planned for what the doctors told us to fear: I could lose my voice as a result of my tumor-removal surgery; I could lose control over half my face. We planned for my limited mobility. We planned for worse. We weren't even then yet married, but we were already steeling ourselves for the suddenly plausible bleakness of my uncertain adulthood — and, without missing a beat, we were doing it together.

As news of my diagnosis spread at work, my wide-eyed colleagues and students came by my office and classroom to nervously offer me hugs. When we touched, I noticed that I somehow weighed more on them — perhaps a burden of having become the tangible embodiment of premature mortality, or universal injustice, in the arms of people who have never had to touch, or stay in touch, with it before. But, her shoulders, so delicate, bore the burden of my new disease so readily.

One night, months after my initial tumor-removal surgery and radiation treatment, she and I were laying in bed. It was early spring and enough residual radiation had left my body that I was safe for her to touch again.

Life was returning to us and to our adopted city after our, and Boston's, most terrible winter. That night it was dark in my apartment, save for the blue glow of a streetlamp outside that shone through the blinds and onto my messy bed, making a Starry, Starry, Night scene of swirling aquamarines and blacks on the twisted white bed sheets. I wanted to thank her for carrying my burden, and for being part of the team of family and medical professionals who saved my life. But the lump swelling in my throat would never let me say those things. I wanted to tell her that I understood how unfair my Cancer was to her too, and that she didn't have to take all of this on; and that it hurt me to think of how this stupid disease was changing my role in her life story from a man who once brought with him opportunity, to one who now represented tragedy. But, I could never get any of that out — not in person, not this close. Spooned together in the Starry, Starry, Night scene, I got quiet, and found what I thought would be the best, most personally achievable way for me to say all of it:

"I don't want to be a sinking ship for you," I told her.

She wrapped herself around my arm, like she does when she doesn't want us to get up from some place comfortable, and told me what to this day we keep our fingers crossed will remain true:

"You're going to be OK. I know it."

*

Back at the Mexican restaurant, she is entirely uninterested in the shrimp on my seafood plate, but is nevertheless helping me to break off all of their attached tails. We are waiting for her entrée to arrive, and she is arranging the prepared shrimp in a perfect crescent around the perimeter of my plate. There was a time after my tumor-removal surgery when I wasn't able to move my neck or lift my arms. I then desperately needed this help, and more, to eat. But, I don't need it anymore. She offers it now for other reasons; I've proposed marriage and she said yes.

So, it turns out she was right. I am OK.

Hell yes, another round. This beer deserves a coaster.

*

Cancer is like a Kraken that swims deep in the bloodstreams of each of us, and surfaces, whenever it pleases, just to sink our ships. Six months after my Cancer diagnosis, my father got one too. And six weeks after that, early one morning, Cancer finished its horrible mission to take him from us, forever. My mother and I sat stunned and helpless in the painfully quiet hospice room.

The morning that your father passes, your swollen heart does not beat, and it does not yet break—first it drones, static and hollow, like the slack-jawed and empty hum of an off-the-hook land-line. Nothing comes in. Nothing goes out. The world, and people's consoling words, and your own ideas about spirituality and afterlife are all washed out in the sad and crushing din of your world forever changing. I had no line to, or from, anyone in the living world—except for her. From the hospice parking lot, I called my beautiful best friend at the job she had found for herself in faraway Boston, just to be near me. I told her that he was gone. And then, when I couldn't cry anymore for the beatless heart and the crushing din, she found her own secret place, somewhere in the ladies' room of an office tower a thousand miles away, and she cried for me.

*

Shortly before he passed, and only weeks before my wedding, my father and I stood at the kitchen counter to prepare what turned out to be our last meal at home together. While we were chopping and peeling, we talked about the food, and how to cook the shrimp. We talked about the interstate highway system. We talked about college football coaches' exorbitant salaries. We talked about everything; and we did it by talking with each other about nothing. That night, before we finished making our last home-cooked meal, he looked off into the distance and became quiet. I knew that look. He was wrestling with the lumps in his throat too. His hands over an old family cutting board, he gave me his last piece of fatherly advice:

"You know, this has gotta be a wedding, not a wedding-plus-a-funeral..."

I knew what he meant.

He meant that we weren't gonna be sinking ships for her.

*

We're nearing the end of our Mexican dinner and I've come to the same realization I do every time that I eat at a place like this: that I must be good for about twice as much beer, but only half as much burrito as the average Mexican male. My soon-to-be bride and I are talking about appointing our future household, and *entertaining*, and serving trays, and all the specialty tools that we've heard New Englanders use for serving shellfish.

All the time, my father's last piece of advice turns over and over in my head. On the one hand, it was specifically about the importance of a woman's wedding day. But I've since taken it to mean something more. Over a year that has given me plenty of reasons to think hard about dying, I've taken those last words as his final charge to me to prioritize celebrations of living first. The man of the house may fall ill, but he must never go dark.

She tells me that she thinks we need real wine glasses because the commemorative plastic cups and coffee mugs that I use for just about everything won't cut it when we're hosting Thanksgiving dinners. "Most people don't drink alcohol from coffee mugs," she says, and I shrug to concede the point. The accoutrements of entertaining, I think to myself — however ridiculous their names, or narrow or specialized their functions might be — all signify reverence for living the shared moments of their use, which is where I've come to believe the man of the house should turn his attention when circumstances surround him with the inevitable and airy night. I tell her that I agree, and quietly decide that I also want an oyster knife — not because I know how to use it, but because I don't think anyone's ever bought one for a funeral before.

Over dinner, I want to tell her all of this. And I want to tell her that she and our future family together is the bright bursting light upon which my father trained my gaze in his and my shared year of adult darkness. But even thinking about that — and the Fourth of July, and Cancer — puts the lumps right back into my throat.

I look across the table at her and my distant, dewy-eyed gaze catches her off guard again.

"You okay?" she asks.

I have so many answers to that question, none of which I will be able to get out — not in-person, not this close. So, I deflect. I add a serving pitcher to my *entertaining* wish list, "you know, for cocktails," I tell her.

She laughs. "Yeah, that's a good idea. But you want to pick out kitchen stuff? What happened to you?"

I get quiet. The lumps in my throat are swelling. I've got to find the best, most personally achievable way to say it.

"You did *Kaboom*."

The Aviary

RANA AWDISH

At time when it seemed everyone needed me, I chose to be devoted to something that didn't need me at all. I chose birds. As our world contracted, their small, borderless lives became something I could orient my own life around. Within our marriage, we had our individual worlds, and they kept us wrapped in weighty responsibility. I had the vast, blighted hospital and everyone's leaden grief. He had constant emails, pressurized calls, and reopening playbooks to urgently draft for the city. We shared a child—who had gained independence by means of our distraction—and announced himself only when hungry, much like the cats. But only the house and the yard functioned as shared spaces. The birds were a third thing and, I believed, marriages required third things. We had other shared subjects on which our mutual gaze could land, of course, with a pandemic paralyzing the world and Black bodies suffocating on cement. But none that felt quite so unburdened of gravity. The birds provided a focus for escape, an opportunity for unselfing. And I believed that our relationship and our sanity depended upon our unselfing.

The news abstractly reported mounting death tolls, while the hospital ran very concretely short on body bags and large, white, refrigerated morgue trunks parked indefinitely outside, blocking natural light from entering the first-floor windows. Daily actions were resonant with reminders of the frailty of our bodies. The compulsive hand-washing, masking and sanitizing all indicators that we were at constant risk of being overtaken by something very small, invisible and seemingly insignificant. Insignificant or deadly, depending on the case. You couldn't be sure. It felt as if we had stepped off some platform and were suspended in a moment of groundlessness, uncertain of whether we would plummet and crash or instead transcend our bodies, become weightless and limitless.

The birds began as my diversion, but I slowly drew the others in by buying binoculars for my son and supplying a book of North American birds my husband could reference. In the morning we would sit in cushioned chairs at the bay window, watching the sparrows, robins and finches feed in the garden. Those gentle minutes of close attention, warmed by coffee and the early sunlight, softened the frayed edges of our nerves. When we were feeling playful, we ascribed personalities and narrated mini battles between them. Two mourning doves were clearly in love, and the blue jay was aggressive despite his singular beauty. A vibrant cardinal perched itself so high in the maple, we thought the leaves had begun to change, until we used the binoculars to look more closely. Wishful thinking, that the season would be changing so quickly.

It was essential in those moments not to allow the larger world in. There would be no checking phones, rehashing news reports or discussing the day that lay ahead. We huddled in our cottony pajamas and disheveled hair and for a moment, our apprehension about boundaries was neutralized. The birds came together in the garden, they ate together and they left, freely.

My husband took a sip of coffee and broke all the rules by stating, "I want you to prepare yourself. I have some serious news."

I looked toward him, to study his face.

"What is it?" What news would he have received before me? If someone had been sick, I would have known first. Since the pandemic had started, I'd become many people's first call. Lawyers are rarely the first call, unless they are criminal attorneys, which he was not. Why would he have waited until morning to tell me something he clearly knew the night before?

By the time he said, "The last time I was at Home Depot," I knew it was about the birds. My eyebrows raised with irritation and disbelief that he'd coopted a technique for delivering serious news to families of dying patients for this discussion.

"They didn't have ANY bird food. Fortunately, I have a surplus in my trunk," he said. I was not surprised. It was his character to anticipate what we needed, secure it and then stockpile backup supplies. "But the way the birds go through it..." he trailed off before adding, "Don't worry, I'm sure I can find some online."

As he got up to go to the kitchen for more coffee, he smoothed the right side of his dark hair back with his hand. The uneven haircut was my fault, and it bothered him endlessly, though all he said when he studied it in the mirror was, "Thank you, this is much better than it was." I was more accountable for his appearance lately, beyond even the lopsided haircut. I'd been feeding him out of distraction and boredom, and we all took in more than our bodies needed, as a kind of consolation for being undernourished in other ways.

Looking outside, I thought how differently we approached our shared space. Where he viewed it as his to deliberately plan and landscape, I favored a passive acceptance of what was to be. He ensured each boxwood was hedged symmetrically and that each miniature spruce was perfectly conical. I favored the untamable wisteria with its tangled vines the animals could climb and encouraged moss to grow in the cracks of the pavement by watering it unnecessarily. Later, when hollows and superficial tunnels appeared in the yard, burrowed by an unseen rodent-mammal, he was offended by its supposed trespassing.

"There is a mole-thing, and it's going to ruin the yard!" he yelled through the door.

"It's the outside. The outside is squarely his, not yours." I tried to remind him without looking in his direction. Then, deciding there was something more important to say, walked toward the door, "Did you ever consider that maybe your need to be in control was actually the problem?"

He stepped toward me, still holding a trowel dripping in mud.

"You're siding with the mole?" He was incredulous. "It never even occurred to me that you would side with the mole on this." He shook his head as if I had disrupted his entire belief system.

I shrugged, uncommitted to a side. "Just let him be," I said.

A month prior, when families of squirrels and chipmunks took up residence in the attic, I'd been entertained by their pattering and busyness above my head, though I couldn't admit that out loud. The whole world was so still and quiet, except for them. They went on about their business, entirely unbothered, and I couldn't imagine their presence was at all dangerous, though the word infestation seemed intent on suggesting otherwise. The company he hired to remove them and seal the gaps in the siding promised they would be relocated humanely.

"I won't stop putting out food for the birds, even if that was the cause," I thought it should be said, to preempt any discussion.

"We go through a fifty-pound bag of birdseed a week," my husband explained to the man on the ladder.

The man raised his eyebrows and nodded in a way that suggested he'd been married a while.

"Sure," he said. "Now that the holes are sealed putting out bird food is fine." The mask he wore hid his smile, but I knew the expression. It was how you regarded the penguins at the zoo. He knew we were just making the best of our artificial habitat.

When I first met my husband, I was drawn to his secure confidence. I had just begun my fellowship training in critical care medicine and was immersed in a world of uncertainty—and frequently unsolvable problems. I was learning how to be proximate to suffering, and the inevitability of death.

He was working as an attorney in a law firm, where his entire existence was dependent upon his ability to plan for and control outcomes through strategy and negotiations. He was highly skilled, and it gave him a sense of himself and his own agency that was grounding. It never struck me as an arrogance, his belief that he had the right to reorder the world around him. I just wanted him to rewind the reel and talk me through every event and choice that had made the ground underneath him so solid. I wanted to know the nuances of that other experience, and to contrast it against all the moments I'd been taught to fit myself into the spaces the world left available, and not to expect accommodation. To invite others in and not expect that they leave, even if they begin to damage the walls.

When the lived spaces within our home began feeling too familiar, and with the world around us in despair, he repurposed an upstairs bedroom as his home office. In redecorating, he was drawn to the clean lines and sharp, predictable edges of midcentury modern furniture. Needing a large work surface as well as a place to read, he set two substantial Miesian desks at right angles to each other and an Eames recliner in the far corner. That the furniture was sturdy enough to outlast us didn't bother him. He enjoyed the way words like heirloom and legacy sounded in sentences. For the time being, each piece created order and offered some sort of architectural protection against the exigency of threat. In that space at least, he was barricaded against the messiness of uncertainty. As he worked, he was surrounded by reminders of his successes, all the other times things had gone exactly to plan. When he wasn't busy, he could still be reminded that he was sad.

In reclaiming an upstairs bedroom, he vacated the downstairs study allowing it to become solely mine. It had French doors I could close, which seemed essential at the time. We sourced an old writing desk with nooks and cubbyholes where I could tuck away cards, journals, colored pens and spools of twine. I was writing letters to everyone then, sending notes of encouragement that could more accurately be described as distress signals. I decorated the room as a counterbalance to the world. Every surface was cheery and comforting, with a bright cerulean sofa, covered in velvet, and an ochre ottoman. I latticed old Persian rugs on the floor. When he asked what style I was going for, I replied, "Maximalism. Obviously." We covered the walls in my brightly colored, figurative paintings and filled the shelves with my favorite books. I disassembled an old ballgown into yards of fabric and sewed pillows and reupholstered the desk chair in the sunny floral material.

We began referring to it as my apartment though everyone took to it. In the afternoon, the cats napped on the long oak window seat.

Taking in the finished room he smiled said, "Well, this is probably the closest I'll ever get to knowing what it is like inside of your head," hugging me from the side so that we could look at everything from the same point of view. It was true, every thought I had developed around was somewhere in one of those books, every dream or nightmare had made it into a painting. It was all there waiting to be understood, for someone to make sense of it all.

Instead of feeling seen or understood, I heard myself thinking, *If I die, you'll sit in here to feel close to me*. Death felt so imminent then.

The redecorating was a transparent attempt to make myself comfortable at home, when I preferred being at the hospital. Strange that an impersonal, plague-infested, hundred-year-old brick building would bring me any comfort, but there was a coherence there that wasn't available to me at home. If I felt edgy or angry or grief-stricken, it was contextualized within the experience we were all sharing. Though I felt all those things at home, I was estranged from any experience that could validate those feelings, or anyone who understood my trauma. At home the trivial worries of the neighbors, and the bland unstructured boredom of the children, mocked my grief. I couldn't bring myself to contribute to their conversations or revise their interpretations of the news. I couldn't bring myself to care about anything that anyone on the outside cared about.

Also, the garden was blooming which seemed odd, and people took bike rides and casually jogged through the neighborhood. I was glad for them that they hadn't seen what we had, and I was frustrated that it allowed them to maintain their denial and resistance to the scale of the losses, and the heavy burden we'd all incurred in caring for the sick. It was as if their ability to remain untouched was enough to invalidate our suffering somehow. What was hardest was that seeing them out forced me to acknowledge the thing that had fundamentally shifted in me. It now hurt more to watch people live their lives than to watch people die. It was as if sitting with death and impermanence for so long had created in me a kind of acceptance of death that I couldn't extend to others simply living. Our lives had become so intertwined, so interdependent, and yet we were unwilling to acknowledge our complicity in each other's pain.

"The mole has burrowed holes in your vegetable garden." He was trying to get me to switch sides.

"Probably helps with aeration of the soil. I bet the plants like it," I mused.

"No, the moles eat the roots and then the plants die. You can't want that. It's your summer garden," he said protectively.

"It's just that none of this is a space that I can control." I looked down at the holes in the garden and thought *not here too.*

"They just come together, they keep meeting here, it's not up to us to keep them apart, it's pointless to even try," I said.

"Sure you can, you can try. We can call the mole guy."

"That won't fix anything," I replied, annoyed that everything was so solvable to him. "Everything might still be ruined; you have to accept that. No one can keep it from happening," I tried to keep from crying.

"I'm confused. Are we still talking about the moles?" he asked.

"Possibly not," I sighed. "But it's all the same anyway." I sat down on the grass, releasing my weight into the ground.

"You can't fix everything?" he offered.

"Yep." I took a deep breath in so that I could get the rest out all at once before I lost the will to communicate honestly. "You know, we had a patient who needed a ventilator, he wasn't very old, mid-sixties. Before going on the vent, he wanted to make sure he wasn't taking it from someone else, someone younger with a better chance of survival. He said, 'You don't put me on that unless you're sure you have enough,' and it made me so sad and no one gets it."

"I'm sorry. That's awful," he said, shaking his head as if he already wished to give the story back to me to hold.

"And people are like, riding bikes," I gestured towards the street. "Like how? How can they be doing that? Explain that to me."

"They aren't trying to hurt you by riding their bikes, they just don't know. None of us can know."

"Well he died anyway. But he died in character. He died a good person who was willing to sacrifice for others. Better than these people," I said, throwing my hands in the air and generally gesturing at everyone else.

"Everyone's just trying to get by the best they can. It's hard for everyone in different ways," he said.

"It's not the same! Their suffering is not the same," knowing that wasn't what he was saying but fighting mostly with myself.

We sat quietly and for long enough that the birds and small animals began wandering back.

"How about you sit, and I will fill the bird feeders?" he said, and I nodded.

I watched as he walked between the trees, carrying the heavy tin barrel of birdseed across the yard. I was never sure if it was out of love and a genuine desire to unburden me, or an attempt to be needed, that he chose to keep the bird food in a container that I couldn't lift. Either way it was too heavy, so feeding them had become his responsibility.

Once he'd finished filling the first two birdhouses, a chipmunk emerged from the maple tree where he'd been hiding. He hung upside down, holding onto the feeder's rounded edge, happily filling his cheeks with seed. I thought how difficult it would be for me to eat suspended upside down, how well-adapted he was for his world. He then scurried down the thick trunk and across the yard; I watched as he approached the house. He paused to look directly at me before slowly climbing the drainpipe, deliberately squeezing his way between pieces of siding and into our attic.

Moro

CLAIRE CASTENEDA

These are the primitive reflexes the baby is born with: stick a bottle in her mouth and she suckles. This is called the rooting reflex. Shove your finger in her palm and she curls her fingers. This is the grasp reflex. Trick her into believing you've let go and she reaches for you. This is the Moro reflex. Stand her on a flat surface and she will take a step. This is the walking reflex. She is born knowing how to eat, how to reach, that she should fear hitting the ground even though she cannot see it yet.

All lights but the one on the wall beside the crib are turned off. The shades are pulled up knee high, leaving enough light on the floor to cross over from the doorway. Her eyes are open and she lies quietly, and it occurs to me that it is possible to be too young to be afraid of the dark.

I haven't seen her mom since she was admitted. Baby arrived in the evening; an hour later mom said she was going home to change clothes, and it is now hospital day three. She said she would be reachable by phone and true to her word, she has been, sometimes, but she has not been back to visit. I remember what she looks like, but it bothers me that I don't remember what color her eyes are. Perhaps she needs a break, perhaps this baby came sooner than she expected and thirty-some days later, this is her only chance to tie up the loose ends of her old life. I wonder if there are paychecks left uncollected, violent television left unwatched. Maybe she'd been counting on just one more night of good sleep. It may be dozens of nights before she rests for six straight hours. Even then, I suppose that no new mother gets the same sleep that she once had for at least another ten years.

Baby is a sky-blue fleece burrito with a bald head. I think she is pretty, though I know she is not, with her skinny thighs and skin translucent enough to see the vein running across her scalp to meet the IV line in her head. She is on her back, eyes no longer as sunken as the day she came and wide open, watching the ceiling. For all the millions of dollars that went into this children's hospital, there are no hanging mobiles of seahorses or stars. I wonder if in this stillness she can feel the earth move, if she's listening to cold air slam itself against the far window. The children's hospital is huge, new, towering, beautiful, with private rooms that are clean and safe. The walls are every shade of blue and there is a whiteboard in the corner with her name written across it in big bubble letters and "Goal for today: gain weight." The emptiness swallows the colorful walls whole, the baby's soft nasal breathing an isolated whistle in the dark. There is no way to know for sure, but I think this is the loneliest place in the world.

I unlatch the side of the crib, rolling her to face me as I lift her up. She can see maybe thirteen inches from her nose at most and is staring at my face, picking up cues. In a few months, she will use this information to cry for food, show discomfort, demand to be held. At two months she will start to smile to tell us she is pleased. Today, she is not yet able to smile, not really, not at others, though she does to herself when she farts. When I realize this, I tickle her belly to make her fart, and the two of us giggle together in her giant, empty room.

I drape a towel over my shoulder and cradle her head in the crook of my elbow, realizing I only know how to hold a baby from having gone to an elementary school covered end-to-end with pictures of the Virgin Mary holding baby Jesus. She feels the end of the bottle hit her palette and her eyelids start to droop, and for the next fifteen minutes I hold her, hold the bottle, listen to the wind hurl flecks of ice at the window and imagine various iterations of her life stretched out in front of us on a maze of unwinding streets. On one, she is never first in four square but gets ice cream after dinner for being a good loser. On another, she braids her sister's blonde hair. On another, she tells the sitter that she can't fall asleep unless she's been tucked in.

These are the maternal reflexes a woman is born with: there is only one. It is not a reflex that tells her how to hold the baby. It does not help wake her every 2-3 hours to breastfeed. It does not tell her how and when to soothe, when to walk away. No white matter highway connects the uterus to the region of the brain involved in choosing between her family and her career. She has only a lactation reflex that triggers dilation of the milk ducts when the baby cries. This is the letdown reflex.

I push us back and forth in the chair, watching scaffolding outside swaying in the winter wind, thinking about letdown. Even the Virgin Mary had it.

Logic says the baby is more durable than she looks. After all, people have been raising people since there were ever people to begin with. My eyes, however, say that she is no more than an unwrapped fleece away from hypothermia, a missed bottle away from hunger, an unwashed hand away from sepsis. Part of me wants to believe all women are wired to nurture, and I think it is there in our construction – hips like rebar folded into soft sides, voices pitched for nighttime lullabies. I imagine, when I rock her, that this is how it must feel to be a great lake or a sequoia, to be so a part of the present as to be unmoored from it. But women, I know, are not trees or landmarks. We are not separated through childbirth into wire mothers and cloth mothers. All babies grow up to be children who grow up to be adults who are too heavy to be carried. While she drifts in her milk-sleep I tell her I'm sorry she came into the world at this particular time, the age of building walls and life after runaway warming and unflinching certitude from everyone at once about right and wrong, good and bad. I apologize that for all the money and cleverness our species has amassed, we spend so much of it making sitcoms and specialty coffee drinks. "On the day you arrived, I said your mom was a bad mom," I say. "I'm sorry for that the most."

She is asleep.

I lower her back into the crib, fully swaddled, set her softly on her disposable mattress pad and pull up the gate. She lets out a tiny baby fart, smiles a tiny baby smile in her sleep. The screen above her head plays a lullaby that a dormant corner of my brain thinks might be an old Disney song. I've wrapped her up tight as a sleeping bag and she is still too young to roll, so I back slowly away, toe-heel, toe-heel, confident but not certain she will be okay at least for another hour. "Goodnight," I say, though it's one-thirty in the afternoon, and I call her by name, the first two syllables low and round and the last lilting and sweet. It suits her. One day she will recognize it. When I get back to the workroom, I let my attending know that she is eating well today, then I sit down at the phone and dial. The other end rings in another county, another town, and I am begging her mother to pick up.

The Awful Grace: Reflections

KATHARINE MARSDEN

Anatomy

I held her hand when we cracked her chest.
When we stole her lungs, I held it.

We lifted out her heart, and we cut into her stomach
and we took her skin.
While I held her hand.

They were covered. Gloved.
Encased in white fabric and sealed behind plastic
they resembled nothing.
But today,
today we pulled the shroud back.
We uncovered her hands.

Her nails are neat.
Were some of her last hours spent waiting for an appointment
Or was it only after that
someone filed and shaped and cut and polished?
She was gone.
Was it important to her?
or to them?
For someone to take that time,
it must have meant something.

We've taken her apart now.
Nothing is where it is supposed to be.
Her lungs and her heart and
her skin is gone.
So, what made her decide to give this?

It can't have been reckless. It must have been
rooted.

Anchored to something.
If I asked her to choose
To choose something like a star,
what would she tell me?
What made her certain?

I held her hand again today,
palm to palm.
I hope she forgives
the pieces of herself that I have
cut and pulled and torn
and lost.

But I am beginning to believe
I know something.
Maybe even something significant.

I think she would forgive me because whoever else,
she was generous.
And whatever else,
I've been holding her hands the whole time.

So.
I have a number of wishes for her,
but the only one worth saying is this:
I hope the last circuit her brain created,
Her very last memory
Was quiet.
I hope it was peace.

A reflection on the donor from my first-year anatomy class.

Surgery

We don't usually hold their hands.
At all.
Not when we meet
when we prepare
when we call time.

Not when they breathe deep
or go under.
And not when the first cut
is drawn across.

The symphony starts well before
they arrive.
Cacophony disguising euphony.
Where each plays a role
all at once.
Propelled around the room
along a current
from one task to the next.

It is an exacting choreography.
Steps I don't know.
To a beat I can't hear.
And the person I know best
Will not remember me
as more than a pair of eyes
under a blue cap.
Or a voice in the distance.

The role I occupy in this play
is a small one.
More Rosencrantz
than even Horatio.

But they will stay with me.

And I will remember
what lies behind their ribs;
and the color of their eyes.

Their children
their hope,
their history.

All that they brought with them
Into this place that is
Incongruous and
Unfamiliar and
Foreign
to them.

And to me.

You can see it in
Their eyes as we tell them to
cross the gap
onto what could be called an altar.

Where we will all make an offering-
Of trust and faith,
Of knowledge and skill.

We begin with
A moment of quiet

The breath before going underwater.

And we are, all of us, submerged.

A reflection on the first days of my surgical rotatio

Pathology

At the side of the bed, I held his hand
Reached out and touched
Briefly.
To say farewell, although
I had not known him.

The calls come
When they come.
And we must go and visit.
We must make
A declaration.

She was alone, when we arrived.
Waiting for us
To lay to rest
The question of living.

A question they had,
for themselves,
answered already.

The room is dark
and quiet
and still.
When the ritual begins.

It is a laying on of hands.

In some ways a blessing.

We listen to airless lungs
And hear a pulseless heart.
And check for reflexes
Where nerves have
gone powerless.

This completed, we must

Turn away from him.
And speak to her.
It is complete.
We can tell her that

This life is past.

This fight is over.

Although it is not my
tragedy, I find myself
nearly overcome.

Although I wish to,
I cannot reach out and
take her hand.

The hand that would
feel meaning in being held.

But we are here with her.
Sitting in the darkness in silence.
Keeping company
and holding vigil.

There are those who
believe we are all composites.
Amalgams.
That every bright eye,
Every inspiration,
Can be seen and weighed
and measured.
That all we are is contained
By the vessels in which we reside.

Perhaps they are right.
Perhaps they are wrong.
I claim no special knowledge.

But I can say this.
Drawn in green marker
on a board
across from the bed:
"No matter how far
You go.
I will always
Love you."

That part is true.

A reflection on visiting with a recently deceased patient.

Radium Emanation

I don't understand
What I am seeing.
This one looks like a dancer.
And there, a vaulted ceiling.
A full skirt swinging wide.
Maybe I am getting the right impression
– it is the chest I'm looking at.
Perhaps they are paired after all, heart and soul.
Mother tells ghost stories
that start the same way.
Space is left – by the great
or the terrible –
a shadow rushes there.

This is what is left for shadow readers.
A picture overexposed
– light around the frame
of the closed door.

That might not be far off.
Voices echo in a hollow place
– replaying words spoken before.

Perhaps these are they.

It's all shadows.
But the demarcation
of place has meaning.

I'm seeing shadows cast by someone –
but not themselves.

Even if I am cracking open their chest
and peering inside.
Looking beyond the barrier or skin And into the bone.

Am I losing the meaning?

Maybe.
Or am I finding a thread,
The truth of one's narrative.

At this moment, though,
it looks like a dancer.

I know what it is,
What I should see.
And I know who it is
but I don't know what they are.

The deepest heart tells me nothing about that.

A reflection on a chest x-ray during my first semester of medical school.

Positron Emission

These four pillars of inflammation: Rubor. Calor. Dolor. Tumor.
Red. Hot. Painful. Swollen.

The body's response to damage
and to threat.
The meshwork that makes us all knows its enemy,
seeks it and marks it out.

For twenty centuries,
For nearly two thousand years,
These have held.

And now I stare at a map
Where bright spots in the darkness Show this same devastation
From a different angle.
Through a different window.
In a different color.

Tumors glow.
It was once a surprise to me.
But there they are –
Bright against the darkness.
Flares against a night sky.

Because we have harnessed
vision beyond our own sight
I know what this is.
And what it signifies.
I know where it is.
And what has been destroyed.

But, in this gain, I also sense a loss. And wonder
Have I lost the context –
by understanding the content?
As I find what I am looking for,
Perhaps I am losing beauty in what there is to see.

Am I failing to see the Soul
where it resides?

Upon reflection, I disagree
with myself.
I am looking –
unraveling a secret
someone keeps without complicity.

And although they signify
nothing good.
The whole of us found a way
to force a show of themselves.

Thus, we still oppose the fates
and perhaps preserve
those threads of a life.

And have not forgotten the soul
in such a seeking.

A reflection on learning to interpret radiology results in practice, during my M2 year

Magnetic Resonance

It is there and gone
In the space of a second.
Moving through the topography
Of the brain.
The tumor appears from nowhere And disappears into nothing.

Glioblastoma.

It barely sounds like a word.
But there it is.
A tumor of glial cells.

Abnormal growth of
nerve cells of the brain.

And although we speak often
In public of
Cancer warriors, and survivors
This particular journey
Will likely be brief.
Barely enough time for armor.

He fell off his bicycle.
That was the beginning.
In the emergency room,
The physician noticed a troubling sign.

An hour later, a new diagnosis.
And an entirely new life marked by surgery, medication, and radiation.

I meet this man – hopeful.
Finally leaving the hospital.
He says he is tired,
but plans to fight.
We discuss his treatment, the plan, and send him on his way.

Two weeks later, he returns.
Altered.
Even I, who know him least, can see There has been a change.
And not for the better.

He asks us about a cure, about a trial,
about a scientist on an island in the Pacific.

He cannot stand, he cannot walk.
It is difficult to understand what he understands
From our conversation.
But that is ultimately irrelevant.

For we must begin where the patient resides.
There is nothing before this.

While his is a personal disaster. None of us are thinking clearly,
He is distanced and disconnected. And we are only people, as he is.

This is not cause
And ensuing effect.

And none of us are gifted with prophecy.

We may fail
or we may succeed.
Much of it is beyond us –
Out of our control.

But what we can do, is seek to understand
And to be understood.
We can walk with you,
as far as the road takes us.

Although we can promise nothing.
Because medicine is both a science and an art
Mystery and magic flow through it
And the outcome is not always what we await.

The magnets that told us where this tumor lived.
What structures it had eaten through,
They resonated,

Our words do too.

A reflection on a patient with Glioblastoma, a conversation with my sister and from reading the reflections of Dr. Scott-Connor on the presentation "Words Matter" during my M3 year

Nothing has happened.

She is standing in front of me
And I am without words.

Or plan.

Just do it.
Say it.
Push the words
Past your lips.
And let them breathe in the world.

It has to be done
It must come to pass.
And you must be
The one
To do it.

So, let the words fall
Now.
We have lost him.

[Lost is an inexact word.
Does it mean no return?
Ruination?
Absence?
Has it simply gone beyond reach?

There's an ownership to lost.
So then there's a fault.
How did it come to be lost?
Did it slip through your fingers?]

It is my duty to be clear

"He died."
I say, and she screams.

Stop.

This is only pretend.
We're only playing at grief
And love
And hate
And fear.
Today is imaginary
but
Tomorrow
it will be real.

No one is hurt today.
The news I impart
Has no impact.
It is an illusion
Ephemeral.

A scenario
On brightly colored paper.
Blue, green and gold.

When I am done here
The world will reset,
the next of us
Will begin.

Nothing of this is true
Or permanent.

Except for me.

The fear I feel is real
The dread at creating a fracture
Of before and after.

Breathe.

When the time comes

For me to tear open the seams of the world
For a stranger.
I hope I call on what blood I have From my grandfather -

Whose words these are:
“We who are finite
huddle together in finitude
and we seek to find
that which is infinite.”

It is he who has gone.
Not you who have lost him.

But more than that,
“He has slipped out of the window
of this world and he has gone home.”

A reflection on learning how to “break bad news” during my M2 year, with quotes borrowed from my grandfather, Jay Monroe Jensen, M.D.

Ghost of a Shadow

I am Tiresias
Not Cassandra.
When I predict the future
I will be believed.
Although, so far
I have not yet seen it
Come to pass.

It shocks me every time
But my words
Now
Carry weight.

A refection on knowing bad news, during my M2 and M3 year.

Gaze

MIRANDA SCHENE

She lies back, gazing at him,
While I discuss her treatment plan
and he leans into my words,
she smiles like a young lover,
watching a long quiet sunset.

I wonder how she's feeling–
She shifts only a little,
and hardly even blinks at him,
or lets her mouth corners fall
from that shy settled smile.

Her head sinks into the pillow
and I wonder how much she hears,
while "*option...prognostic...alleviate...*"
blow around her bed
like so many dying leaves.

Her indifference weighs on me:
I'm part of the scenery to her.
A sparrow perched on the window
that her husband tends to,
Hoping it will sing them a pretty song.

I wonder what she's thinking,
What her tiny smile implies.
It looks a bit like love, but
it could also be sorrow, pity, hope,
Joy, weariness, or resignation.

Or maybe she just thinks he's handsome.
I don't really think he is,
But luckily, she has stopped listening to me.

Vietnam Surgeon

LIANA MEFFERT

Every Christmas I'm surrounded by
a thousand pendulous ornaments
galvanizing the glow of another
Only to return to rice paddies & kerosene fumes
to find my Grandpa—where he always is
and also other places he won't or cannot name
rested in a backdrop of incandescent green

I ask him for the story about triaging soldiers
in D'nang he can't recall so he tells me
about fixing mitral stenosis in the locals,
mimes sticking a finger through the valve
to make space, sewing up the edges
like cinching a purse string, shrugs
life was as malleable as a heart in two hands,
which is to say it took to shape easy as red wrapping
or blood splashing on sandals, something to wade through
when the pressure wouldn't rise & feeling in the dark
for leaky wounds felt like plugging holes in the hull
of a sinking ship and was never enough
like the cap-full of tequila from Father Perez
with plenty of holy water to drown us all
even the boy who survived
because living was the consolation prize

The story was a riddle. If there aren't enough
units of blood or time to save everyone…& I know
if he remembers anything at all, it's what he chose

Editorial Board

Bruce P. Brown, MD is the founding editor-in-chief for The Examined Life Journal. His literary work has appeared in The Annals of Internal Medicine, Kalends and Hospital Drive. He is an emeritus radiologist and internist at the University of Iowa in Iowa City, Iowa.

As a mother of two young children and a practicing physician, **Brittany Bettendorf** often sees people at their best and worst; she is intrigued by the everyday moments amidst which a life plays out. Brittany uses writing to explore difficult questions in an attempt to understand human relationships. Her essays have appeared in the Wall Street Journal and on WUWM Milwaukee Public Radio's Lake Effect. She is currently an MFA student in University of Iowa's Nonfiction Writing Program.

Cate Dicharry, MFA, is the director of the Writing and Humanities Program at the University of Iowa Carver College of Medicine and has an MFA in Creative Writing from the University of California, Riverside. Her debut novel was published by Unnamed Press in 2015, and her writing has appeared in Electric Literature, Literary Hub, The Nervous Breakdown, Role/Reboot, and elsewhere.

Serena J. Fox (Night Shift Poems, 2009) is an intensive care physician at Mount Sinai Beth Israel Medical Center, NYC. She believes deeply that poetry and humanities have essential roles in the teaching of medicine, ethics, human rights and caregiving. Her poems have appeared in the Paris Review, Journal of the American Medical Association (JAMA), and the Western Humanities Review.

Kerri Goers is a Neonatal Nurse Practitioner at the University of Iowa Stead Family Children's Hospital. She received her Bachelor of Arts degree from Luther College, her Masters of Science in Nursing from The University of Iowa College of Nursing, and her Post-Masters Neonatal Certification from Rush University College of Nursing. She has a Writing Certificate from The University of Iowa and is working on her Masters of Fine Arts at The Bennington Writing Seminars.

Carol EH Scott-Conner is professor and chair emeritus of the Department of Surgery at the University of Iowa Carver College of Medicine. She has written numerous textbooks, three monographs on writing, and two volumes of short stories. Her short fiction explores the interactions between physicians and patients. A perennial student, she is enrolled in the Narrative Medicine and Creative Writing graduate programs at Lenoir-Rhyne University.

Editorial Readers

Linda Ayres-Frederick, Phoenix Theatre's Artistic Director since 1985, has enjoyed a rewarding career as an actor, director, producer, critic and playwright. Twice granted the Shubert Playwriting Fellowship, Linda's plays have received over 20 productions in NYC, San Francisco, Edinburgh, France and Alaska. Her work has been published in: Poets on Parnassus; The Squaw Review; SF Bay Times; Westside Observer; Bay One-Acts Anthologies; Yale University Graduate-Professional. Linda resides in San Francisco with her life partner.

Roy Carlson is an otolaryngologist in private practice in the NJ suburbs of Philadelphia. He has written a study on James Joyce and is interested in the relation of narrative theory to medicine.

Diane DeBok has an MFA in nonfiction writing from the University of Iowa. She is an occasional blogger for Bur Oak Land Trust in Iowa City. Her work has appeared in From the Edge of the Prairie, and her short story, "Knowing What to See," will appear in that publication in November 2020. An Editor and Content Manager at the University of Iowa, Diane is also a freelance writer and editor.

Roberta Hartling Gates has been published in literary magazines such as Confrontation, Fourth Genre, and the Beloit Fiction Journal, as well as two anthologies. She was a runner-up in Solstice's 2017 short story contest, a Narrative finalist in 2013, and a Nelson Algren finalist in 2002. In addition, a collection of her short stories was a finalist in the Gold Wake Press contest in 2020 and a semifinalist for Hidden River's Eludia Award in 2019. She has an MFA from the Vermont College of Fine Arts.

Kerri Goers is a Neonatal Nurse Practitioner at the University of Iowa Stead Family Children's Hospital. She received her Bachelor of Arts degree from Luther College, her Masters of Science in Nursing from The University of Iowa College of Nursing, and her Post-Masters Neonatal Certification from Rush University College of Nursing. She has a Writing Certificate from The University of Iowa and is working on her Masters of Fine Arts at The Bennington Writing Seminars.

Rachel Hammer, MD, MFA is a new Assistant Professor of Psychiatry and Internal Medicine at Tulane University. She completed an MFA in Creative Nonfiction at Seattle Pacific University while in medical school at Mayo Clinic.

Brian Olshansky, MD, cardiac electrophysiologist, professor emeritus of medicine, is a member of the editorial board since inception of The Examined Life Journal. After graduating from Carleton College and University of Arizona medical school, he completed training at NYU/Bellevue, University of Iowa and University of Alabama. Brian has directed two electrophysiology training programs. A creative writer for over 20 years, he has been affiliated with the University of Iowa creative writing program for 15 years from which The Examined Life Journal emerged. Aside from writing, Brian has diverse interests ranging from technical and mechanistic aspects of cardiology to holistic issues regarding medical care and the doctor-patient relationship.

Steven Phillips has been a writer, director, and creative director for film, video, and large-scale events, which he has staged around the world. Now retired, he teaches and volunteers with a number of public humanities initiatives in the New York area. Steven holds advanced degrees in Literature and American Studies from the University of Chicago and Columbia, as well as an MFA in film from NYU's Tisch School of the Arts.

Ann Rushton lives and writes in Iowa City. Her work has appeared online and in print journals. She is currently working on a novel and is represented by Writers House.

Alok Sachdeva is a sleep medicine physician in Brighton, Michigan. He believes that writing improves healthcare by enhancing our understanding of one another's experiences. Alok has worked with The Examined Life Journal since 2011.

Jennifer Stern's short fiction has appeared in Colorado Review, Hobart, Briar Cliff Review, Blue Mesa Review, and Gulf Stream among other journals, has been nominated for the Pushcart Prize, received honorable mention by Glimmer Train, and been anthologized in The Masters Review, as selected by Kevin Brockmeier. She holds an MFA from Warren Wilson College. She is also a physician.

John William Stout holds degrees from PLY & the Iowa Writers' Workshop and teaches rhetoric at the University of Iowa. His work has been nominated for Best New Poets and his poems have been published in the New England Review, Lana Turner Journal, Prelude, Iowa Review Online, Horsethief, Omniverse, Tulane Review, Canada Quarterly, Poetry is Dead, Saxifrage, and elsewhere. The Dream of Zukofsky was a semifinalist and finalist for the Omnidawn Chapbook Competition in 2018 and 2017, respectively.

David Ray Vance is the author of two collections of poetry: Vitreous (Del Sol Press, 2007), and Stupor (Elixir Press, 2014). He earned a PhD in Literature and Creative Writing at the University of Houston and is an Associate Professor in the Creative Writing Program at The University of Texas at San Antonio, where he serves as Creative Writing Program Director.

Lindsey Vella, MFA, is a graduate of the University of Michigan and Iowa Writers' Workshop. She is originally from Detroit and now lives and works in Iowa City. Her poems have appeared in Bat City Review, Tupelo Quarterly, Black Warrior Review, Birdfeast, and Sugar House Review.

Contributors

Rana Awdish is a Critical Care Physician in Detroit, Michigan and the author of the critically-acclaimed memoir In Shock, My Journey from Death to Recovery and the Redemptive Power of Hope.

Allison Baxter is a high school English as a Second Language teacher in Chicagoland. She lives near Chicago with her husband, daughter, and a grumpy dog. She writes a mystery series based in Chicago neighborhoods, the first of which is Death in Logan Square. This story is based on a character in that series.

Jo Ann Benda, MD, trained as an Obstetrician/Gynecologist as well as a Pathologist. Her experiences in a tertiary care hospital as clinician and patient have been subjects of her poetry. She also writes about the natural world and life experiences away from her work life.

Corinne Carland is a 4th year medical student at Tufts University and Maine Medical Center. She recently completed a research year through the Sarnoff Fellowship at Stanford.

Erik Carlson is a third-year medical student at Loyola University Chicago Stritch School of Medicine.

Claire Castaneda is a fourth year medical student at the Carver College of Medicine. Her interests include geriatrics, palliative care, fiction writing, and photographing her elderly cat, Ernest, in fashionable hats. Her work has previously been published in The Examined Life.

Joanne M. Clarkson's poetry collection, The Fates, won the Bright Hill Press annual contest and was published in 2017. Her chapbook, Believing the Body, from Gribble Press came out in 2014. Her poems have been published in journals such as American Journal of Nursing. Clarkson has a master's degree in Library Science, and worked as a professional librarian. After caring for her mother, she re-careered as a Registered Nurse specializing in hospice care.

Lee Cooper works as a biotechnology investor and entrepreneur in Cambridge, Massachusetts, helping to bring new medicines to patients. Lee is passionate about teaching and communicating the human aspects of healthcare innovation and ethics. His writing and speaking draw from both professional experiences in healthcare and from personal experiences as a patient. Lee lives in the Boston area with his wife and son.

David HC Correll works as a teacher, researcher, and writer in the greater Boston area. He is originally from Cedar Falls, Iowa.

Kristine Crane is a writer and journalist in Gainesville Florida, where she also teaches journalism and digital storytelling at the University of Florida. She holds an MFA in nonfiction from Pacific University. Previous essays and digital stories have been published in River Teeth's Beautiful Things, and The Florida Review. She is originally from Iowa City. She is a monthly columnist and associate editor of the online publication The American in Rome.

Joy Cutler is a playwright, performer and jewelry designer. Her staged plays, solo shows, and radio plays have been produced in the U.S. and Germany in theaters, schools, medical conferences, performance salons and the occasional living room. Joy currently works as a Standardized Patient at medical colleges in Philadelphia, using her theater experience to train healthcare students in medical and empathy skills.

Philip DiGiacomo's work has appeared in The Nervous Breakdown, 1888 The Cost of Paper, Fiction on The Web, Halfway Down the Stairs, Story and Grit, Fish Food Magazine, Literary Manhattan, The Examined Life Journal, Fleas on the Dog, and The Bethlehem Writers Group. He is a former painter and actor from New York. He studied with Lou Mathews and Colette Sartor at UCLA.

Linnet Drury is 17 and lives in Oxford, England. She is a sixth form student in year 12 at Oxford Spires Academy. She has been a top 100 winner in the Foyle Poetry Competition, long-listed for the Tower prize and has won local poetry competitions. She is a member of a group organized by Kate Clanchy who has set up a poetry workshop over Zoom which focuses on poems about the pandemic, the lock-down in England and how the times have changed their lives.

Dina Elenbogen is a widely published and award-winning poet, author of the poetry collection, Apples of the Earth (Spuyten Duyvil, NY) and the memoir, Drawn from Water (BkMkPress, University of Missouri.) Her work has appeared in numerous anthologies and literary magazines. She has just completed an essay collection entitled Eating and Drinking with Sages. Dina has an MFA in poetry from the Iowa Writer's Workshop and teaches creative writing at the University of Chicago.

Gwen Erkonen is currently an assistant professor of pediatric critical care at Texas Children's Hospital in Houston. She works in both the cardiac and medical intensive care units. Her research interests focus on narrative medicine and medical humanities. She is mother to four incredible children.

Alec Feuerbach is an emergency medicine resident and writer living in Brooklyn. He recently graduated from the Icahn School of Medicine at Mount Sinai and received a degree in Spanish Language and Literature from the University of Denver. Raised in Colorado, he loves hiking, skiing, and, of course, reading.

Erin FitzGerald is a palliative medicine physician and medical educator honored to care for under-served and sometimes under-cherished humans often at the end of their lives. She lives in the Land of Enchantment with her partner and son and their two rowdy mutts.

Katy Giebenhain is the author of Sharps Cabaret (Mercer University Press). Her creative writing MPhil is from University of South Wales. Her poems have appeared in Intima: A Journal of Narrative Medicine, The Healing Muse, The Glasgow Review of Books, the National Academy of Medicine's Expressions of Clinician Well-Being Online Gallery and elsewhere.

James W. Girardy serves as a Clinical Associate Professor of Surgery at University of Illinois College of Medicine-Rockford with a focus on Ethics & Humanities. He retired from clinical activity after 32 years as a General & Critical Care Surgeon.

Gail Goepfert is a poet, photographer, and teacher. She is an associate editor of RHINO Poetry and the author of a chapbook, A Mind on Pain (Finishing Line Press, 2015) and two books, Tapping Roots (Kelsay Books, 2018) and Get Up Said the World (Červená Barva Press, 2020). Recent publications include Night Heron Barks, Journal of Compressed Arts, Open: Journal of Arts and Letters, SWWIM, Rogue Agent, and Beloit Poetry Journal.

Kerri Goers is a Neonatal Nurse Practitioner at the University of Iowa Stead Family Children's Hospital. She received her Bachelor of Arts degree from Luther College, her Masters of Science in Nursing from The University of Iowa College of Nursing, and her Post-Masters Neonatal Certification from Rush University College of Nursing. She has a Writing Certificate from The University of Iowa and is working on her Masters of Fine Arts at The Bennington Writing Seminars.

Jan Grossman's poems have appeared or are forthcoming in Salmagundi, Poet Lore, The South Carolina Review, Potomac Review, Poetry East, The Midwest Quarterly, THINK, Tampa Review, Slant, Atlanta Review, The Worcester Review, Third Wednesday, and Plainsongs, among other journals.

Rebecca Grossman-Kahn is a resident physician at the University of Minnesota. The piece that appears in this issue was shaped by her trip to Poland and Germany as a FASPE fellow in 2017. Her professional interests include medical education, clinical ethics and narrative medicine. She is a corresponding member of Pegasus Physician Writers at Stanford. When not at the hospital or writing, she can be found listening to samba music and touring historic houses.

Ann Howells edited Illya's Honey from 1999 to 2017. Publications include the books Under a Lone Star (Village Books Press), Cattlemen and Cadillacs (editor, Dallas Poets Community Press), So Long As We Speak Their Names (Kelsay Books), and Painting the Pinwheel Sky (Assure Press). She also has four chapbooks, including Black Crow in Flight (Editor's Choice, Main Street Rag) and Softly Beating Wings, winner William D. Barney Contest (Blackbead Books). Her poems have recently appeared in Chiron Review, Slant, and San Pedro River Review.

Kain Kim studied English Literature at Johns Hopkins University before teaching language classes in North Macedonia as a Fulbright Fellow. She has previously worked on several projects in healthcare education with the Johns Hopkins Hospital and the Narrative Medicine department at Columbia University, and is currently in the process of applying to medical school.

Richard Kravitz is a psychiatrist In New Haven, CT. He works at the VA Hospital in West Haven, CT and teaches in the Department of Psychiatry at the Yale School of Medicine. His poems have appeared in a variety of medical journals.

Elizabeth Lanphier has previously published poetry with The Examined Life Journal (as Elizabeth Alexandra) and the Intima (forthcoming), and looks forward to continuing to be a reader and contributor within medical humanities creative spaces. She is primarily a social and political philosopher and bioethicist who engages with the arts and creative expression in ethics scholarship and teaching.

Andrea L. Lingle lives in the Western North Carolina mountains with her family. She loves to play in her garden to varied success, read philosophy she may or may not understand, and walk her dogs. She is a writer and lay theologian for the Missional Wisdom Foundation. Her books include Credulous and Into a Reluctant Sunrise.

Katharine Marsden is a third-year medical student at the Carver College of Medicine. Originally from Salt Lake City, Utah. She studied history at the University of Chicago.

Eileen McGorry practiced as a Registered Nurse for forty years. She has been published in The Examined Life Journal, eChapbook and The American Journal of Nursing. Her essay, "Destination Nursing," won first prize for nonfiction in the Writers on the Sound Conference contest in 2008. She lives in Olympia Washington with her husband, Ron.

Michael McGuire was born and raised and has lived in or near much of his life; he divides his time; his horse is nondescript, his dog is dead. Naturally, McGuire regrets not having passed his life in academia, for the alternative has proven somewhat varied, even unpredictable.

Kevin McKim is currently a Neonatal-Perinatal Medicine fellow in his 3rd year, training at Stanford in California. He completed medical school through Temple University at St. Luke's University Hospital in Bethlehem, PA in 2015, and finished pediatric residency at Cohens Children's Medical Center in Queens, NY in 2018. He enjoys spending his time post-call learning new recipes, maintaining his reef tank, and hiking through local California parks.

Liana Meffert is a second-year medical student at Carver College of Medicine. She has previously been awarded an Academy of American Poets Poetry Prize, Stanford's Irvin David Yalom Literary Award, University of Iowa's Carol A. Bowman Creative Writing Award, and an honorable mention for the William Carlos Williams Poetry Award.

Caryn Mirriam-Goldberg, PhD, Kansas Poet Laureate Emerita is the author of 24 books, including How Time Moves: New & Selected Poems, Miriam's Well, a novel, Needle in the Bone, a non-fiction book on the Holocaus, The Sky Begins At Your Feet, a memoir on cancer and community. Founder of Transformative Language Arts, Mirriam-Goldberg leads writing workshops widely, coaches people on writing and right livelihood and consults with businesses and organizations on creativity.

Gabe Montesanti is a queer, Midwestern roller derby player. She earned her BA in mathematics and studio art from Kalamazoo College and her MFA in Creative Nonfiction from Washington University in St. Louis. She skates for Arch Rival Roller Derby in St. Louis under the name Joan of Spark. Her first book, Brace for Impact, a memoir about coming out, coming of age, and roller derby, will be published by The Dial Press in 2022.

Maureen Neal is a retired teacher of English whose previous essays have appeared in High Country News and in several academic journals. Her current work focuses on the ethical and spiritual issues involved in caretaking and caregiving.

Tamara Nicholl-Smith's poetry has been featured on two Albuquerque city bus panels, one parking meter, numerous radio shows, a spoken-word classical piano fusion CD, and in several publications, most recently in Enchantment of the Ordinary put out by Mutablis Press, Kyoto Journal Issue 95, and Catholic Arts Today. She lives Houston, TX, enjoys puns, and likes her bourbon neat.

Slavena Salve Nissan is a 2020 graduate of the Icahn School of Medicine at Mount Sinai. She is a lifelong lover of all things storytelling and is deeply interested in the intersection of the arts with health/illness. Her poetry has been published in Doximity, Pulse, Hektoen International, and The Pharos.

Michael Oppenheim works and writes in Lexington, Kentucky.

Robin Perls-Shultis is a teacher, wife, mom, stepmom, and friend. She has been writing since she was eleven and has recently started sending her writing out into the world. She is in remission from ovarian cancer and is generally very grateful to be here.

Sheri Reda, M.A., M.A.R., M.L.I.S, is a writer, educator, presenter, with certifications as a mediator, spiritual director, and master life-cycle celebrant. Sheri is a steering committee member of the Narrative Medicine Committee at Advocate Healthcare Park Ridge, Illinois, a board member at the CG Jung center in Evanston, Illinois, and a member of the Chicago Conservation Corps. She has presented present talks, workshops, and seminars at the Examined Life conference and elsewhere.

Paul Rousseau is a semi-retired physician and writer, published or forthcoming in The Healing Muse, Blood and Thunder, Intima: A Journal of Narrative Medicine, The Human Touch, Months To Years, Cleaning up Glitter, Burningword Literary Journal, The Centifictionist, Prometheus Dreaming, Dr. T. J. Eckleburg Review, Another Chicago Magazine, JAMA, Annals of Internal Medicine, Canadian Medical Association Journal, Tendon, and others. He is a lover of dogs.

Hanna Saltzman is a resident physician in pediatrics at the University of Utah. She is a graduate of the University of Michigan Medical School and Williams College. She lives in Salt Lake City.

Miranda Schene is a third year MD/PhD student at the University of Iowa Carver College of Medicine, just beginning her research training in Molecular Medicine. When she isn't studying or writing, she enjoys playing with her cat and biking around the local parks.

Desiree Schippers grew up in the rural community of Colby, Kansas and graduated with degrees in English Creative Writing and Gerontology from Kansas State University. She enjoys film, Sonic cheese sticks, and long walks to the bathroom. She is currently a Kott Gerontology Scholar pursuing her MFA in Documentary Film at Northwestern University.

Carol EH Scott-Conner is professor and chair emeritus of the Department of Surgery at the University of Iowa Carver College of Medicine. She has written numerous textbooks, three monographs on writing, and two volumes of short stories. Her short fiction explores the interactions between physicians and patients. A perennial student, she is enrolled in the Narrative Medicine and Creative Writing graduate programs at Lenoir-Rhyne University.

Rosanna Staffa is an Italian-born author, published by The Sun, Tampa Review, Mud Season Review and Blood Orange Review among many others. She received 2nd place Honorable Mention in Tiferet 2019 Writing Contest and New Millennium 47 Writing Award, and ws nominated for the Pushcart Prize in 2019. She has recently completed a novel, and holds a PhD in Modern Foreign Languages from Statale University in Milan as well as an MFA in Fiction from Spalding University.

Travis Stephens is a tugboat captain who resides with his family in California. A graduate of University of Wisconsin-Eau Claire, recent wrting credits include: Gyroscope Review, 2River, Sheila-Na-Gig, Tiny Seed Literary Journal, Raw Art Review, Gravitas and The Dead Mule School of Southern Literature.

Christine Stewart-Nuñez Poet and memoirist Christine Stewart-Nuñez is the author of Postcard on Parchment (2008), Keeping Them Alive (2010), Untrussed (2016), and Bluewords Greening (2016), winner of the 2018 Whirling Prize. She is a Professor in the English Department at South Dakota State University and the South Dakota Poet Laureate.

Jacob Taxis is a palliative care chaplain and ordained Lutheran minister. He counts kayaking and reading a worn volume of James Wright among life's greatest pleasures. Jake lives with his wife, Greta, in Milwaukee, where the two first met as film students.

Kathryn Trueblood has been awarded the Goldenberg Prize for Fiction and the Red Hen Press Story Award. Her work is situated firmly in the medical humanities. Her most recent book, Take Daily As Needed, treats parenting while chronically ill with the desperado humor the subject deserves (University of New Mexico Press, 2019). Her previous novel, The Baby Lottery, dealt with the repercussions of infertility in a female friend group (a Book Sense Pick in 2007).

Elliot Wilner is a retired neurologist, living in Bethesda, MD. Since his retirement he has—with his wife's forbearance—indulged in a long-deferred dalliance with creative writing. Several of his stories and essays have been published in literary magazines, including The Examined Life Journal.

Amy Zimmerman is a writer and current MFA student at the University of Washington. She previously worked as a reporter at The Daily Beast. Her creative writing has appeared in Fourth Genre and Hayden's Ferry Review, and is forthcoming from Gigantic Sequins. Originally from New York City, she currently lives in Seattle.